1998 Cumulative Supplement

Purchasing Manager's
DESK BOOK
OF
PURCHASING LAW

Third Edition

1998 Cumulative Supplement

Purchasing Manager's
DESK BOOK
—— of ——
PURCHASING LAW

Third Edition

DONALD B. KING

JAMES J. RITTERSKAMP, JR.

PRENTICE HALL
PARAMUS, NEW JERSEY 07652

Library of Congress Cataloging-in-Publication Data

King, Donald Barnett.
    Purchasing manager's desk book of purchasing law.—3rd ed. /
Donald B. King. James J. Ritterskamp, Jr.
      p.   cm.
    Includes index.
    ISBN 0-13-959669-0 paper
    1. Sales—United States. 2. Contracts—United States.
3. Purchasing agents—Legal status, laws, etc.—United States.
I. Ritterskamp, James J. II. Title.
KF915.R58'   1997
346.7307'2—dc21   97-30492
                                                                                       CIP

© 1999 by Prentice Hall, Inc.
All rights reserved. No part of this book may be reproduced, in any form or by any means, without permission in writing from the publisher.

    This publication is designed to provide accurate and authoritative information in regard to the subject matter covered. It is sold with the understanding that the publisher is not engaged in rendering legal, accounting, or other professional service. If legal advice or other expert assistance is required, the services of a competent professional person should be sought.

—*From a Declaration of Principles jointly adopted by a Committee of the American Bar Association and a Committee of Publishers and Associations.*

ISBN 0-13-959669-0

Printed in the United States of America

10 9 8 7 6 5 4 3 2 1

ATTENTION: CORPORATIONS AND SCHOOLS

Prentice Hall books are available at quantity discounts with bulk purchase for educational, business, or sales promotional use. For information, please write to: Prentice Hall Career & Personal Development Special Sales, 240 Frisch Court, Paramus, NJ 07652. Please supply: title of book, ISBN number, quantity, how the book will be used, date needed.

PRENTICE HALL
Paramus, New Jersey 07652

A Simon & Schuster Company

On the World Wide Web at http://www.phdirect.com

Prentice Hall International (UK) Limited, *London*
Prentice Hall of Australia Pty. Limited, *Sydney*
Prentice Hall Canada, Inc., *Toronto*
Prentice Hall Hispanoamericana, S.A., *Mexico*
Prentice Hall of India Private Limited, *New Delhi*
Prentice Hall of Japan, Inc., *Tokyo*
Simon & Schuster Asia Pte., Ltd., *Singapore*
Editora Prentice-Hall do Brasil, Ltda., *Rio de Janeiro*

This supplement is dedicated to my classmates over the years (Pullman Elementary, Junior, and High Schools, Washington State University, Harvard Law School, New York University and Saint Louis University).

Acknowledgments

This Supplement, which reflects recent diverse developments affecting purchasing law, is made possible not only by the author's efforts alone but also by the cooperative efforts of work with others who have done specialized research. I am pleased to acknowledge at this time the overall and individualized efforts of Mr. Lingling Zou, Juris Doctor, Member of the New York State Bar, who was my faculty research assistant and for his writings on world trade and regional country law; Mr. Joseph Keaveny, for his writing dealing with purchases from bankrupt companies and purchasing for such companies; Mr. Thierry Guastavino, for his input on corrupt practices; and Mr. Thomas Burton, for his work generally and on electronic signatures and purchases of computer software and services.

As always, there is a well-deserved acknowledgment to Mary Dougherty for her fine skills as faculty secretary with the computers and word processors.

About the Authors

Donald B. King has taught commercial law for thirty-nine years. During this time he has written or edited twelve books, and over forty articles and essays. The *Commercial Transactions* casebook he first coedited in 1968 is now in its fifth edition. He has coauthored a book on Sales Law and has written books on "Consumer Protection Experiment in Sweden" and "Consumer Protection in Chinese." Professor King also was the editor of books on "Commercial and Consumer Law from an International Perspective" and "Essays on Comparative Commercial and Consumer Law." His teaching has been concentrated in the fields of commercial law, consumer law, secured transactions, products liability, and comparative law. He has taught at the University of Washington, Dickinson Law School, Wayne State University, and Saint Louis University. He also was a Visiting Professor at the University of Cincinnati, Stetson Law School, and Sichuan University in China.

He is founder and Honorary President of the International Academy of Commercial and Consumer Law, a select group of sixty international authorities. He has done comparative research and given lectures on commercial and consumer law in a number of countries throughout the world.

He received his Bachelor of Science degree in psychology from Washington State University and his Juris Doctor from Harvard Law School. Professor King has also earned a Masters from New York University and a Masters in psychiatric social work from Saint Louis University. He is a member of the Missouri, Washington State, and Supreme Court bars, is an elected member of the American Law Institute and was recently given the honor of "Life Member," an honor held by less than 600 lawyers out of the 985,900 lawyers in the United States. Professor King was elected President of the Central States Law School Association for 1995, which consists of over forty law schools from thirteen states. The Saint Louis University Du Bourg Society has named him an Honorary Dean, Honorary Vice President, and Honorary Trustee. He was appointed as a visiting scholar at Harvard Law School for 1998.

James J. Ritterskamp, Jr. coauthored and contributed to several books on purchasing and wrote a monthly column, *Ritterskamp Views the Law,* which was carried in numerous purchasing magazines, including *Purchasing Management, Midwest Purchasing,* the *St. Louis Purchaser, Purchasing Professional,* and the *New South Purchaser.* He was best known for his legal seminars conducted for the National Association of Purchasing Management, for Regional Purchasing Management Associations, and for private organizations throughout the country.

He served as president of numerous professional associations, including the Purchasing Management Association of St. Louis, the National Association of Educational Buyers, the National Association of College Stores, and the National Association of College and University Business Officers. He taught accounting, law purchasing, and economics at Washington University and Vassar College.

He received his Juris Doctor degree from the School for Law of Washington University in St. Louis, and held various academic posts at the Illinois Institute of Technology in Chicago, The University of Chicago, and Vassar College in New York. In 1986, he came out of retirement to become President of Rocky Mountain College in Billings, Montana, for one year.

Preface

With the *Purchasing Manager's Deskbook of Purchasing Law, Third Edition,* published in 1997, most of the recent developments in law could be incorporated in it. Nevertheless, the continued developments of the law and purchasing make it necessary to issue this Supplement. The necessity and desirability of providing the purchasing manager with the most recent developments is apparent.

In this Supplement, several major developments are dealt with in more detail:

- Purchasing Manager's Staff: Discrimination Suits
- Purchasing Manager's Staff: Americans with Disabilities Act
- Purchasing Manager's Staff: Religious Discrimination
- Purchasing Manager's Staff: Pregnancy Discrimination
- Purchasing Manager's Staff: National Origin
- Purchasing Manager's Staff: Sexual Harassment
- The World Trade Organization and Its Effects on Purchasing
- European Community Organization and Laws
- North American Free Trade Association
- Corrupt Practices Treaty
- Licensing of Technology New UCC Proposals
- Bankruptcy and Purchasing

- Countertrade
- Letters of Credit Developments

As one can readily see, these developments represent a balance between domestic and international laws. In addition, there are several items in the appendix that may be of some value to the purchasing manager:

1. Rules and Procedures for Dispute Resolution (American Arbitration Association)
2. Convention on the International Sale of Goods
3. State Department Notes on Convention Provisions
4. Seller and Purchaser Clauses for Foreign Trade

Contents

Acknowledgments	vii
About the Authors	ix
Preface	xi

Supplement to Chapter II
THE ROLE OF YOUR LEGAL COUNSEL — 1

- Introduction — 1
- Alternative Dispute Resolution — 2
- Reeling in Legal Bills — 3

Supplement to Chapter VII
PERSONAL LIABILITIES OF THE AGENT — 5

- Business Use of an Automobile — 5

Supplement to Chapter VIII
LIABILITIES OF A PURCHASING MANAGER REGARDING THE STAFF — 7

- Discrimination Generally — 7
- Age Discrimination and the Purchasing Manager — 8
- Disability Discrimination — 9
- Pregnancy Discrimination — 16
- National Origin Discrimination — 18
- Religious Discrimination — 19
- Sexual Harassment — 20

Legal Remedies	27
Recent Supreme Court Decisions	29

Supplement to Chapter X
Purchasing Ethics and the Law — 33

MultiLateral Treaty on Commercial Bribery	33

Supplement to Chapter XXII
LETTERS OF CREDIT — 37

Bank's Duty to Raise All Discrepancies	38
Modified Time Period for Bank Examination of Documents	38
"New" Standard for Bank Examination of Documents	39
A Rule for Seeking Waivers of Discrepancies	39
Letters of Credit: Tips for Buyers	40
Standby Letter of Credit	41

Supplement to Chapter XXV
BUYER'S SPECIAL REMEDIES — 45

Bankruptcy and Purchasers	45
Types of Bankruptcy	47
Executory Contracts	48

Supplement to Chapter XXVIII
COMPUTER PURCHASES AND CONTROVERSIES — 55

U.C.C. Article 2B Proposals, and Current Digital Signature Issues	55
What Is and Is Not Covered by Article 2B	56
Attribution Procedures and Use of Digital Signature Technology	67
Electronic Notaries or Certification Authorities	70
State Legislation Addressing the Use of Digital Signatures	72

Supplement to Chapter XXXI
Purchasing from Foreign Vendors   77

    Countertrade   77
    Counterpurchase   78
    Compensation   78
    Switch Trading   79

Chapter XXXIA
**PURCHASING UNDER WORLD TRADE ORGANIZATION
AND REGIONAL INTEGRATION ARRANGEMENTS**   81

    Basic Systems   81
    Multilateralism or Regionalism?   82
    The Composition and Nature of GATT and WTO   85
    How WTO Works   87
    Basic Principles of the WTO Trading System   89
    Main Substantive Rules of WTO Trading System   91
    The Uruguay Round Impact   101
    Benefits to the United States Economy   103
    North American Free Trade Agreement   105
    Key NAFTA Provisions   109
    NAFTA Rules of Origin   112
    NAFTA Customs Administration and Procedures   117
    NAFTA's Impact   120
    The European Union   121
    What Is the European Union?   122
    How the European Union Works   124
    EU Commercial Rules   128
    United States—EU Relations   135
    Regional Economic Cooperations in Asia   137
    Asia Pacific Economic Cooperation   139
    ASEAN Free Trade Area (AFTA)   147
    Conclusions   150
    Selected Bibliography on World Trade and Regionalism   151

Supplement of Chapter XXXIII
CULTURAL-LEGAL PROBLEMS IN FOREIGN PURCHASING   **153**

    Business Feng Shui   153

Appendix A

    ADDITIONAL INFORMATION   155

Appendix B

    UNITED NATIONS CONVENTION ON CONTRACTS FOR THE INTERNATIONAL SALE OF GOODS: OFFICIAL ENGLISH TEXT   157

Appendix C

    LEGAL ANALYSIS OF THE CONVENTION ON CONTRACTS FOR THE INTERNATIONAL SALE OF GOODS   191

Appendix D

    SELLER AND PURCHASER CLAUSES FOR FOREIGN TRADE   217

Appendix E

    RULES AND PROCEDURES FOR DISPUTE SETTLEMENT   225

CUMULATIVE INDEX   253

Supplement to Chapter II

The Role of Your Legal Counsel

INTRODUCTION

Purchasing managers may someday confront the prospect of being subjected to a deposition by an attorney. Business people generally seek to avoid such deposition. It is sometimes suspected that the purpose behind the notice of deposition of a high-ranking corporate executive is to induce a settlement in exchange for canceling the deposition or to increase settlement value. If a manager does not have relevant information on the matter at hand, has only a passing involvement, or if the lack of other relevant discovery makes it premature for the other litigant to pursue information from such him, the manager should seek protective orders from the court to prevent the deposition. Courts will consider the following factors in its protective order decision: whether the manager really has no information on the subject matter; whether some other available person could testify about the matter in controversy; whether existing discovery has laid a foundation to involve the manager; whether the information sought form the executive is relevant or likely to lead to admissible evidence.

ALTERNATIVE DISPUTE RESOLUTION

There are four ways in which legal disputes are settled: by the attorneys themselves; good judicial administration and case management; direct judicial action; and alternative dispute resolution. However, attorneys settle usually because of external pressure imposed by the progress of the case. Good judicial administration entails control of the discovery process, effectively conducting pretrial hearings and setting a firm date for the trial of the case. Direct judicial action includes three types: the trial judge can conduct a settlement conference, or can send the case to another judge for a settlement conference, or the trial judge can conduct a summary jury trial. Alternative dispute resolution has not been utilized enough but is gaining popularity among lawyers, clients, and courts. More and more courts adopted rules that place more emphasis on the use of alternative dispute resolution (ADR).

Mediation returns control of a lawsuit to the parties involved in the lawsuit. In mediation, the parties actually talk to each other again, with the helpful direction of a skilled mediator. The parties control what is disclosed to each other. Moreover, the parties get some measure of control over the time that is wasted in preparing for trial. When a case settles, it is frequently long before any trial date.

Beyond mediation, ADR might take the form of arbitration, mini-trial, or any variation of these procedures on which the parties agree. Arbitration is a process in which each side presents its case at a hearing to a neutral for a final and binding decision. Mini-trial is a structured settlement procedure in which attorneys present their best case in an abbreviated form with experts; if appropriate, before senior executives of the companies involved and a neutral party who chairs the presentation. After the presentation, the senior executives meet for a settlement discussion. In the event that the senior executives are unable to settle the dispute, the neutral may be empowered to mediate and/or provide a nonbinding advisory opinion regarding the likely outcome if the case were litigated. Advisory arbitration in most respects mirrors traditional arbitration. It differs, however, in focusing on specific issues in a dispute and deciding them in an award that is not binding on the parties. Other ADR methods include fact-finding, investigation of a dispute by a neutral who issues findings and a nonbinding report, and med-arb, which combines the two primary processes.

REELING IN LEGAL BILLS

Courts are beginning to look askance at the huge cuts lawyers take in contingent fee cases and are cutting them down to size. Judges in some states have expanded their authority to rein in legal fees to mass settlements as well as class settlements. The judges are dusting off ethical rules that limit lawyers to charging "reasonable" fees, no matter what their contracts say. Lawyers are being required to tell their clients upfront that hourly rates may save them a lot of money. In suits ranging from recent tobacco litigation to ordinary fender-benders, clients are beginning to get some relief from staggering legal fees.

Several factors appear to be driving the new scrutiny: clients are bolder, lawyers are more willing to sue peers, and in some jurisdictions, conservative judges are railing against the contingent system. Amid the growing scrutiny, more lawyers are voluntarily reducing contingent fees, because they would otherwise be considered excessive.

For years, contingent fees have been debated, portrayed either as a righteous exercise in making justice available to the poor or a way to pick clients' pockets. Lawyers say they are entitled to a premium over hourly rates to compensate them for taking such a risk. Proposals to limit contingent fees, in Congress and in many states, have been blocked by trial lawyers.

With the rapid development of computer technology, the legal profession is now in a restructuring period. Lawyers and clients are now talking about alternative pricing to bring legal fees more in line with the lawyers' value of the work product, rather than the hours they spend producing the work. The most popular alternative billing methods are: fixed fees, blended rates, and discounted hourly rates.

Flat fees are typically used for matters such as simple wills, bankruptcy/collection work, personal tax returns, residential closings, and securitization. Fixed fees are also often used in litigation defense practices handling a heavy volume of small cases. Fixed fees are sometimes based on volume—as the volume goes up, the fees per case go down.

Blended hourly rates are variations on standard hourly rates. Instead of specific hourly rates for individual timekeepers, one rate applies to all hours billed on a matter. For example, the hourly rate would be the average of those timekeepers involved on a specific matter. If the standard hourly rates a partner is $225, an associate $100, and a paralegal $50, the client would be charged $110 per hour for time spent by any of the timekeepers under the blended system.

Many clients like split-fee billing because the firm shares in the risk. Usually, the firm receives a reduced hourly rate for the work. The client and the lawyer agree on the desired result before the work is undertaken. If a favorable result is achieved, the firm gets an additional fee. If a result achieved is less than the minimum agreed upon, the firm receives only its reduced hourly rate. This method is typically used in defense litigation, tax and securities matters, and acquisitions, but it could be adapted to other types of work.

Unit billing assigns a time value, to be billed at hourly rates, to a specific task. Unit billing has been popular for years because it simplifies recording hours and minimizes lost time for inadequate recordkeeping. This method is often used in insurance defense litigation.

Result-oriented pricing does not involve hourly rates and is therefore a more subjective approach. Some of the subjective factors considered in value billing are time and labor involved, customary fees for similar work, the difficulty and complexity of the matter, the level of expertise required, the experience and reputation of the lawyer, what is at stake, and the results obtained. This type of pricing arrangement is common when the firm has a reputation for expertise or influence in a particular area.

Supplement to Chapter VII

Personal Liabilities of the Agent

BUSINESS USE OF AN AUTOMOBILE

In many cases, when people are traveling on business or vacation in a town away from home, they rent a car. Liability insurance is provided by the car rental company. The person who has rented the car also has his or her own liability coverage. This is not an "either/or" situation, rather, both coverages apply.

In most states there is a pronounced effort by car rental agents to sell collision insurance. Such insurance has a very profit margin similar to credit life insurance for a merchant in retail sales. To protect his/her own assets, one renting a vehicle certainly ought to have coverage for any damage to the car that is rented. In one case, *Allstate v. Alamo,* the driver did not by the collision damage waiver (CDW) coverage and was involved in a significant collision the same day he rented a purple Lincoln Town Car worth $30,000. After deducting for the salvage, Alamo sent him a statement for $13, 840.62 requesting that he put the invoice number on his check and use the enclosed envelope to make prompt payment. To avoid such incident, it is strongly urged that the some form of CDW be in place.

However, a CDW is not always necessary. Some employers tell their business traveling employees not to buy a CDW since such a charge can not be cost justified on a company-wide loss experience. Some credit card companies, for their Gold or Business Accounts, will include collision coverage if the charges for the rental are put on the credit card. Moreover, the driver's own coverage may include the collision on the rental car.

Supplement to Chapter VIII

Liabilities of a Purchasing Manager Regarding the Staff

DISCRIMINATION GENERALLY

Discrimination comes in many forms. Courts are not hesitant to expand the anti-discrimination laws to new forms of discrimination. The job-bias law explicitly protects current employees and job applicants from retaliation after they claim they were victims of discrimination. The U.S. Supreme Court has ruled that the federal job-bias law applies to former workers who have accused a former employer of discrimination. Therefore, workers can file lawsuits charging their former employers with giving bad references or other forms of retaliation.

    With the popularity of computers and E-mails in offices, a new kind of discrimination lawsuits has emerged. Employers could be liable for racially or sexually offensive or inappropriate E-mail messages posted on the company E-mail system by employees. Employers should initiate E-mail use compliance policies and rules and train their employees on avoiding abusing E-mail privileges. Some employers may take disciplinary actions on violators of E-mail policies, such as termination, suspension without pay, revoke pay increases previously awarded, or suspend the severance benefits of an employee who was no longer working for the company but still have access to the company E-mail systems.

However, courts will not go as far as some people wish. In one lawsuit, the employee charged that a contentious job-performance review with her boss was so stressful that it triggered a painful medical condition and demanded that her employer assign her to a new boss. The Seventh Circuit Court ruled that she was not entitled to a transfer. The court reasoned that the Americans with Disabilities Act (ADA), which requires employers to make "reasonable accommodations" for disabled workers, does not require them to transfer people to new supervisors. The ADA does not protect people from the general stresses of the workplace.

AGE DISCRIMINATION AND THE PURCHASING MANAGER

The U.S. Supreme Court recently ruled favorably to the older workers. In 1994, a worker accepted a termination agreement and signed a waiver of employment claims against her employer. In return she was paid $6,258 over four months. After the last payment, she, then 41, sued her employer, charging violations of the Age Discrimination in Employment Act. The law covers workers 40 and older. The lower federal courts dismissed the case because she had ratified the termination agreement by accepting the severance pay.

However, the Supreme Court ruled that older workers who seemingly sign away their rights to sued their bosses for age discrimination when they accept buyout packages may be able to reclaim that right under certain circumstances. Ousted employees can still sue if the waivers they sign releasing their employers from employment claim fail to comply with federal disclosure requirements. The employer in this case had failed to comply with the Older Workers Benefit Protection Act in three ways. She was allowed 14 days, instead of 21 days required by the statute. She was not given seven days after signing the release to change her mind, as required by law. Nor did the release, as required, specifically refer to rights or claims arising under law. Therefore, the waivers signed by the employee were invalid.

It is clear that employers will not be able to purchase silence from discharged workers with defective waivers. If employers want immunity from age discrimination lawsuits, they will have to comply with the clear and specific requirements of the law. However, employers may be able to force discharged workers to repay severance benefits. Courts might order that damages for age discrimination be reduced by the amount of a severance payment.

DISABILITY DISCRIMINATION

Title I of the ADA prohibits private employers, state and local governments, employment agencies and labor unions from discriminating against qualified individuals with disabilities in job application procedures, hiring, firing, advancement, compensation, job training, and other terms, conditions and privileges of employment.

If you have a disability and are qualified to do a job, the ADA protects you from job discrimination on the basis of your disability. Under the ADA, you have a disability if you have a physical or mental impairment that substantially limits a major life activity. The ADA also protects you if you have a history of such a disability, or if an employer believes that you have such a disability.

To be protected under the ADA, you must have a record of, or be regarded as having a substantial, as opposed to a minor, impairment. A substantial impairment is one that significantly limits or restricts a major life activity such as hearing, seeing, speaking, walking, breathing, performing manual tasks, caring for oneself, learning or working.

If you have a disability, you must also be qualified to perform the essential functions or duties of a job, with reasonable accommodation, in order to be protected from job discrimination by the ADA. This means two things. First, you must satisfy the employer's requirements for the job, such as education, employment experience, skills or licenses.

Second, you must be able to perform the essential functions of the job with reasonable accommodation. Essential functions are the fundamental job duties that you must be able to perform on your own or with the help of a reasonable accommodation. An employer cannot refuse to hire you because your disability prevents you from performing duties that are not essential to the job.

Employees and applicants currently engaging in the illegal use of drugs are not covered by the ADA, when an employer acts on the basis of such use. Tests for illegal drugs are not subject to the ADA's restrictions on medical examinations. Employers may hold illegal drug users and alcoholics to the same performance standards as other employees.

Job discrimination against people with disabilities is illegal if practiced by:

- private employers
- state and local governments
- employment agencies
- labor organizations
- labor-management committees

The part of the ADA enforced by the EEOC outlaws job discrimination by all employers, including State and local government employers, with 25 or more employees after July 26, 1992, and all employers, including State and local government employers, with 15 or more employees after July 26, 1994.

Another part of the ADA, enforced by the U.S. Department of Justice (DOJ), prohibits discrimination in State and local government programs and activities, including discrimination by all State and local governments, regardless of the number of employees, after January 26, 1992.

Because the ADA establishes overlapping responsibilities in both EEOC and DOJ for employment by State and local governments, the Federal enforcement effort is coordinated by EEOC and DOJ to avoid duplication in investigative and enforcement activities. In addition, since some private and governmental employers are already covered by nondiscrimination and affirmative action requirements under the Rehabilitation Act of 1973, EEOC, DOJ, and the Department of Labor similarly coordinate the enforcement effort under the ADA and the Rehabilitation Act.

The ADA makes it unlawful to discriminate in all employment practices such as: recruitment, firing, hiring, training, job assignments, promotions, pay, benefits, lay off, leave, all other employment related activities. It is also unlawful for an employer to retaliate against you for asserting your rights under the ADA. The Act also protects you if you are a victim of discrimination because of your family, business, social or other relationship or association with an individual with a disability.

Reasonable accommodation is any change or adjustment to a job or work environment that permits a qualified applicant or employee with a disability to participate in the job application process, to perform the essential functions of a job, or to enjoy benefits and privileges of employment equal to those enjoyed by employees without disabilities. For example, reasonable accommodation may include:

- providing or modifying equipment or devices
- job restructuring
- part-time or modified work schedules
- reassignment to a vacant position
- adjusting or modifying examinations, training materials, or policies
- providing readers and interpreters
- making the workplace readily accessible to and usable by people with disabilities

An employer is required to provide a reasonable accommodation to a qualified applicant or employee with a disability unless the employer can show that the accommodation would be an undue hardship—that is, that it would require significant difficulty or expense.

Reasonable accommodation may include, but is not limited to:

- Making existing facilities used by employees readily accessible to and usable by persons with disabilities.
- Job restructuring, modifying work schedules, reassignment to a vacant position.
- Acquiring or modifying equipment or devices, adjusting modifying examinations, training materials, or policies, and providing qualified readers or interpreters.

An employer is required to make an accommodation to the known disability of a qualified applicant or employee if it would not impose an "undue hardship" on the operation of the employer's business. Undue hardship is defined as an action requiring significant difficulty or expense when considered in light of factors such as an employer's size, financial resources and the nature and structure of its operation.

An employer is not required to lower quality or production standards to make an accommodation, nor is an employer obligated to provide personal use items such as glasses or hearing aids.

Caveat Nota: If a person is applying for a job, the prospective employer cannot ask if he or she is disabled or ask about the nature or severity of the disability. An employer can ask if he or she can perform the duties of the job with or without reasonable accommodation. An employer can also ask one to describe or to demonstrate how, with or without reasonable accommodation, one will perform the duties of the job. An employer cannot require a person to take a medical examination before being offered a job. Following a job offer, an employer can condition the offer on one's passing a required medical examination, but only if all entering employees for that job category have to take the examination. However, an employer cannot reject one because of information about the disability revealed by the medical examination, unless the reasons for rejection are job-related and necessary for the conduct of the employer's business. The employer cannot refuse to hire a person because of his or her disability if one can perform the essential functions of the job with an accommodation.

Once you have been hired and started work, your employer cannot require that you take a medical examination or ask questions about your disability unless they are related to your job and necessary for the conduct of your employer's business. Your employer may conduct voluntary medical examinations that are part of an employee health program, and may provide medical information required by State workers' compensation laws to the agencies that administer such laws. The results of all medical examinations must be kept confidential, and maintained in separate medical files.

Enforcement

The U.S. Equal Employment Opportunity Commission issued regulations to enforce the provisions of Title I of the ADA on July 26, 1991. The provisions originally took effect on July 26, 1992, and covered employers with 25 or more employees. On July 26, 1994, the threshold dropped to include employers with 15 or more employees.

If you think you have been discriminated against in employment on the basis of disability after July 26, 1992, you should contact the U.S. Equal Employment Opportunity Commission. A charge of discrimination generally must be filed within 180 days of the alleged discrimination. You may have up to 300 days to file a charge if there is a State or local law that provides relief for discrimination on the basis of disability. However, to protect your rights, it is best to contact EEOC promptly if discrimination is suspected.

You may file a charge of discrimination on the basis of disability by contacting any EEOC field office, located in cities throughout the United States. If you have been discriminated against, you are entitled to a remedy that will place you in the position you would have been in if the discrimination had never occurred. You may be entitled to hiring, promotion, reinstatement, back pay, or reasonable accommodation, including reassignment. You may also be entitled to attorney's fees.

Although the EEOC can only process ADA charges based on actions occurring on or after July 26, 1992, you may already be protected by State or local laws or by other current federal laws. EEOC field offices can refer you to the agencies that enforce those laws. The EEOC conducts an active technical assistance program to promote voluntary compliance with the ADA. This program is designed to help people with disabilities understand their rights and to help employers understand their responsibilities under the law.

The Commission also recognizes that differences and disputes about ADA requirements may arise between employers and people with disabilities as a result of misunderstandings. Such disputes frequently can be resolved more effectively through informal negotiation or mediation procedures, rather than through the formal enforcement process of the ADA. Accordingly, EEOC will encourage efforts of employers and individuals with disabilities to settle such differences through alternative methods of dispute resolution, providing that such efforts do not deprive any individual of legal rights provided by the statute.

Caveat Nota:

1. If you think you will need a reasonable accommodation to participate in the application process or to perform essential job functions, you should inform the employer that an accommodation will be needed. Employers are required to provide reasonable accommodation only for the physical or mental limitations of a qualified individual with a disability of which they are aware. Generally, it is the responsibility of the employee to inform the employer that an accommodation is needed. The ADA requires that the employer provide the accommodation unless to do so would impose an undue hardship on the operation of the employer's business. If the cost of providing the needed accommodation would be an undue hardship, the employee must be given the choice of providing the accommodation or paying for the portion of the accommodation that causes the undue hardship.

2. An employer cannot make up the cost of providing a reasonable accommodation by lowering your salary or paying you less than other employees in similar positions. The requirement to provide reasonable accommodation covers all services, programs, and non-work facilities provided by the employer. If making an existing facility accessible would be an undue hardship, the employer must provide a comparable facility that will enable a person with a disability to enjoy benefits and privileges of employment similar to those enjoyed by other employees, unless to do so would be an undue hardship.

3. The ADA does not require that an employer hire an applicant with a disability over other applicants because the person has a disability.

4. The ADA only prohibits discrimination on the basis of disability. It makes it unlawful to refuse to hire a qualified applicant with a disability because he is disabled or because a reasonable accommodation is required to make it possible for this person to perform essential job functions.

5. The ADA permits an employer to refuse to hire an individual if she poses a direct threat to the health or safety of herself or others. A direct threat means a significant risk of substantial harm. The determination that there is a direct threat must be based on objective, factual evidence regarding an individual's present ability to perform essential functions of a job.

6. An employer cannot refuse to hire you because of a slightly increased risk or because of fears that there might be a significant risk sometime in the future. The employer must also consider whether a risk can be eliminated or reduced to an acceptable level with a reasonable accommodation.

7. The ADA does not affect pre-existing condition clauses contained in health insurance policies even though such clauses may adversely affect employees with disabilities more than other employees.

8. The ADA only requires that an employer provide employees with disabilities equal access to whatever health insurance coverage is offered to other employees.

9. The ADA makes it unlawful to discriminate against an individual, whether disabled or not, because of a relationship or association with an individual with a known disability.

10. The legislative history indicates that Congress intended the ADA to protect persons with AIDS and HIV disease from discrimination.

PREGNANCY DISCRIMINATION

The Pregnancy Discrimination Act is an amendment to Title VII of the Civil Rights Act of 1964. Discrimination on the basis of pregnancy, childbirth or related medical conditions constitutes unlawful sex discrimination under Title VII. Women affected by pregnancy or related conditions must be treated in the same manner as other applicants or employees with similar abilities or limitations.

An employer cannot refuse to hire a woman because of her pregnancy-related condition as long as she is able to perform the major functions of her job. An employer cannot refuse to hire her because of its prejudices against pregnant workers or the prejudices of co-workers, clients or customers.

An employer may not single out pregnancy-related conditions for special procedures to determine an employee's ability to work. However, an employer may use any procedure used to screen other employees' ability to work. For example, if an employer requires its employees to submit a doctor's statement concerning their inability to work before granting leave or paying sick benefits, the employer may require employees affected by pregnancy related conditions to submit such statements.

If an employee is temporarily unable to perform her job due to pregnancy, the employer must treat her the same as any other temporarily disabled employee; for example, by providing modified tasks, alternative assignments, and disability leave or leave without pay. Pregnant employees must be permitted to work as long as they are able to perform their jobs. If an employee has been absent from work as a result of a pregnancy related condition and recovers, her employer may not require her to remain on leave until the baby's birth. An employer may not have a rule that prohibits an employee from returning to work for a predetermined length of time after childbirth.

Employers must hold open a job for a pregnancy related absence the same length of time jobs are held open for employees on sick or disability leave. Any health insurance provided by an employer must cover expenses for pregnancy related conditions on the same basis as costs for other medical conditions. Health insurance for expenses arising from abortion is not required, except where the life of the mother is endangered. Pregnancy-related expenses should be reimbursed exactly as those incurred for other medical conditions, whether payment is on a fixed basis or a percentage of reasonable and customary charge basis.

The amounts payable by the insurance provider can be limited only to the same extent as costs for other conditions. No additional, increased or larger deductible can be imposed. If a health insurance plan excludes benefit payments for pre-existing conditions when the insured's coverage becomes effective, benefits can be denied for medical costs arising from an existing pregnancy.

Employers must provide the same level of health benefits for spouses of male employees as they do for spouses of female employees. Pregnancy-related benefits cannot be limited to married employees. In an all-female workforce or job classification, benefits must be provided for pregnancy related conditions if benefits are provided for other medical conditions.

If an employer provides any benefits to workers on leave, the employer must provide the same benefits for those on leave for pregnancy related conditions. Employees with pregnancy-related disabilities must be treated the same as other temporarily disabled employees for accrual and crediting of seniority, vacation calculation, pay increases and temporary disability benefits.

NATIONAL ORIGIN DISCRIMINATION

Title VII of the Civil Rights Act of 1964 protects individuals against employment discrimination on the basis of national origin as well as race, color, religion and sex. It is unlawful to discriminate against any employee or applicant because of the individual's national origin. No one can be denied equal employment opportunity because of birthplace, ancestry, culture, or linguistic characteristics common to a specific ethnic group. Equal employment opportunity cannot be denied because of marriage or association with persons of a national origin group; membership or association with specific ethnic promotion groups; attendance or participation in schools, churches, temples or mosques generally associated with a national origin group; or a surname associated with a national origin group.

A rule requiring employees to speak only English at all times on the job may violate Title VII, unless an employer shows it is necessary for conducting business. If an employer believes the English-only rule is critical for business purposes, employees have to be told when they must speak English and the consequences for violating the rule. Any negative employment decision based on breaking the English-only rule will be considered evidence of discrimination if the employer did not tell employees of the rule.

An employer must show a legitimate nondiscriminatory reason for the denial of employment opportunity because of an individual's accent or manner of speaking. Investigations will focus on the qualifications of the person and whether his or her accent or manner of speaking had a detrimental effect on job performance. Requiring employees or applicants to be fluent in English may violate Title VII if the rule is adopted to exclude individuals of a particular national origin and is not related to job performance.

Harassment on the basis of national origin is a violation of Title VII. An ethnic slur or other verbal or physical conduct because of an individual's nationality constitute harassment if they create an intimidating, hostile or offensive working environment, unreasonably interfere with work performance or negatively affect an individual's employment opportunities.

Employers have a responsibility to maintain a workplace free of national origin harassment. Employers may be responsible for any on-the-job harassment by their agents and supervisory employees, regardless of whether the acts were authorized or specifically forbidden by the employer. Under certain circumstances, an employer may be responsible for the acts of non employees who harass their employees at work.

The Immigration Reform and Control Act of 1986 (IRCA) requires employers to prove all employees hired after November 6, 1986, are legally authorized to work in the United States. IRCA also prohibits discrimination based on national origin or citizenship. An employer who singles out individuals of a particular national origin or individuals who appear to be foreign to provide employment verification may have violated both IRCA and Title VII. Employers who impose citizenship requirements or give preference to U.S. citizens in hiring or employment opportunities may have violated IRCA, unless these are legal or contractual requirements for particular jobs. Employers also may have violated Title VII if a requirement or preference has the purpose or effect of discriminating against individuals of a particular national origin.

RELIGIOUS DISCRIMINATION

Title VII of the Civil Rights Act of 1964 prohibits employers from discriminating against individuals because of their religion in hiring, firing, and other terms and conditions of employment. The Act also requires employers to reasonably accommodate the religious practices of an employee or prospective employee, unless to do so would create an undue hardship upon the employer. Flexible scheduling, voluntary substitutions or swaps, job reassignments and lateral transfers are examples of accommodating an employee's religious beliefs.

Employers cannot schedule examinations or other selection activities in conflict with a current or prospective employee's religious needs, inquire about an applicant's future availability at certain times, maintain a restrictive dress code, or refuse to allow observance of a Sabbath or religious holiday, unless the employer can prove that not doing so would cause an undue hardship.

An employer can claim undue hardship when accommodating an employee's religious practices if allowing such practices requires more than ordinary administrative costs. Undue hardship also may be shown if changing a bona fide seniority system to accommodate one employee's religious practices denies another employee the job or shift preference guaranteed by the seniority system. An employee whose religious practices prohibit payment of union dues to a labor organization cannot be required to pay the dues, but may pay an equal sum to a charitable organization.

Mandatory "new age" training programs, designed to improve employee motivation, cooperation or productivity through meditation, yoga, biofeedback or other practices, may conflict with the non-discriminatory provisions of Title VII. Employers must accommodate any employee who gives notice that these programs are inconsistent with the employee's religious beliefs, whether or not the employer believes there is a religious basis for the employee's objection.

SEXUAL HARASSMENT

Sexual harassment is a form of sex discrimination that violates Title VII of the Civil Rights Act of 1964. Unwelcome sexual advances, requests for sexual favors, and other verbal or physical conduct of a sexual nature constitutes sexual harassment when submission to or rejection of this conduct explicitly or implicitly affects an individual's employment, unreasonably interferes with an individual's work performance or creates an intimidating, hostile or offensive work environment.

Sexual harassment can occur in a variety of circumstances, including but not limited to the following:

- The victim as well as the harasser may be a woman or a man. The victim does not have to be of the opposite sex. In *Oncale v. Sundowner Offshore Services, et al.*, the Supreme Court specifically ruled that men's sexualized subordination of other men is a violation of Title VII of the 1964 Civil Rights Act.
- The harasser can be the victim's supervisor, an agent of the employer, a supervisor in another area, a co-worker, or a non-employee.
- The victim does not have to be the person harassed but could be anyone affected by the offensive conduct.
- Unlawful sexual harassment may occur without economic injury to or discharge of the victim.
- The harasser's conduct must be unwelcome.

It is helpful for the victim to directly inform the harasser that the conduct is unwelcome and must stop. The victim should use any employer complaint mechanism or grievance system available. When investigating allegations of sexual harassment, EEOC looks at the whole record: the circumstances, such as the nature of the sexual advances, and the context in which the alleged incidents occurred. A determination on the allegations is made from the facts on a case-by-case basis.

Prevention is the best tool to eliminate sexual harassment in the workplace. Employers are encouraged to take steps necessary to prevent sexual harassment from occurring. They should clearly communicate to employees that sexual harassment will not be tolerated. They can do so by establishing an effective complaint or grievance process and taking immediate and appropriate action when an employee complains.

Although sexual harassment has been a pervasive problem for women throughout history, only in the past two decades have feminist litigators won definition of sexual harassment as a form of sex discrimination and have women come forward in droves to demand remedies and institutional change. In the United States, sexual harassment in employment, housing (harassment by a landlord or building manager), or academia is illegal.

Women around the world are beginning to tell their stories and expose the pervasiveness of sexual harassment in their societies. A 1992 International Labor Organization survey of 23 countries revealed what women already know—that sexual harassment is a major problem for women all over the world. Sexual harassment affects women's mental and physical health as well as their social and economic status. The level of tolerance for sexual harassment varies from culture to culture; there is incidence of, and remedies for, sexual harassment in a variety of countries.

Any of the following unwanted behaviors may constitute sexual harassment:

- leering
- wolf whistles
- discussion of one's partner's sexual inadequacies
- sexual innuendo
- comments about women's bodies
- accidentally brushing sexual parts of the body
- lewd and threatening letters
- tales of sexual exploitation
- graphic descriptions of pornography
- pressure for dates
- sexually explicit gestures
- unwelcome touching and hugging
- sexual sneak attacks, (e.g., grabbing breasts or buttocks)

- sabotaging women's work
- sexist and insulting graffiti
- demanding, "Hey, baby, give me a smile"
- inappropriate invitations (e.g., hot tub)
- sexist jokes and cartoons
- hostile put-downs of women
- exaggerated, mocking 'courtesy'
- public humiliation
- obscene phone calls
- displaying pornography in the workplace
- insisting that workers wear revealing clothes
- inappropriate gifts (ex. lingerie)
- hooting, sucking, lip-smacking, & animal noises
- pressing or rubbing up against the victim
- sexual assault
- soliciting sexual services
- stalking
- leaning over, invading a person's space
- indecent exposure

Sexual harassment is not mutual and is unwelcome. It is rude, demeaning behavior and is usually about the abuse of power. In fact, sexual harassment psychologically hurts the women involved and the work atmosphere. According to the National Council for Research on Women, women are 9 times more likely than men to quit their jobs, 5 times more likely to transfer, and 3 times more likely to lose jobs because of harassment. There may be serious economic consequences as a result of sexual harassment. A woman's job status may be jeopardized and she may lose wages if she is fired or takes extended leave to avoid the harasser.

The 1994 Merit Systems Protection Board Study of sexual harassment noted that women in traditionally male-dominated occupations such as construction, policing, the military are more likely to be harassed. Additionally, other studies have found that harassment is more commonly found in female-dominated workplaces where majority of women earn low wages and the management is predominantly male.

Victims of sexual harassment may file legal claim even if they (she/he) has tolerated the behavior for fear of retaliation or losing their jobs. The law remains unclear whether a woman "who is not herself the object of sexual harassment might still have a hostile environment claim." Offensive and demeaning behavior does not have to be tangibly detrimental (e.g., wage loss, passed promotion) to the job to be considered sexual harassment.

Employers are responsible for the conduct of supervisors and managers. Employers also have a responsibility to protect their employees from harassment by non-employees (e.g., customers, vendors, suppliers, etc). Managers are liable for sexual harassment between co-workers if they knew or should have known about it and took no steps to stop it. The existence of a company grievance procedure alone does not automatically insulate employers from liability. Employers should also take responsibility to take action against sexual harassment once they are aware it is occurring.

An effective sexual harassment policy stresses the illegality of sexual harassment and delineates a clear and appropriate complaint process while ensuring the confidentiality for the victim. Additionally, such a policy encourages witnesses or victims to report the behavior immediately and mentions that retaliation against persons reporting harassment is illegal and will not be tolerated.

Once finalized, an organization's sexual harassment policy should be distributed to all employees and a copy posted in an accessible and prominent location. Employers should also consider scheduling seminars or workshops on sexual harassment to promote company-wide knowledge of the policy.

Many states have drafted state prevention model policies for employer use. Other employer resources concerning may be obtained from federal employment discrimination enforcement agencies such as the Equal Employment Opportunity Commission (EEOC) and state fair employment agencies, or national organizations combating sexual harassment.

Ignoring problems of sexual harassment can cost the average company up to $6.7 million a year in low productivity, low morale, and employee turnover and absenteeism, not including litigation or other legal costs. Following clear and proactive formal policies against sexual harassment in the workplace is one way to prevent lawsuits and drops in productivity and efficiency.

If possible, and if the harassment is not too severe or violent, directly confronting the harasser may be useful. Also, although having protested is not necessary for a claim, it would strongly strengthen a claim. The following steps have been recommended for women who believe they are sexually harassed:

1. Do the unexpected: Name the behavior. Whatever he's just done, say it, and be specific.

2. Hold the harasser accountable for his actions. Don't make excuses for him; don't pretend it didn't really happen. Take charge of the encounter and let people know what he did. Privacy protects harassers, but visibility undermines them.

3. Make honest, direct statements. Speak the truth (no threats, no insults, no obscenities, no appeasing verbal fluff and padding). Be serious, straightforward, and blunt.

4. Demand that the harassment stop.

5. Make it clear that all women have the right to be free from sexual harassment. Objecting to harassment is a matter of principle.

6. Stick to your own agenda. Don't respond to the harasser's excuses or diversionary tactics.

7. His behavior is the issue. Say what you have to say, and repeat it if he persists.

8. Reinforce your statements with strong, self-respecting body language: eye contact, head up, shoulders back, a strong, serious stance. Don't smile. Timid, submissive body language will undermine your message.

9. Respond at the appropriate level. Use a combined verbal and physical response to physical harassment.

10. End the interaction on your own terms, with a strong closing statement: "You heard me. Stop harassing women."

An employee may also file an internal complaint through the appropriate avenues offered by the organization's policy on sexual harassment if it has one. If the victim is a union member, reporting the harassment to the union steward may garner support and secure a potential ally. According to the National Labor Relations Act, unions must represent and aid their members in stopping sexual harassment, a form of discrimination. There are strict limits on filing grievances. They must be filed with six months of the date of the incident you are complaining about. If the union is uncooperative, the victim may file a complaint (also within those six months) with the NLRB (National Labor Relations Board).

Documenting the harassment is important for use as evidence in a case or complaint. The employee is advised to:

- Photograph or keep copies of any offensive material at the workplace.

- Keep a journal with detailed information on instances of sexual harassment. Note the dates, conversation, frequency of offensive encounters, etc.

- Tell other people, including personal friends and co-workers if possible.

- Obtain copies of one's work records (including performance evaluations) and keep these copies at home.

LEGAL REMEDIES

If an employee decides to file a complaint with an outside agency, it is advisable for the employee to consult an attorney, although one is not required to retain counsel in order to file. Attorney referrals can be obtained by contacting local (e.g., women's centers, rape crisis centers) or national women's organizations, one's union (if member), specialized employee interest groups, law schools, legal aid community services, state Fair Employment Practice (FEP) agencies, or state Equal Employment Opportunity Commission (EEOC) offices. In addition, friends and professional contacts may know suitable attorneys.

The employee is advised to interview all attorneys who may potentially represent him or her. At the very least, any attorney chosen must specialize or have experience in employment discrimination law. Ask the attorney if she/he has prior experience dealing with sexual harassment cases, and what the outcomes of those cases were. Pay attention to the attorney's demeanor and to your "gut" feeling about this person. Once you retain an attorney, pay attention to how she/he treats your case. Are your phone calls returned within a reasonable time frame? Does your attorney take your concerns into consideration as she/he develops your case?

The following remedies are available:

- **Filing your claim with the EEOC (under Title VII of the 1964 Civil Rights Act).** One must file a claim with the EEOC within 180 days of the last incident of harassment to begin the process for obtaining relief under Title VII. An EEOC claim can be filed in a manner to protect the victim's identity. Title VII covers all public and private employers in the United States, as well as U.S. Citizens working for a U.S. company based in a foreign country. Complaints can be filed through EEOC district offices are located across the United States. The Civil Rights Act covers only companies with 15 or more employees. State fair employment agencies (FEP) laws may be more generous and extend to smaller companies.

The EEOC conducts its own investigation of the company or organization. Through the investigation, the EEOC determines whether or not harassment occurred, whether harassment is provable in court, and whether other employees have suffered from sexual harassment as well. Upon finishing the investigation, the EEOC makes a determination. If the EEOC finds in the favor of the victim (agrees one was harassed), it can pursue (settle) the case (happens in less than 1 percent of cases filed) or issue a 'right-to-sue' letter so one or one's lawyer can file a lawsuit independently. If the investigation finds one was not harassed, one can appeal the EEOC's finding.

The EEOC investigation can be lengthy and take over a year. If an employee wishes, he or she can skip the EEOC investigation, but one must at least file a claim with the agency before one can obtain the right to sue letter that allows one to enter court. Few sexual harassment cases get to federal court, and those that do can take years. Victims who win sexual harassment cases in federal court can receive the following remedies: attorneys fees; reinstatement of promotion; compensatory and punitive damages; pay for lost wages and benefits; injunctive relief (changes in workplace policy and practice to prevent future harassment). The amount of damages awarded depends on the size of the company.

- **Employee claim filing under state Fair Employment Practice (FEP) statutes.** States statutes are modeled after Title VII. Most states have a Fair Employment Practice agency located in the state capital that is responsible for enforcing state statutes banning sex discrimination. Most states also have an investigative process that varies. Be aware that some states have weak FEP laws that provide for little or no remedy at all. Time limits for filing claims with FEP agencies range from six months to one year. Most FEP agencies do not protect the victim's identity.

  Filing a common law tort suit allows victims to: receive money for compensatory damages (personal injury, lost wages, or health care expenses), or money from punitive damages (money awarded to victim in order to punish company). Assault and battery or wrongful discharge cases can also file this suit. Confidentiality is not guaranteed, nor is the woman protected from company retaliation.

The EEOC and state fair employment practice agencies will first attempt to settle your case out of court. Dual filing with more than one agency (both EEOC and state or local agency) is also an option. They sometimes work together or share information on cases. But the EEOC has a huge backlog and is likely to refer cases to local agencies or local FEP automatically. If the harassment crosses over into the criminal realm (e.g., sexual assault and rape), an employee may report the incident(s) to the police.

RECENT SUPREME COURT DECISIONS

In the area of sex discrimination, the United States Supreme Court handed down some decisions in June of 1998 which have implications for the purchasing agent or manager in the handling of his office staff. These decisions in effect make it easier for an employee to sue for sexual discrimination. At the same time they provide some insights for how to prevent some problems and liabilities.

On one case, *Faragher v. City of Boca Raton,* the Court placed a heavier burden on the employer to see that sexual discrimination is not occurring in the company or office or place of employment. In this case the charge was that two supervisors had created a sexually hostile atmosphere by uninvited and offensive touching, lewd remarks, and speaking of women in offensive terms. Even though upper management may have issued clear policies, it still may be liable for the harassing acts of supervisory personnel. This is so even though it has no knowledge of such acts. Thus the vicarious liability stated in *Burlington Industries* was reaffirmed. On the other hand, the affirmative defense was also reiterated.

1. Reasonable care to prevent any sexually harassing behavior, and

2. That the employee failed to take advantage of preventive or protective opportunities provided by the employer or to avoid harm otherwise. It should be noted that this affirmative defense is not available to the company if the supervisors' harassment culminates in discharge, demotion, or an undesirable reassignment.

In another case, *Burlington Industries v. Ellerth*, the Supreme Court held that an employee could sue for sexual harassment even though there was no actual job related harm. Indeed, in this case, while the employee refused all of the mid-level manager's advances, she was promoted! The Court noted that under agency law, a master is subject to liability for the torts of his servants committed while acting in the scope of their employment. An employer is liable if it is negligent, if it knew, or should have known, of the tort occurrence. It also is vicariously liable for the tort of an agent who was aided in accomplishing it because of the existence of the agency relations. At the same time, the Court did require that the employee did use effective complaint procedures offered by the company. An employer is subject to vicarious liability to a victimized employee for an actionable hostile environment created by a supervisor with immediate (or successively higher) authority over the employee. When no tangible employment action is taken, a defending employer may raise an affirmative defense to liability or damages, subject to proof by a preponderance of the evidence, see Fed. Rule. Civ. Proc. 8(c). The defense comprises two necessary elements: (a) that the employer exercised reasonable care to prevent and correct promptly any sexually harassing behavior, and (b) that the plaintiff employee unreasonably failed to take advantage of any preventive or corrective opportunities provided by the employer or to avoid harm otherwise.

Caveat Nota: The establishment of effective complaint procedures within the office and company is most desirable and those that have been established should be reviewed for effectiveness. Employees should be given a clear statement as procedures to follow if they feel there has been any harassment. Often a suit can be prevented. While they do not offer a company complete protection, their non-use by the employee may give it a defense. The subject of sex discrimination was given widespread public attention in 1998 with the decision of a federal district court judge dismissing the case brought by Paula Jones against President Clinton for sexual harassment. He was the Governor (Chief Executive) and she was a state employee at the time. One of the grounds of the dismissal was that she suffered no job-related harm; she was not dismissed or punished in any way on the job. This part of the District court's decision has now become most questionable in light of the Supreme Court's decision in the *Burlington Industries* case. The other grounds of the District Court's opinion that there was no sexual discrimination because this was a single act, not a series of acts over time, may have some validity, but hardly should be relied upon since other legal liability may be present from even a single outrageous act.

The employee may still bring other common law actions based on the single act, such as assault or intentional infliction of mental harm. Furthermore, authorities are not in complete agreement that a series of acts is absolutely necessary for sexual harassment.

Caveat Bene: The definition of what actually constitutes sexual harassment is still somewhat "murky" or unclear. Efforts and policies should seek to prevent even single occasions of sexual harassment. The lack of clarity in some aspects of the law combined with some natural interaction in the office between employees makes this a murky and uncertain area of the law.

Supplement to Chapter X

Purchasing Ethics and the Law

MULTILATERAL TREATY ON COMMERCIAL BRIBERY

For 20 years, ever since Congress made it a crime for American citizens to bribe foreign officials, U.S. business leaders have complained of having to fight uphill against competitors. Other industrial countries allow commercial bribery as a necessary part of winning foreign contracts, they pointed out, and some even make bribes tax deductible. Only the United States explicitly outlaws bribery of foreign officials.

Now, after a bruising diplomatic campaign by the past three administrations, the United States has finally scored a major breakthrough—a commitment from the world's other big industrial countries to adopt anti-bribery laws of their own. After arduous negotiations that were completed only at the 11th hour yesterday, the European and Asian members of the 29-nation Organization for Economic Cooperation and Development announced that they had agreed to a treaty setting the end of 1998 as the deadline for each country to adopt the anti-corruption rules.

The pact, to be signed by Cabinet members from the OECD nations in a ceremony here in mid-December, is seen as an important step in leveling the playing field for U.S. and overseas companies seeking contracts with foreign governments. It is a sign of greater willingness by other industrial countries to confront international crime and corruption—the spread of which constitutes a major threat to the global economy. The pact would help keep democratic countries from being weakened by corruption. The pact symbolized the way many countries around the world are coming to grips with the problem by finally acknowledging that it has seriously undermined their economies and the rule of law. The treaty means countries will no longer be rewarding the disease of corruption and are bringing out into the open a taboo that has been undercutting the global economy.

One of the greatest difficulties negotiators had faced was in defining who was a foreign public official. Some countries had objected to including parliamentary officials and officials of political parties. The final sticking point was whether to include legislators and political party leaders among the officials whom it would be illegal to bribe. Some countries, particularly in Europe, resisted the U.S. demand that all be included. U.S. sources said the final bargain includes legislators and party officials in countries with one-party political systems in which the party and the government are essentially identical. Final work on the OECD treaty comes at a time or arising awareness of corruption's cost to advanced and developing nations alike.

The Commerce Department says that since mid-1994, it has cataloged significant allegations of bribery by foreign companies in 139 international commercial contracts valued at $64 billion. U.S. companies lost 36 of those contracts, valued at $11 billion, and the department said this represented only a fraction of total U.S. losses on such contracts. The cost buying influence has escalated, experts say, because with global trade expanding, officials in developing countries are demanding much larger bribes in return for business contracts. The average price of bribery has risen to 10 percent to 15 percent of a contract's value.

The OECD treaty includes these major provisions:

- Member countries will adopt definitions of what constitutes bribery of a foreign official that closely parallel the United States' Foreign Corrupt Practices Act.
- Nations signing the treaty will impose criminal penalties on those who bribe foreign public officials that are comparable to the penalties for bribing public officials in their own countries.
- The proceeds of bribes and the profits of any bribe-induced transactions can be seized and confiscated, again paralleling terms of the U.S. act.

One potential weakness of the OECD treaty is that the legal principles that undergird the treaty define criminal bribery only in terms of illicit payments to public officials "to obtain or retain business." This narrow definition, by excluding other bribes, leaves serious consequences of corruption unaddressed. The definition should include bribes to evade taxes, manipulate the judicial process, or avoid regulations, such as those aimed at protecting the environment or public health and safety. The G-7 leaders should seek an expanded definition of bribery to include in treaty language and in national implementing legislation.

Implementing legislation for the pact is to be before national parliaments by next April and to be adopted by the end of 1998, although supporters concede that new resistance may arise as individual parliaments take up the agreement. Some European business leaders argue that they need the freedom to pay bribes to offset the power of larger U.S. companies and the economic and diplomatic help that those companies often get from their national government. Japan could also be a problem. Its decision-making process is slow, and an OECD source said the Japanese "say it's virtually impossible to get the criminal code changed, it's almost in stone." Except for public pressure, the OECD will have no direct power to see that anti-bribery laws are enforced. It will be a continuing process. OECD will monitor enforcement and assess it. Any deficiencies will be reported.

Supplement to Chapter XXII

Letters of Credit

Documentary letters of credit help reduce the risk of foreign trade transactions. Documentary handling of payments gives the buyer power of disposal over the goods because the documents are handed over only on or after payment. The documents provide the vendor with confirmation that the quantity, quality, and nature of the goods delivered are the same as that determined in the contract. There are two payment types:

1. Payment against documentary collection, including documents against payment. Documents against acceptance.
2. Payment using letter of credit.

The development is based on ICC Uniform Customs and Practice for Documentary Credits (1993 revision) from the International Chamber of Commerce and ensures integrated credit management for exports.

The 1993 revision [of the UCP] came into effect on January 1, 1994. The UCP is a set of standard terms, which only applies if incorporated by reference into a documentary credit. That is not to suggest that few credits adopt the UCP. One commentator has estimated that some 95% of credits worldwide are issued subject to the UCP. For credits which adopt the UCP, Article 5 of the UCC serves merely to fill the lacuna left by the incomplete coverage of the UCP. In other words, the UCP governs on those issues with which it is in conflict with the UCC except for those UCC provisions out of which parties cannot contract.

The UCP is a set of standard terms drafted by bankers for bankers. The very parties documentary credits are designed to serve, exporters and importers, are not directly represented at the drafting table. The Working Group that prepared the revision had ten members—bankers, bank lawyers and two law professors.

The principal changes in the 1993 revision fall into four further categories as follows:

1. a bank's duty to raise all discrepancies;

2. a modified time period for bank examination of documents;

3. a "new" standard for bank examination of documents; and

4. a rule for seeking the waiver of discrepancies.

BANK'S DUTY TO RAISE ALL DISCREPANCIES

Two obligations arise upon receipt of the documents tendered under the credit by the issuing and/or confirming bank (if any) or a nominated bank acting on their behalf. First, the relevant bank must examine the documents to determine whether they conform to the terms of the credit. Second, it must decide what to do if discrepancies are found. The 1993 revision attempts to clarify the banks' duties in each case.

MODIFIED TIME PERIOD FOR BANK EXAMINATION OF DOCUMENTS

Discrepancies in tendered documents are an everyday occurrence. In the great majority of cases the discrepancies are remedied, apparently, by either the beneficiary obtaining changed and conforming documents or the applicant electing to waive the discrepancies.

Previously, a bank had a reasonable time to examine the documents and then had to give its notice of rejection, if any, "without delay." These were cumulative periods. Now a bank still has a reasonable time to examine the documents and still has to give its notice without delay but the examination and the giving of the notice are together subject to the seven banking day limit.

"NEW" STANDARD FOR BANK EXAMINATION OF DOCUMENTS

Article 13(a) now provides two new sentences. "Compliance of the stipulated documents shall be determined by international standard banking practice as reflected in these Articles. Documents not stipulated in the Credit will not be examined by banks."

A RULE FOR SEEKING WAIVERS OF DISCREPANCIES

[I]n the United States this practice of seeking waivers of discrepancies has been described as "a common and perhaps universal banking practice." Applicants waive the discrepancies and accept the documents in about 90% of the cases in which they are consulted, doubtless because most defects are minor and technical. In the words of one of the witnesses, "[this practice] saves everyone a lot of time and trouble." The Court of Appeals in *Bankers Trust* held that such consultation with the applicant was permissible under the UCP and that the time reasonably spent in doing so is to be included in the reasonable time allowed for the examination under the UCP. U.S. practice is the same.

This almost universal practice has not been enshrined in article 14(c).

LETTERS OF CREDIT: TIPS FOR BUYERS

Purchasing managers should pay attention to the following aspects:

1. Before opening a L/C (letter of credit), the buyer should reach agreement with the seller on all particulars of payment procedures, schedules of shipment, type of goods to be sent, and documents to be supplied by the supplier.

2. When choosing the type of L/C to be used, the buyer should take into account standard payment methods in the country of the seller.

3. When opening a letter of credit, the buyer should keep the details of the purchase short and concise.

4. The buyer should be prepared to amend or renegotiate terms of the L/C with the seller. This is a common procedure in international trade. On irrevocable L/Cs, the most common type, amendments may be made only if all parties involved in the L/C agree.

5. The buyer can eliminate exchange risk involved with import credits in foreign currencies by purchasing foreign exchange on the forward markets.

6. The buyer should use a bank experienced in foreign trade as the L/C issuing bank.

7. The validation time stated on the L/C should give the seller ample time to produce the goods or to pull them out of stock.

8. The buyer should be aware that an L/C is not fail-safe. Banks are only responsible for the documents exchanged and not the goods shipped. Documents in conformity with L/C specifications cannot be rejected on grounds that the goods were not delivered as specified in the contract. The goods shipped may not in fact be the goods ordered and paid for.

9. Purchase contracts and other agreements pertaining to the sale between the buyer and seller are not the concern of the issuing bank. Only the terms of the L/C are binding on the bank.

10. Documents specified in the L/C should include those the buyer requires for customs clearance.

STANDBY LETTER OF CREDIT

Standby letters of credit are frequently used as a form of payment guarantee or as payment enhancement in the case of nonperformance under a contractual obligation. Their importance is reflected in their yearly volume, estimated in excess of $300 billion worldwide. The prolific use of standby letters of credit in recent decades has led international bankers to formulate a separate set of rules to govern their use. Those rules were modeled on the UCP and were embodied in the International Standby Practices (ISP).

The International Standby Practices (ISP) provides separate rules for standby letters of credit in the same sense that the Uniform customs and Practice for Documentary Credits and the Uniform Rules for Demand Guarantees do for commercial letters of credit and independent bank guarantees. The ISP reflects standby practice and states it so as to assure the worldwide integrity of standbys.

The need for standby rules has long been apparent. While the UCP did a great deal to reinforce the independence and documentary character of the standby, the UCP is not fully applicable to standbys as is recognized in UCP Article 1. Not only are some provisions inappropriate for standbys (such as the force majeure and installment drawing rules), but many critical issues affecting standbys are not addressed because the UCP understandably focuses on commercial letters of credit.

Even the least complex standbys issued subject to the UCP (those calling for presentation of only a draft) pose problems not addressed by it. More complex standbys (e.g. those involving longer terms or automatic extensions, transfer on demand, requests that the beneficiary issue its own undertaking to another, and the like) require much more sophisticated treatment.

The ISP differs from the UCP in style and approach because its audience is not only bankers and merchants but the broader range of those actively involved in standby law and practice—rating agencies, corporate treasurers and credit managers, government officials, a wide variety of regulators, and a host of other sophisticated users as well as their counsel. Because standbys are often intended to be available in the event of disputes or insolvency, their text is subject to a type of scrutiny not encountered by commercial letters of credit. As a result, the ISP is also written to provide guidance to lawyers and judges in the interpretation of standby practice.

While the ISP is more complex than the UCP, it is intended to make the text of standbys more simple, standardized, and streamlined, and to provide clear and widely accepted answers to common problems. The language of the rules is more precise to make the standby more dependable when a drawing or honor is questioned. Although the ISP can be varied by the text of a standby, it provides neutral rules acceptable in the majority of situations and a useful starting point for negotiations in other situations. It will save parties considerable time and expense in negotiating and drafting standby terms.

The ISP rules are generally consistent with the UCP rules because standby and commercial practices are generally the same. As a result, there are basic similarities with the UCP on fundamental issues. The differences result either from different practices, different problems, or the need for more precision. In addition, the ISP proposes basic definitions should the standby permit or require presentation of documents by electronic means. Since standbys infrequently require presentation of negotiable documents, standby practice is currently more conducive to electronic presentations, and it is expected that the welcome participation of S.W.I.F.T. (Society for World-Wide International Funds Transfer) in the ISP project will accelerate the use of this means of presentation.

Like the UCP and the URDG, the ISP will apply to any independent undertaking issued subject to it. This approach avoids the impractical (and often impossible) task of identifying and distinguishing standbys from independent guarantees and, in many cases, commercial letters of credit and independent guarantees.

The ISP is designed to be compatible with the UN Convention on Independent Guarantees and Standby Letters of Credit and with local law, whether statutory or judicial and to embody standard letter of credit practice under that law. Where these rules conflict with that law on issues such as assignment of proceeds of a letter of credit or transfer by operation of law, applicable law will, of course, control. Nonetheless, most of these issues are rarely addressed by local law and progressive commercial law will often look to the type of balanced solution afforded by the ISP for guidance in such situations, especially with respect to cross border undertakings. As a result, it is expected that the ISP will complement local law rather than conflict with it.

Supplement to Chapter XXV

Buyer's Special Remedies

BANKRUPTCY AND PURCHASERS*

The purchaser may confront many problems when a seller files for bankruptcy. Those general problems as well as some of the specific problems will be discussed. In a society where there are an increasing number of bankruptcies, resulting in a closing of businesses or reorganizations, it is important for the purchasing manager to have both an overall view and specific insights as to his/her rights in a bankruptcy situation. Some background is useful to better understand what bankruptcy is and how it works.

Bankruptcy law proper can be traced back to the days of Roman law. It was transplanted to England in 1592. The early English bankruptcy statutes, which were limited to debtors of an ill-defined "merchant" class, and which provided solely for involuntary petitions, and were viciously punitive from the perspective of the debtor. They tried to prevent the debtor from secreting assets, and they offered no discharge or relief. Bankruptcy law applied only to merchants and the discharge

---

* Acknowledgment: Joseph Keaveny.

given merchants began as an element of a debt collection device that included capital punishment. The death penalty was the stick; the discharge was the carrot. They were part of the same package. A discharge was granted to merchants who were totally honest and forthright with their creditors. However, a merchant that tried to hide assets from the creditors in an effort to avoid paying them were issued severe penalties, up to and including the death penalty.

The discharge for merchant debtors began not as a substantive right, but as a procedural device to facilitate the gathering of evidence about the debtor's assets. Early English bankruptcy could only be started by the creditors; the voluntary bankruptcy petition was unknown. Bankruptcy was a collective remedy that enabled creditors to gather together and divide among themselves assets of a common merchant debtor.

During the 18th century, bankruptcy law underwent a change. Instead of being a way for creditors to overcome a debtor who tried to evade them, it was a way to sort out the affairs of a merchant who failed, but who may have been unlucky rather than dishonest. Non-merchants, on the other hand, could be put in debtor's prison for their inability to pay their bills. Congress passed the first bankruptcy act in 1800 and it was repealed in 1803. The Bankruptcy Act of 1800 was designed to enable the creditors to collect the assets of an insolvent merchant.

There was no bankruptcy statute until 1841. The Bankruptcy Statute of 1841 provided relief for the debtors. It however was repealed in 18 months because it proved unexpectedly favorable to debtors. Another statute was passed in 1867 and still another was passed in 1898. The Bankruptcy Act of 1898 was, however, the first that showed any staying power. It lasted until 1979. The Bankruptcy Act of 1898 accommodated both the creditors' desire for an effective means of gathering and selling the assets of their debtor and the interests of insolvent individuals in securing a discharge for past indebtedness.

A new Bankruptcy Code was passed by Congress in 1978 as part of the Bankruptcy Reform Act of 1978 and became effective in 1979. It confided many of the judicial developments in bankruptcy law. In addition, it created a new bankruptcy court and gave new bankruptcy judges greatly expanded powers.

The history of bankruptcy and insolvency laws has shown the individual's right to discharge past indebtedness and obtain a financial fresh start. This was cut back somewhat in 1984 because of perceived abuses under the 1978 Bankruptcy Code and intense lobbying by consumer lenders. Nevertheless, the basic principle that individuals are entitled to a fresh start has become uncontroversial.

TYPES OF BANKRUPTCY

The two most basic types of bankruptcy for business are Chapters 7 and 11 of the Bankruptcy Code. A Chapter 7 bankruptcy proceeding involves liquidating all of the assets of the debtor and giving each creditor their pro-rata share of the proceeds. This chapter is used when the business is hopelessly insolvent.

A Chapter 11 bankruptcy allows firms that should remain intact to survive, even though their debt obligations need to be dramatically restructured. The three tests that the court will look at in approving a Chapter 11 reorganization are:

1. The plan must be "fair and equitable."
2. The plan must be "feasible."
3. The plan must meet the "best interests of the creditors."

The firm will put together a plan addressing the above criteria, submit it into court, and if the court approves, conduct it into business. In the basic bankruptcy process, the person or corporation in charge of gathering together the assets of the estate and distributing them to the claimants is called the "trustee." The principal duties of the trustee include collecting the property of the estate, reducing it to money, and applying the proceeds to payment of expenses and the claims of creditors, in a specified order. In collecting the property of the estate, the trustee steps into the shoes of the debtor and also the debtor's creditors for many purposes.

It is wrong to simply assume the trustee represents the debtor. In many respects, the trustee can be seen as an agent for the unsecured creditors, and one can state that the basic part of the job of the trustee is to maximize the assets available for payment to general unsecured creditors. This can be substantiated by the fact that, while an interim trustee is appointed by the United States Trustee promptly after a Chapter 7 case is commenced, the unsecured creditors have the power of electing their own, permanent trustee by voting.

In a Chapter 11 (reorganization) case, if a trustee is not appointed, the debtor, as a "debtor-in-possession," continues to operate the business. Much of the process of negotiation in reorganization under Chapter 11 seems to assume that the debtor-in-possession will represent the debtor and negotiate with the creditors.

EXECUTORY CONTRACTS

Section 365 of the Bankruptcy Code deals with the trustee's relations to a particular type of asset: "executory contracts and unexpired leases." The legislative history suggests only that "it generally includes contracts on which performance remains due to some extent on both sides. An executory contract for purposes of bankruptcy is a contract on which performance remains due, to some material extent, on the part of both contracting parties. The failure of either side to fulfill its remaining performance obligations would constitute a material breach. This would justify the other party's failure to complete its unperformed obligations under the contract.

One can see from the brief legislative description of executory contracts that they are nothing more than mixed assets and liabilities arising out of the same transaction. An unperformed contract contains both: an asset (the performance promised by the other side) and a liability (the performance promised to the other side). Once the contract is no longer executory, it means that one (or both) sides have substantially finished their performance.

For example, assume that the contract is that Acme promises to deliver goods to purchaser, who is to pay for them. Once Acme delivers the goods, from Acme's perspective the contract is just as asset. It is an account receivable from the purchaser. The purchaser's obligation to pay Acme is a traditional asset that, if Acme files for bankruptcy, would be brought into the estate.

Conversely, once Acme has delivered the goods, the contract is, from the purchaser's perspective, a liability. The purchaser now simply owes money to Acme. If the purchaser filed for bankruptcy, Acme would need to pursue the path of a general, unsecured creditor of the purchaser in the bankruptcy proceeding.

Before either side has performed, however, both sides have a contingent asset (e.g., the obligation promised by the other side), and a contingent liability (e.g., the obligation promised to the other side). The combination of an unperformed asset and liability in the same contract is the special attribute of an executory contract.

Each party to the contract can choose to perform the contract or breach the contract. If that party decides to breach the contract, they must suffer the consequences under the contract theory that is often espoused. The decision whether to do so will turn on whether the performance one is promised is worth more than the return performance one must give, or conversely, whether that performance is worth less than what one must give in return. Of course, there may in some cases be questions raised as to the lack of good faith in the performance. It may well be that the thought of a right to breach is gradually becoming less accepted.

In the case of *In Re Crippen,* 877 F.2d 594, the Court noted, " While bankruptcy courts have the power to allow debtors to escape burdensome contracts by rejecting them, bankruptcy courts do not have the power to rewrite contracts to allow debtors to continue to perform on more favorable terms."

Outside of bankruptcy, it may not make sense to breach the contract, either because the contract is enforceable by injunction or because one has to consider the damage claim that would result. In some cases, there might be liability for a breach of good faith or fraud, which may result in punitive damages as well.

In a situation such as bankruptcy, however, where the party contemplating breach is insolvent, and a breach will result in a money damage claim, the resulting claim may only be worth a fraction of the face amount and breach by the insolvent party, may be in the best interests of the other creditors. The purchasing manager may find him or herself in any one of several situations. Consider the following examples:

1. Cash Deposit on Goods. The buyer has a contract to purchase 1,000 widgets from seller at $6.00 per widget, to be shipped June 1. The buyer sends a $500 security deposit May 1. The seller files for bankruptcy May 15. On the filing of bankruptcy, the trustee must decide if he will assume the contract or reject it. For buyer's purchasing manager this means that it is up to the trustee to decide if a valid contract exists. This decision will determine whether purchasing manager obtains the widgets from seller of whether purchasing manager must find another source for his/her widgets.

If the trustee must provide the widgets to buyer at a cost that exceeds sale price, he/she will reject the contract. In this case, the buyer would be an unsecured general creditor of vendor. The buyer would have a claim against vendor's bankruptcy estate for the $500 security deposit and any money damage as a result of the breach. He/she would share in the pro-rata distribution with all of the other general unsecured creditors. For the buyer's purchasing manager, this means that he/she must find another source for his/her widgets. He/she may pursue the seller for any damage that resulted from the rejected contract (i.e., increased cost), but realistically, the costs associated with filing suit and the probability of obtaining payment of any awarded judgement would preclude the buyer from pursuing this course.

If the trustee can provide the widgets to the buyer at a cost below the sale price, he/she will assume the contract. In this case, the bankrupt estate will provide the widgets and expect to be paid the balance due of $5,500. This transaction, being profitable, would increase the size of the bankrupt estate for the benefit of the other creditors. For the purchasing manager, this means that he/she will obtain the widgets as though business was being conducting as usual.

2. Prepayment of Entire Contract Price. The seller contracts to sell 1,000 widgets to the buyer at $6.00 per widget and to ship them over a period of time. The buyer prepays the seller the entire contract price. Before any widgets are shipped and before the seller obtains the widgets, the seller files for bankruptcy.

The buyer would have a claim against the seller's bankruptcy estate. It is not an executory contract. The seller could not possibly honor the contract because he/she does not have the widgets on hand to perform the contract. For the buyer's purchasing manager, this means he/she must find another source for his/her widgets and submit a claim to the bankruptcy court for $6,000.00.

3. Title to Machinery Passes When Identified to Contract. The buyer's purchasing manager orders a large piece of machinery from Manufacturer on June 1 and the order is accepted. On June 5, the buyer files bankruptcy. The contract specifies that title will pass when the machine has been identified to the contract and the buyer will pick up machine on June 10. This is not an executory contract.

The machine is really the buyer's and the manufacturer has a claim against the bankruptcy estate as a general creditor. This means that for the purchasing manager of the bankrupt company, the machine will become available to be used as if no bankruptcy had been filed.

However, if the contract stated that the manufacturer retains title until paid in full, the manufacturer would be a secured creditor under the Uniform Commercial Code and be entitled to payment before the general creditors. But for the purchasing manager of the bankrupt company, it would mean that he/she could pick up the machine on June 10 and continue to conduct business as usual.

4. Title to Machinery Passes When Identified to Contract. The buyer's purchasing manager orders a large piece of machinery from Manufacturer on June 1. The manufacturer files for bankruptcy on June 5. The contract specifies that title will pass when the machine has been identified to the contract and the buyer will pick up machine on June 10. The decision to assume or reject the contract would lie with the bankruptcy trustee based on the ability to perform the contract and the overall profitability of the contract.

5. Installment Payment on Delivered Goods. The seller enters into a contract with the buyer on June 1, to sell 100,000 widgets to the buyer at a price of $500,000. The widgets are to be delivered on July 1, and payment is to be made at $100,000 per month for five months beginning August 1. On June 15, the buyer files for bankruptcy. If the seller does not ship the widgets, it is liable for the breach. The danger to the seller is not only for damages, but the breach may be viewed as a termination of the contract and a violation of the automatic stay.

If the seller ships the widgets, and the buyer assumes the contract after shipment, the seller would be paid in full. If the seller ships the widgets, and the buyer rejects the contract, the seller gets a claim against the estate. It is probably a priority claim because the seller put assets into the estate post-bankruptcy. Generally, in a Chapter 7 Bankruptcy, the creditors will file claims with the trustee. The trustee will collect all of the assets of the bankrupt company, liquidate them, pay the secured creditors, and allocate any money leftover to the unsecured creditors.

In a Chapter 11 Reorganization Plan, upon filing of the bankruptcy petition, the status of the company is basically frozen. The company continues to operate. Any business that is transacted after the filing of the petition is as though no bankruptcy was filed and the business as usual. Any business transacted before the filing is the subject of negotiation between the debtor-in-possession and the creditors.

This means for the purchasing manager of a company that is undergoing Chapter 11 Reorganization, his/her credit status should be improved. Any vendor should by comfortable working with a company with a supervised plan to remedy its financial past. It is also a violation of the automatic stay for a company to take retaliatory measures against a company for filing a Chapter 11 Reorganization.

For a purchasing manager of a company that is in a business relationship with a company undergoing a Chapter 11 Reorganization there is a finite amount of exposure. Any previous balance will be the subject of negotiations and any future dealings should be carried on as business as usual.

Obviously, bankruptcy law is a complex matter and the purchasing manager should confirm decisions with corporate counsel.

Supplement to Chapter XXVIII

Computer Purchases and Controversies*

U.C.C. ARTICLE 2B PROPOSALS, AND CURRENT DIGITAL SIGNATURE ISSUES (REPLACES ARTICLE 2B PARAGRAPH ON PAGE 483 OF ORIGINAL TEXT)

The current Article 2 of the Uniform Commercial Code (UCC) is not sufficient to handle transactions involving the sale and licensing of computer software. Under current law, several courts have even held that such transactions involving computer software do not fall within Article 2 of the UCC. These courts hold that such sales are not transactions in goods, but rather are transactions for services. This holding is common when the software contract entails substantial services (i.e., when the contract is for custom designed software).

Software contracts differ from contracts involving ordinary goods in two important features: 1) software contracts transfer intangible goods; and 2) software contracts often entail a license of rights to use rather than a sale. There needs to be a shift from case law to the legislative front to tackle these differences and resolve the problem of the scope of Article 2.

---

*Acknowledgment: Thomas J. Burton, J. D., Saint Louis University.

Early in the 1990s, several studies were conducted to develop uniform law treatment of software contracts, either in or outside the UCC. By 1992, the National Conference of Commissioners on Uniform State Laws (NCCUSL) and the American Law Institute (ALI) had combined forces to form a draft committee to address the issues under a revision of Article 2 of the UCC. After considerable consultation and review with groups in the software and information industry, the Article 2 drafting committee decided to adopt a "hub and spoke" structure for revising Article 2. Under this structure, software licensing and sales would be treated under separate sub-articles ("spokes") of Article 2 ("hub"). The "spokes" would be subject to the general commercial contract law principles of the "hub." However, because of developments in cyberspace technology and other areas, the information industry groups pressured the Draft Committee to drop a separate treatment of software sales under the UCC and focus on the "unique character" of software licensing and other transactions involving information as opposed to actual goods. Under the current structure, Article 2 applies to the "sale of goods" in general, Article 2A covers "leases" of goods, and the proposed Article 2B handles the special treatment of software and information licensing.

WHAT IS AND IS NOT COVERED BY ARTICLE 2B

Software Contracts and Licenses to Use Information

The proposed Article 2B covers software contracts and related agreements to support, maintain, or modify software. The article also applies to licensing of information, which was previously governed by common law and coexisted with copyright law. According to Article 2B, "Information" not only includes software, but also data, text, images, sounds, mask works, and works of authorship. For example, components of multimedia products such as film, music, and books in digital format are "information" within the scope of Article 2B, if they are licensed. While this article certainly encompasses commercial software transactions, a purchasing manager will find that Article 2B provisions also govern the use of information such as supplier catalogs which can be accessed electronically or on-line, but are subject to licensing agreements.

Applicable to Licensing Transactions, But Not to Sales

For transactions involving information other than computer software, Article 2B creates a distinction between transactions involving a license and transactions involving the unrestricted sale of a copy. This leaves undisturbed major segments of the information industry that may not need treatment in a uniform law, such as contracts involving an unrestricted sale of a copy of a book, a newspaper, or even an instruction manual, where use of the copy has not been contractually conditioned. In this situation, the information provider authorizes the sale, but relies on copyright or other law to restrict use of the information in the copy. So a purchasing manager procuring a bound instruction manual from a manufacturer may not be subject to any restrictions on the use of that manual, except as provided under federal copyright laws.

Caveat Nota: Very limited copying of copyrighted material is permissible for teaching purposes under the copyright law's "Fair Use" provision. In determining whether the unauthorized reproduction is a fair use, the court weighs the following factors:

- The purpose and character of the use, including whether such use is of a commercial nature or is for nonprofit educational purposes.
- The nature of the copyrighted work (i.e., is the manual actually for entertainment rather than instructional purpose).
- The amount and substantiality of the portion used in relation to the copyrighted work as a whole; and the effect of the use upon the potential market for or value of the copyrighted work.

Caveat Bene: To avoid copyright law's relatively restrictive rights for production, if a purchasing manager anticipates needing to have extra copies of manuals or needs to reproduce sections from such manuals for training users, the purchasing manager should provide for extra copies of manuals in the original contract.

Where the purchasing transaction involves an intangible (i.e., digital data or images), a license often accompanies the sale of a copy of the licensed subject matter. For example, a purchasing manager may procure the same instruction manual on a diskette or download it from the manufacturer's website. In this instance, Article 2B provisions provide uniform express limits on the rights and privileges to use this licensed information.

With the exception of some limited types of software products noted below, computer software transactions (licenses or sales) are subject to either express or implied limitations on the use, distribution, modification, and copying of the software. The uniform provisions of Article 2B encompasses these important limitations because modern technology makes copying, modification, and other uses of software easier to achieve in forms that can yield commercially harmful results.

Just as a car dealer can choose to structure the disposition of a car as a sale, in which case Article 2 applies, or as a lease, in which case Article 2A applies; so can owners of information structure their transactions as a sale, in which case the common law will apply, or as a license, in which case Article 2B will apply.

Explicit Exclusions

Because Article 2B covers transactions that traditionally were governed by common law, certain exclusions were necessary to corral the broad scope of proposed uniform law. Article 2B-103(b)(1) yields control of rights and remedies of subject matter covered by other U.C.C. Articles. For example, if the purchasing manager's transaction involves only the sale of goods (i.e., computer hardware or accompanying instruction manuals), that subject matter is still governed by Article 2. However, if the sale of goods is bundled with the sale of software or licensed information, the transaction is split. That part of the transaction dealing with software or information, including issues dealing with the media containing the information (i.e., diskettes), its packaging, and its documentation is governed by Article 2B. Alternatively, the purchasing manager and the supplier can agree to have Article 2B, or other applicable law, apply to the transaction as a whole. See Article 2B-103(c)(3).

Generally, bundled software does not include computer programs embedded in the good, and sold as an integral part of that good. If the software is embedded, Article 2 (Sale) or Article 2A (Lease) will apply to the transaction. Article 2B applies to embedded software only if the product is a copy of an embedded program (e.g., a diskette), is a computer (e.g., operating system loaded in memory or on a hard drive), or is a product whose primary purpose is to provide access to the program. For example, if a purchasing manager buys televisions for company video conferencing purposes, that transaction is not governed by Article 2B because the primary purpose of the televisions' embedded software is for video reception and not for software processing. However, this scenario may change as Internet or information processing activities migrate from stand alone computers to cable TV stations. As software is added to future televisions to support their expanding purpose, Article 2B may cover this transaction as well.

Article 2B does not apply if the license or software contract is only a minor part of or is incidental to a services contract or otherwise excluded transaction. The court would not be required to follow a predominate purpose test for this service transaction to determine what law is applied. The court would simply weigh whether it would be too difficult, confusing, and unwieldy to apply Article 2B to that minor part of the transaction that concerns licensed information.

A possible scenario for a purchasing manager may entail specifying in a contract that the vendor deliver the software configuration and diagnostics (licensed information) for the robotic controllers to be installed on the company's assembly lines. The requested data may be used for in-house tracking and be a minor part of the actual procurement and installation of the controllers. On the other hand, if the licensed information was incidental to an otherwise excluded transaction such as blueprints from an architect or legal memo from an attorney, Article 2B would not apply to the underlying service contract. Of course, if the services relate to an independent contractor hired to develop, support, modify, or maintain specialized software (i.e., for the company's data processing system), then Article 2B would govern the contractual relationship since it directly relates to a software contract. Other service contracts for employment or entertainment (i.e., actors or musical groups) are specifically excluded from Article 2B coverage.

Information attributable to core banking, payment, and financial service activities is excluded from Article 2B. Other UCC or federal or state laws govern these activities including electronic money substitutes or payment systems. However, as banks or other institutions enter into fields identical to that of information industries (i.e., online systems such as America OnLine), then Article 2B will govern the licensing of information or software provided. As far as existing or developing state laws related to electronic contracting, Article 2B contract formation rules apply unless an applicable federal regulation preempts (i.e., bank's electronic notarization of contracts govern by Article 2B).

Implicit Limitations (Article 2B Default Rules)

In an attempt to clarify the existing law or industry practice concerning software and information licensing, Article 2B establishes default or fallback rules that will apply if parties do not otherwise contract. The rights in information transferred by a contract are limited to the rights existing at the time of the transfer. Where not expressly limited in the contract, the rights granted include those essential to the licensee's use of the information. So if a purchasing manager licenses a multimedia program containing proprietary photo or art clips, the company has the right to transfer and modify the media to fit into company business proposals unless the licensor of the software has expressly excluded modification rights.

Another default rule provides that the licensee has no rights to updates, maintenance, or improvements unless that has been specifically provided in the contract. In addition, if a license does not identify the number of simultaneous users, Article 2B calls for a commercial reasonableness test to be used to determine the allowable number of users. That test requires a court to look at what number of users is reasonable in light of the commercial circumstances existing at the time the licensing agreement was formed. Under this test, simultaneous users are multiple users accessing the same computer program from different computer terminals. The program may have been copied for each desktop computer or loaded on a central server where multiple users can separately access the program (i.e., a network site license for a word processing program). For example, a purchasing manager may buy the latest Microsoft Windows Word program (i.e., word processing application) with the intention of placing in on a network for the company's hundred employees to use. However, if the license does not specify the number of simultaneous users under the site license contract, then the court may view the commercial standard to be ten users for a normal site license contract. As unlikely as this is to occur, the purchasing manager should still ensure that the desired number is specified. Likewise, any claims to future updates or corrections must be specified in the contract.

In other cases, Article 2B default rules are used to reflect a public policy choice rather than industry practice, and parties who do not contract around them will be bound by that choice. For example, although the software industry routinely excludes consequential damages, the default rule in Article 2B, as in law traditionally, makes consequential damages available to an aggrieved party. So if Microsoft does not explicitly preclude against consequential damages on its software shrink-wrap license or in its contract with a purchasing manager, the company may be liable for damage to a computer system resulting from the installation of its latest software operating system.

Electronic Contract Formation and Validation

One of the primary goals of the drafters of Article 2B was to provide uniform contract formation and validation rules for the now prevalent electronic commerce practices. Currently, electronic contracting may not be effective under common law or under Article 2 or 2A. Article 2B provides "electronic" provisions to handle issues relating to writing, signature, and manifesting assent requirements for an electronic contract. In keeping with statutes of fraud requirements, Article 2B expands the idea of a writing and a signature to include, respectively, a record and an authentication. A record is defined to be information stored on a tangible or electronic medium (i.e., on a diskette or in computer memory) and retrievable in perceivable form. Authentication of the record calls for some sort of electronic symbol, sound, or record encryption that substitutes for a signature. To manifest assent to a record or electronic contract, the accepting party or electronic agent must have an opportunity to review the record or be knowledgeable of it before authenticating the record. The accepting party can also demonstrate assent by affirmatively responding to instructions provided in the record, including terms that indicate that the person or agent had an opportunity to decline. For example, an affirmative response by a vendor to purchasing manager's E-mail procurement request for computer software upgrades and instructions for accepting the offer would be an enforceable electronic contract under Article 2B.

Article 2B does not dictate the attribution procedure for establishing that an electronic authentication, record, message, or performance is that of the respective party or for detecting changes or errors in content. Article 2B simply requires that the attribution procedures, whether established by agreement or adopted by the parties or whether established by default state law or regulation, be commercially reasonable. This requirement protects parties who lack knowledge of technology, and prevents a dominating party from overreaching in establishing attribution procedures in the negotiation process. For instance, assume Boeing's attribution procedures with its major aircraft parts suppliers did not require any security devices, and relied only on a vendor's E-mail address as an authentication identifier. An outside hacker cracks the computer system and uses the procedure to cause unwanted parts to be ordered, manufactured, and delivered, resulting in huge losses to Boeing's suppliers. The suppliers would be liable for those losses unless the procedures were deemed commercially unreasonable. Commercial unreasonableness is gauged on the agreement, the current technology, the types of transactions affected by the procedure, and other variables. Using these factors, it is likely that Boeing's attribution procedure would be deemed unreasonable and that the company would be accountable for the losses.

Caveat Nota: Although the commercial reasonableness test called for in Article 2B balances the bargaining power between a dominate party contracting with a less powerful buyer, a purchasing manager should still be knowledgeable of the security or attribution procedures identified in a contract. Should the contract not identify an attribution procedure, the purchasing manager, wishing to contract electronically, should be aware of any applicable law or regulation for electronic contracting within the state where the licensor resides. As of July 1998, sixteen states have passed digital or electronic statutes, and eighteen other states are considering similar legislation.

As previously noted, Article 2B authorizes an "electronic agent" or automated computer system to bind a human principal in a contract formation where the automated system has been affirmatively selected, used, or programmed for the purpose of automatically initiating or accepting offers. The terms of the contract are determined under Article 2B-207, but do not include terms provided by the requesting individual in a manner to which the electronic agent could not react. For example, a purchasing manager may electronically tap into a supplier's online sales and inventory computer system to order parts. By clicking on the appropriate menu selections, a purchase order can be completed. The purchasing manager chooses to add a color designation to a part by typing "blue only" after the item name. The supplier's automated system, which is not set up to recognize a color designation, orders the part in green. There is still a contract under Article 2B as the additional condition is ineffective. Conditions clearly outside the capability of the electronic agent to respond does not eliminate the contract reached to automatically request shipment.

Caveat Nota: A purchasing manager who wants an additional condition added to an electronic order with a vendor, should decline or void the automated standard form that has been accessed. Instead, the purchasing manager should either print the form and write in the condition that the electronic agent could not handle, or call the vendor and speak to someone who can accept the special request.

Article 2B handles other unique issues associated with electronic commerce. Where an on-line vendor automatically provides direct marketing to the world through Internet, Article 2B provides that the state law where the licensor's chief executive office is located governs. Otherwise, the vendor would have to comply with the law of fifty states and 170 countries since it will often not be clear where the information is being sent. Some states or countries mandate such compliance through local laws, such as for example, recent amendments to California warranty law applicable to the sale of goods. The Article 2B drafters favor opting for a more stable and identifiable choice of law to facilitate electronic commerce in digital products.

On the other hand, Article 2B combats forum shopping by a licensor operating on the Internet. Article 2B requires that the law of the U.S. location with the most significant relationship to the licensor be used in lieu of the licensor's foreign location when that foreign country's laws place the licensee at a significant disadvantage.

Caveat Bene: A purchasing manager can still provide in a contract that a given state's laws are to be applied in the event of a legal dispute.

Article 2B electronic commerce provisions do not change the substantive content of state statutes or regulations, such as whether a disclaimer can ever be made, what language must be used, and like issues. There are hundreds of potentially relevant statutes that may affect electronic commerce. For transactions governed by Article 2B, the rules of this Article ordinarily supplant the other law (except for certain consumer transactions) as to contractual issues in full and the express preemption for state electronic commerce laws in this article is not necessary.

Shrink-Wrap License and Screen Licenses

Standard forms, including shrink-wrap licenses, are commonly used in commercial and mass-market software transactions. Article 2B provisions govern the enforceability and use of such forms in contract practice. When the process of drafting a law on software licensing began, the validity of shrink-wrap licenses, where the license can only be read after the software is acquired, was in some doubt. Shrink-wrap software is so named because it is often mass-produced and packaged in shrink-wrap cellophane with instructions that indicate opening the package and use of the software constitutes acceptance of the "license" contract inside the box. Of course, one cannot read the license and the rights that it grants or excludes until after the purchase and unwrapping of the product. Ironically, this purchase by the buyer is considered a conduct-based license containing non-negotiated terms. To sustain the enforceability of shrink-wrap licenses, software licensors argue that it is impractical to negotiate and execute a new agreement for each individual software license, especially when mass-market transactions are so prevalent. On the other hand, consumer advocates and others have expressed concern over the use of standard form licenses in mass-market transactions, since consumers may be forced to adhere to surprising or unreasonable terms.

However, there is now some case precedent upholding the validity of shrink-wrap licenses. The U.S. Court of Appeals for the Seventh Circuit held that shrink-wrap licenses are enforceable, unless their terms are objectionable under general contract principles. *ProCD Inc. v. Matthew Zeidenberg and Silken Mountain Web Services Inc.,* 86 F3d 1447 (7th Cir. 1996). Whether this case precedent will be followed in the other circuits is not yet known. Article 2B adopts this recent case law and validates shrink-wrap licenses. Following the test set forth in Section 211 of the Restatement (Second) of Contracts, Article 2B provides that a surprising or oppressive term will not be enforced unless the term was brought to a party's attention and consent was obtained. Article 2B further provides that a party will be bound by the terms of a standard form if it manifests assent to the terms of the form within a reasonable time after using the information or commencing performance under the agreement. For mass-market licenses that include shrink-wrap licenses, terms that are inconsistent with customary industry practices or that conflict with previously negotiated terms may only become part of an agreement if the party that did not prepare the form manifests assent to the terms. According to Article 2B, mass-market or shrink-wrap licenses are to be interpreted according to an objective standard where the terms of the license are to be interpreted whenever reasonable as treating all similarly situated parties in a similar fashion without regard to their knowledge or understanding of the terms of record.

Caveat Nota: Therefore, as long as a software licenser does not exclude a right in the use of the software that would appear to be outlandish within the industry (i.e., preclude use of spell-check function in purchased word processor program), a shrink-wrap license would be considered enforceable.

Caveat Bene: The purchasing manager can override the shrink-wrap license by forming a special contract with the software licensor prior to acceptance of packaged software products.

In a similar fashion, Article 2B supports the enforcement of "screen" or "click-wrap" licenses. These licenses are contracts formed entirely over the Internet. A buyer surfing the Internet encounters a seller's website where the seller's products are advertised. The buyer clicks on a button to indicate a desire to purchase a particular item. The seller's standard license for the product is then displayed on the screen with the option to accept or reject the purchase accordingly. According to Article 2B, if the buyer selects the "I agree to the terms" option, a contract is formed.

Liability for Software Viruses

Article 2B does not expressly allocate liability for introducing a virus into a software program or computer system. Article 2B Reporter notes that there is currently no case law under Article 2 addressing allocation of the risk of viruses between parties to a contract. Instead, liability is deferred to "The Computer Fraud and Abuse Act," 18 USC §1030, which imposes criminal liability for knowingly introducing viruses or harmful code into the computer system of another and causing damage.

Furthermore, software licensers typically warrant that their software is virus free.

Caveat Nota: The purchasing manager should check with a vendor before purchasing software to see if a virus free warranty is provided in the license, especially if the software has a shrink-wrap license where the license terms can not be read until after purchase of the product. If the vendor has not provided such a warranty with the product, the purchasing manager should ask that one be added via a contractual letter from the vendor prior to purchase of the software.

Consequently, the proposed Article 2B, does not treat viruses as a warranty issue. The drafters also reason that the risk of introduction of viruses comes from both sides of the agreement. Viruses may be contained in software or may be introduced when the software is loaded onto a licensee's system.

ATTRIBUTION PROCEDURES AND USE OF DIGITAL SIGNATURE TECHNOLOGY

As previously discussed, the drafters of proposed Article 2B call for an "attribution procedure" to be used to verify the source (i.e., signer) and content (i.e., writing) of an electronic message. While Article 2B drafters have outlined steps to allow for validating electronic commerce and avoiding issues of fraud, they have also been careful not to require that a specific technology (i.e., digital signatures) be used in an attribution procedure. In fact, an attribution procedure may include algorithms, codes, identifying words or numbers, encryption, callback procedures, or any other reasonable security device. With an open-ended definition of attribution procedure and authentication, the proposed Article 2B does not discourage technological innovations that may lead to a superior method for validating an electronic transaction between two parties. However, after more than a decade of scientific research, digital signature technology has been proven to be a secure means to ensure the authenticity and integrity of electronically generated communications as denoted under Article 2B. Purchasing managers who contract over an open, non-secure computer network like the Internet will find it necessary to use available digital signature technology to avoid fraud and any misunderstandings in transactions with vendors, especially when the purchasing manager and vendor have had no prior dealings.

Digital signatures, like their written counterparts, are able to identify the sender by linking the authenticated document back to the signor. By going through the motions of digitally signing, the sender formalizes the agreement, evidences his approval of the agreement, and signals the legal significance of electronically signing. The signatures also protect the documents, which become difficult to alter by third parties that may intercept the digitally signed document. Because messages on the Internet are not sent over a single pathway, but are transmitted over a series of thousands of networks, a message must move from network hub to the next network hub on the Internet before reaching its final destination. The result is that any person with access to any intermediate hub, can intercept, read, or alter an electronic message in a way that is undetectable by the recipient. With the passage of a digital signature act or its equivalent, states have a mechanism for protecting and enforcing digitally signed contracts.

A digital signature is not a scanned replica of a handwritten signature. A digital signature consists of an encrypted or mathematically scrambled document with a string of characters appended to the message that serve to identify the sender and the integrity of the document. Only someone with the proper software can decode the message. Digital signatures are typically generated using a public key or an asymmetric cryptosystem. Asymmetric cryptosystem is based on the use of two software codes, or "public/private" key pair, to send and receive documents. The "private" key is kept secret by its owner and is used to encode the text of a document into the digital signature. The "public" key is made publicly available to persons who may be dealing with the owner or sender of the document and who need to decode the transmission. The public and private keys are mathematically related, but the relationship is so complicated that it is "computationally infeasible" to deduce one key solely from knowledge of the other key. The keys are such that the digital signature created by one key can only be decrypted by the other key. Hence, when used in conjunction with one another, the public/private key system provides complete security.

The following is an example of how a purchasing manager may use digital signature technology to contract with a vendor over the Internet. First, the purchasing manager would need to have purchased the appropriate software and been given a key pair from that software company. SafenSigned software from SecuriSys Corporation is an example of a commercially available digital signature software package. SafenSigned consists of two programs, the SafenSigned File Signer and the Safen-Signed Verifier. After filling out a standard electronic purchase form, the purchasing manager would digitally sign the completed form using the his or her private key (i.e., use selections under SafenSigned File Signer program to digitally sign the appropriate file to be sent over the Internet). This will verify the identity of the purchasing manager because the message will require the purchasing manager's public key for decryption. Next, the purchasing manager then encrypts (i.e., scrambles with unique signature) the document using the recipient's public key, before sending it to the vendor. This is to ensure that only the recipient can read the message. If the purchasing manager wished to broadcast a digitally signed offer to purchase to several vendors, the preceding step would be skipped. The vendor or recipient, upon receiving the document, would then decipher the purchase order form using the recipient's private key and verify the signature using the purchasing manager's public key (i.e., uses SafenSigned File Verifier program to check the digital signature). A successful verification of the digital signature ensures that the purchase order form is truly from the purchasing manager and has not been modified in the distribution channel, either by accident or by malicious attempt. The vendor can assent to the order by following the same steps taken by the purchasing manager. Following Article 2B guidelines, this sequence could be identified in an attribution procedure (i.e., security procedure for signing and authenticating documents) that the purchasing manager and vendor(s) have previously agreed to be enforceable means of authenticating their transactions. Alternatively, depending on the state law of choice, the sequence could also be an enforceable agreement under the state's electronic signature laws. As noted below, those states with comprehensive digital signature laws would require that a licensed certification authority authenticate the transaction to make it an enforceable agreement.

ELECTRONIC NOTARIES OR CERTIFICATION AUTHORITIES

The major problem with the public/private key system is verifying that the sender of the document is who they say they are. The recipient can verify that the message is from the sender by verifying the signature with the sender's public key, but if key pairs are not licensed to any specific individual, the recipient has no way of verifying the actual identity of the sender. If you cannot relate the public key to a real person you can trust, you still cannot trust the document. This is analogous to the situation where you have received a properly signed check but still cannot tell whether or not the check is good, because you do not know what the account holder's signature looks like. This is the reason a digital signature should be notarized. According to the American Bar Association's Guidelines on Digital Signatures, "Some convincing strategy is necessary to reliably associate a particular person or entity to the key pair."

States that have passed comprehensive legislation (e.g., Utah) license and extensively regulate the activities of certification authorities (CAs). The licensed CAs perform substantially the same function as a notary would for written documents, except now that role has exploded as business transactions have moved to the Internet to take advantage of its efficiencies. Generally, a digital signature notarization service issues a digital certificate that ties the registered private/public key pair with the identity information of its owner. The digital certificate is signed by the issuer's digital signature and can be verified using the issuer's public key, which is usually well publicized. This certificate is made publicly available in a "repository" maintained by the CA or someone else. A recipient of a digitally signed message will access the certificate and determine that a public key is associated with a private key possessed by a certain person (i.e., the program manager), obtain a copy of that public key, and then use that public key to decrypt the digitally signed message the recipient (i.e., vendor) received. After verifying both the signature on the message and the certificate notarizing the signature, the party is ensured that the message is truly from the person identified by the information included in the notary certificate. In addition to being a reliable method of identifying the source of an electronic message, a digital signature is also very good evidence that the message has not been tampered with since transmission. Any alteration of a digitally signed message will cause the public key to fail to decipher the digital signature, thus indicating to the recipient that the message has been tampered with since it was digitally signed. Hence, assuming that the CA has effectively verified the identity of the person associated with a public key (i.e., program manager) and assuming that person has exercised reasonable care to prevent the loss or compromise of the private key, the use of digitally signed documents provides an extraordinarily reliable method of validating both the source and the content of an electronic contract.

SecuriSys Corporation provides a certification authorization for its SafenSigned customers. A purchasing manager who has subscribed with SecuriSys and wants to certify his or her digital signature would follow the steps outlined on the company's website, http://www.securisys.com. Essentially, the program manager pays a fee to have SecuriSys verify the public/private key assigned to him or her. A digital certificate is then issued to the program manager. After this, every file the program manager signs will contain a copy of the certificate. The program manager's signature will then be shown as "Notarized" in the SafenSigned File Verifier and will be treated as "Trusted" even if the user has never seen your signature before and has not marked your signature as "Trusted." Because SecuriSys is not necessarily licensed as a certification authority in every state, the company offers the following disclaimer to those relying on its certification: "SecuriSys makes no warranty on the accuracy of the information nor the trustworthiness of the holder of the digital signature notarized. The relying party is advised to use his/her own judgement in deciding whether or not to trust a signature based on the information contained in the digital certificate and other information available. SecuriSys Corporation and its signature notarization services are not responsible for any damages caused by relying on their certificates."

STATE LEGISLATION ADDRESSING THE USE OF DIGITAL SIGNATURES

Over two-thirds of the states have already enacted some form of legislation pertaining to the use of digital signatures. Those states have followed either broad initiatives similar to those outlined in Article 2B, or the more comprehensive Digital Signal Guidelines published by the American Bar Association which specifies the use of digital signatures and ignores other future technological advancements.

The legislation enacted in states such as Florida, Illinois, and Kansas have followed the broader, less governmentally regulated approach to digital signature legislation similar to that proposed by the drafters of the uniform Article 2B act. Such state electronic signature statutes generally provide that an "electronic record" satisfies any rule of law requiring information to be "written" or "in writing." Furthermore, it states that an "electronic signature" satisfies any rule of law requiring a signature. Like Article 2B, these state statutes do not authorize electronic signatures for non-contract based documents such as wills, trusts, powers of attorney, negotiable instruments, or instruments of title. States that have followed this approach recognize the imperfect nature of the technology but also recognize the same is true of written signatures. For instance, the accuracy of expert written signature analysis is dependent on the quality and quantity of the subject's writing samples. Therefore, the ability to authenticate a written signature and link it back to its owner is limited as well. Because of this limitation, common law places the burden of proving the signature's authenticity on the one attempting to enforce the agreement.

Caveat Nota: If a purchasing manager is contracting with a new vendor that has not agreed to a attribution procedure and who resides in a state that does not require certification authorities to authenticate digital signatures, the purchasing manager is advised to print and validate the document with the vendor for evidentiary purposes before assenting to any order. Likewise, if the value of the contract is significant, the purchasing manager may want to get the printed document notarized. In the event of a breach of contract, this will facilitate the purchasing manager who wants to enforce the agreement.

On the other hand, Utah's statute is modeled after the ABA guidelines and calls for strict regulation of private/public key pairs and licensing of certification authorities. Because the Utah statute requires key pairs to be certified, the statute creates the legal presumption that a document with a digital signature was signed by the person registered to use that signature. This places the onus on the individual assigned a digital signature to ensure that the private key does not fall into the possession of someone else. Thus, Utah and other states have made a decision to shift the burden of proof to the holder of the digital signature to challenge its authenticity, rather then the party seeking to enforce the agreement. The rationale for this shift, according to ABA guidelines, is that "a person relying on a digital signature generally has less access to evidence of the authenticity of the signature than the signature's owner."

States implementing comprehensive digital signature laws have also limited the potential liability of certification authorities. For example, the Utah statute specifically prohibits plaintiffs from collecting punitive damages or damages resulting from lost profits and pain and suffering. In addition Utah also allows certification authorities to set their own "reliance limits" or damage limitations. The rationale for providing these liability limitations is to encourage the formation of certification authorities by protecting their various tort liabilities.

Caveat Nota: Until a uniform law like Article 2B is passed by the states, a purchasing manager needs to consult with in-house counsel about state digital signature statutes where the company's vendors reside, especially when electronically contracting with a new vender who has no prior dealings with your company. This is important for ascertaining enforceability and liability issues. In addition, in keeping pace with technological innovations, the state of the new vendor may have adopted a new technology for authenticating electronic transactions. The amendment could have a bearing on the enforceability of any future agreements with the respective vendor.

Caveat Nota: Although a lot of the wrinkles and concerns with the earlier Article 2B drafts have been ironed out, neither the National Conference of Commissioners on Uniform State Laws nor the Drafting Committee have as yet passed or accepted the article in its present form. Until Article 2B is officially accepted, purchasing managers are cautioned about relying on the uniform laws set forth in the proposed article.

The following sources were used in writing this section, and may be referenced for additional information:

Henry Beck, *Uniform Commercial Code Article 2B Licenses,* 517 PLI/Pat 287 (1998). The latest draft of Article 2B can be found at http://www.law.uh.edu/ucc2b, a website maintained by the Reporter for Article 2B, Dean Raymond T. Nimmer, Leonard Childs Professor of Law, University of Houston.

Holly K. Towle, *Proposals to Change the Uniform Commercial Code—Article 2B,* 510 PLI/Pat 233 (1998).

Craig Joyce et al., Copyright Law, (3rd ed. Supp. 1997).

R. J. Robertson, Jr., *Electronic Commerce on the Internet and the Statute of Frauds,* 49 SCLR 787 (1998).

Anthony M. Singer, *Electronic Commerce: Digital Signatures and The Role of the Kansas Digital Signature Act,* 37 WBNLJ 725 (1998).

SecuriSys Corp., *SafenSigned Home Page* (visited July 13, 1998) <http://www.securisys.com>.

Richard Raysman et al., *Devising a Framework for Software Licensing,* 12/10/96 N.Y.L.J. 3, (col. 1) (1998)

Martin H. Samson, *Click-Wrap Agreement Held Enforceable,* 6/30/98 N.Y.L.J. 1, (col. 1) (1998).

Supplement to Chapter XXXI

Purchasing from Foreign Vendors

COUNTERTRADE

When the Soviet Union disintegrated and the market economy system prevailed in central and eastern Europe, many experts thought that countertrade in all its many forms, from sophisticated swaps to downright barter, would go into terminal decline. It did not happen.

New forms of countertrade have emerged. The practice is responding to changed needs by taking on different forms and moving into new regions and relationships. Emerging Asian markets, like Indonesia and Thailand, have developed official countertrade policies. Offset deals—the term used when governments impose countertrade conditions on procurement contracts such as defense deals—are now widely practiced in Western Europe, North America, and the Middle East.

Many of the former centrally planned economies of Eastern Europe are exploring variations on barter as a way of overcoming their lack of foreign exchange to pay for imports from the West. Latin American countries have led the way in debt/equity swaps, which can be considered a form of "financial countertrade." The two most common types of countertrade are known as "counterpurchase" and "compensation" trade. Another less common form is switch trading.

COUNTERPURCHASE

In a counterpurchase arrangement, a private firm agrees to sell products to a sovereign nation and to purchase from the nation goods that are unrelated to the items that it is selling. For example, in a series of transactions between a major U.S. manufacturer of commercial aircraft and the government of Indonesia, the U.S. firm sold jet aircraft to Indonesia and agreed to purchase substantial quantities of Indonesia crystal glassware, cutting tools, leather coats, and canned hams.

In a counterpurchase transaction, each party is paid in currency upon the delivery of its products to the other party. It is common in such transactions for a private firm to be allowed a period of time following the delivery of the goods that it is selling in which to fulfill its purchase obligation. Periods of from three to five years, for example, are not uncommon in counterpurchase obligations imposed by some nations.

Private firms resort to a variety of methods to dispose of goods which they are forced to purchase, but most frequently resell these goods to trading companies or directly to end users, often at a discount. Sometimes the private firm will resell the countertraded goods at a price below that which it paid for them, seeking to offset this loss by larger profits generated by the sale of its own product to the nation.

COMPENSATION

The most common form of countertrade is referred to as "compensation" or "buy-back." In a compensation transaction, a private firm will sell equipment, technology, or even an entire plant to a sovereign nation and agree to purchase a portion of the output produced from the use of the equipment or technology. Compensation transactions frequently involve significantly longer periods of time during which the private firm will be permitted to fulfill its purchase obligation than in counterpurchase. In addition, compensation transactions are generally of larger dollar value than counterpurchase transactions.

Unlike counterpurchase transactions, the products that the private firm purchases in compensation trade are frequently of marketable quality and in demand in the international marketplace. Further, Western firms frequently are able to negotiate a purchase price for the output that is below the world market price so that the firm can earn a profit in reselling the product that it is forced to buy.

SWITCH TRADING

A switch trade is a device used to balance a bilateral clearing agreement. In a bilateral clearing arrangement between Romania and Brazil, for example, Romania may have taken more products from Brazil than Brazil has taken from Romania at the end of the clearing period. In this instance, Brazil will have a "credit" in its "clearing account," or as is frequently described, a surplus of Romanian "clearing dollars." The problem will arise when there are no available Romanian products which Brazil is interested in taking. In the switch trade, Brazil will locate a third party that is interested in purchasing Romanian goods and substitute the third party's purchase of Romanian goods in satisfaction of its own purchase obligation. Technically, Brazil sells its "clearing dollars" to the third party, and the third party uses these credits to pay for exports from Romania. Brazil sells the credits at a discount—discounts of up to 30 percent are not uncommon—and receives hard currency from the third party. It is common for a trading intermediary to assist Brazil in locating the third-party purchaser. This intermediary, known as a "switch trader," would generally receive a portion of the discount for its services.

Chapter XXXIA

Purchasing under World Trade Organization and Regional Integration Arrangements*

BASIC SYSTEMS

Purchasing in these modern times, and even more so in the future, may be affected by developments beyond the borders of the United States. Indeed, even some purchases may be made outside these boundaries. It is important for the purchasing manager to have some understanding of the new systems that affect our trade and pricing.

There are two major systems affecting trade that exist in the world today. One is sometimes called "multilateral." This means that nations throughout the entire world have reached some agreement as to the regulations that may or may not be placed upon the trade, customs and tariffs, and pricing of goods. The "multi" aspect means many nations are

---

* Acknowledgment: Lingling Zou, J.D., Saint Louis University, Member of New York Bar.

involved. The "lateral" aspect means that there is a web of connections between all the various nations throughout the world.

Within this worldwide system of multilateralism, there is some flexibility. For example, different standards may be set for developed, developing, and underdeveloped countries. Also in some situations, plurilateral agreements are allowed. "Pluri" means many but not all and "lateral" means connection. Under such specific agreements, those countries that want to be a part of it consent to it. Other multilateral countries may abstain.

The second major system is called "regional." This is simply a group of countries in a particular region of the world that has formed a system which affects trade, customs and tariffs, and pricing of goods. Such systems may go even further and regulate the quality of goods and set common standards. It is possible, though more rare, for such systems to be even more extensive and set standards for consumer rights and human rights and establish freedom of movement across borders, a common currency, and supernatural government. The European Union is an example—the term "regional" means countries in a given region of the world, but not necessarily all of the countries of that region. Also there may be differing views of what constitutes a region. For example, while NAFTA has Canada, the United States, and Mexico as members, they have been considering the admission of Chile to membership.

MULTILATERALISM OR REGIONALISM?

The post-World War II world economy witnessed two trends: multilateralism and regionalism. On one hand, the world economy has largely been based on the three pillars—IMF (International Monetary Fund), the World Bank, and GATT (General Agreement on Trade and Tariffs). These multilateral frameworks for economic relations have contributed greatly to modern economic growth. During this period, there developed an attitude that multilateral approach of trade liberalization is better than a regional approach, which could become the basis of trade conflicts.

No doubt the integration process of the global economy will continue as advances in industrial technologies lead to greater efficiencies and economies of scale. The conclusion of the trade talks between most of the nations of the world, called the Uruguay Round trade talks, resulted in a new worldwide trade treaty. It also served to create the WTO (World Trade Organization). These are great steps toward furthering global economic integration. More important, WTO trade rules extend to new areas not covered by GATT such as trade in services, trade-related investment measures, and trade-related intellectual property rights.

On the other hand, regional economic integration started early and has become stronger even as global economic interaction is growing tremendously. Both GATT and WTO contemplated the co-existence of global and regional trade arrangements. Article 24 of the GATT sets out the conditions under which its contracting parties allowed to establish FTAs (free trade areas) with other contracting parties. Basically, GATT requires that FTAs may lower trade barriers among themselves, but may not raise trade barriers against non-members. However, the GATT requirements have been weakly applied. Of the more than 60 preferential trade agreements referred to GATT under Article 24 since 1947, none has been ruled in violation of GATT, despite the fact that many of them are discriminatory against non-members of the region.

Caveat Nota: In seeking the best prices, it is necessary to bear in mind the possible differing tariffs between the multilateral and regional systems. Regional economic integration is not a new phenomenon. The modern idea of an economically integrated Europe grew up during the final phases of World War II, first taking shape as the European Coal and Steel Community in 1951 and finally pinnacled as the European Union (EU). The North American Free Trade Agreement (NAFTA) is the expansion of the earlier United States-Canada Free Trade Agreement.

Countries of Africa, Asia, and Latin America also fashioned regional integration arrangements (RIAs) to promote economic and political cooperative self-determination. In Africa, there are the East African Common Market and the South African Development Community that started in 1992. In Asia, there is the Association of Southeast Asian

Nations (ASEAN) and also the South Asian Association for Regional Cooperation that began operations in 1985. Joint development plans have also been initiated in Northeast and Central Asia. The concept of "Great China" economies also caught the imagination of many business people. In the southern Pacific, Australia and New Zealand signed a treaty for "Closer Economic Relations," which establishes a free trade area between the two countries.

Latin America and the Caribbean are replete with their own subregional integration schemes that differ from each other and from either NAFTA or the EU. Some have a rather elaborate institutional structure, such as the Andean Pact countries (Bolivia, Colombia, Ecuador, Peru, and Venezuela), while others are more akin in their structure to NAFTA, such as MERCOSUR (the Southern Cone Common Market, consisting of Argentina, Brazil, Paraguay, Uruguay, and Chile) formed in 1991. In addition, there are other subregional groupings: the Central American Common Market (1960), made up of Costa Rica, El Salvador, Guatemala, Honduras, and Nicaragua and the Caribbean Community and Common Market (1973) with thirteen members (eight of which formed the Organization of Eastern Caribbean States). Over and above these subregional groupings is the Latin American Integration Association (ALADI), established in 1980, with eleven members each belonging to one or another of the subregional groups.

The process of regional integration will continue in the Western Hemisphere as the Northern and Southern Americas expand existing integration arrangements and create new ones. Many of these Latin American trade groups believe their futures lie with NAFTA and actively seek integration with NAFTA. The "Summit of the Americas" initiative is a plan of action to extend NAFTA that is already under discussion with Chile and Argentina. Chile has negotiated free trade agreements separately with Mexico in 1991 and Canada in 1996, and the MERCOSUR countries in 1996.

Other legal mechanisms could also be used to achieve the same result. For example, third world countries, whether from Latin America or Asia, may accede directly to the NAFTA. The NAFTA may merge with existing or newly formed Western Hemispheric RIAs. Indeed, as mentioned previously, regional economic integrations are not limited to geographic confines. Intercontinental integration is also under way. The United States already has a free trade agreement with Israel and may enter into free trade agreements with Australia and New Zealand. The EU may form alliances with MERCOSUR or Southeast Asian countries. In recent years, Asia-Pacific Economic Cooperation (APEC) took on another trend in interregional integration. It encompasses countries from Asia, North and South Americas. Talks of forming a Transatlantic Free Trade Agreement (TAFTA) between EU and NAFTA might also mature some day. African and Asian countries around the Indian Ocean also initiated the "Indian Ocean Economic Realm" concept, a common market uniting Africa's vast resources with Asia's booming industrial power.

Caveat Nota: Both multilateral and regional economic integration arrangements are important for purchasing managers. These arrangements have different rules and benefits. It is equally important to understand rule systems under WTO and the various regional arrangements and to get benefits therefrom. Finally, it should be emphasized that multilateral and regional arrangements are not necessarily in conflict in the overall achievement of prosperity. Up to now, they have mutually contributed to the overall world trade liberalization and world economic development. Combining adequate WTO discipline and enforcement of policies and rules relating to the elimination of trade barriers, free trade areas can be useful building blocks of a world trade regime.

THE COMPOSITION AND NATURE OF GATT AND WTO

The General Agreement on Tariffs and Trade (GATT), a multilateral trade agreement, came into being on January 1, 1948. During more than 50 years, GATT has achieved an impressive record. It has undertaken a total of eight rounds of trade liberalization talks and achieved its main objective of substantially reducing tariff barriers. GATT is aptly dubbed as the "General Agreement on Talks and Talks"! GATT countries also agreed on codes of conduct for nontariff barriers such as subsidies, standards, or government procurement. Under its aegis, the world economy has grown dramatically and world trade has grown even faster. For example, between 1965 and 1990, inflation-adjusted world exports grew by 439 percent, while world production rose 136 percent.

However, the GATT structure has its limitations. Despite its achievement, it remains a set of agreed-upon rules and a forum in which countries discuss and negotiate. It is not a formal institution. GATT trade talks has mostly been successful in tariff reductions, but only minimally successful in the area of non-tariff trade barriers. GATT totally failed in the agricultural products area. Moreover, GATT does not cover trade in services, intellectual property, and investment. Hence, a new round of negotiation was initiated in September 1986 in Punta del Este, Uruguay, the so-called Uruguay Round.

The Uruguay Round resulted in the most comprehensive trade agreement in history, approved by 117 nations in Geneva on December 15, 1993, with the signing ceremony held in Marrakesh, Morocco, in April 1994. The agreement known as the "Final Act" weighed 385 pounds and included over 22,000 pages. Even the basic texts reproduced as part of the Final Act totaled 424 pages.

Most importantly, the Uruguay Round led to the establishment of a new entity, the World Trade Organization (WTO), on January 1, 1995. However, to facilitate the transition between GATT and WTO, GATT combined with WTO. Now part of the WTO is called "GATT 1994." The old GATT is referred to as "GATT 1947." GATT 1994 is contextually co-extensive with, but "legally distinct" from GATT 1947. The WTO as a whole contains agreements in addition to GATT 1994.

The former contracting parties to GATT 1947 may withdraw from GATT and join WTO or they may continue to participate in GATT 1947 and the Tokyo Round agreements while maintaining their WTO membership for one year. Therefore, there is a transitional co-existence of GATT

1947 and WTO Agreement in 1995. The majority of the contracting parties to GATT 1947 have taken on and implemented the obligations of the WTO Agreement. WTO Members may deny benefits to non-WTO Members, including those who remained contracting parties to GATT 1947. After 1995, WTO completely replaced GATT. The United States remained a contracting party of GATT 1947 through the end of 1995, but withdrew from all of the Tokyo Round agreements in early 1995. As of the end of 1996, WTO had 129 members, with an additional 31 governments requesting to join it.

The WTO is not a simple extension of GATT. It completely replaces its predecessor and has a very different character. The WTO is a permanent institution while GATT was a set of rules applied on a "provisional basis." The WTO involves commitments for the entire membership while many of GATT's new agreements had been selectively applied. The WTO dispute settlement system is faster, more automatic, and more assured of implementation of dispute findings than the old GATT system. However, GATT lives on as "GATT 1994," the amended and up-dated version of GATT 1947, which continues to provide the key disciplines affecting international trade in goods.

The main functions of WTO are: to administer and implement the multilateral and plurilateral trade agreements which together make up the WTO; to act as a forum for multilateral trade negotiations; to seek to resolve trade disputes; to oversee national trade policies; and to cooperate with other international institutions involved in global economic policy-making, notably the IMF and the World Bank.

HOW WTO WORKS

In 1995, the focus shifted from GATT to WTO. Some pre-existing GATT 1947 disputes were abandoned and re-filed under WTO, and others have simply not been pursued. All assets and liabilities of GATT were transferred to WTO as of the entry into force of the WTO Agreement. The

WTO Director-General has assumed the GATT Director-General's functions, assisted by four Deputy Directors-General.

The highest authority of WTO is the Ministerial Conference, composed of representatives of all WTO members, which meets every two years and which can make decisions on all matters under any of the multilateral trade agreements. The day-to-day administration of WTO falls to the General Council, which also convenes as the Dispute Settlement Body (DSB) to oversee the dispute settlement procedures and as the Trade Policy Review Board (TPRB) to conduct regular reviews of the trade policies of individual WTO members. The General Council delegates responsibility to three other major bodies—namely the Councils for Trade in Goods, Trade in Services, and Trade-Related Aspects of Intellectual Property Rights.

Three other bodies are established by the Ministerial Conference and report to the General Council. The Committee on Trade and Development is concerned with issues relating to the developing countries and, especially, to the "least-developed" among them. The Committee on Balance of Payment is responsible for consultations between WTO members and countries that take trade-restrictive measures. The Committee on Budget deals with issues relating to WTO's financing and budget. Besides, each of the four plurilateral agreements of WTO—those on civil aircraft, government procurement, dairy products, and bovine meat—establishes its own management bodies which are required to report to the General Council.

The WTO Secretariat is located in Geneva. It has a staff of roughly 450 and a budget of $83 million, with individual contributions calculated on the basis of shares in the total trade conducted by members. The United States' share is approximately 15 percent of the total.

WTO seeks to make decisions by consensus. Where consensus is not possible, the WTO agreement allows for voting on the basis of "one country, one vote." There are four specific voting situations:

1. a majority of three-quarters of WTO members can vote to adopt an interpretation of any of the multilateral trade agreements;

2. by the same majority, the Ministerial Conference may decide to waive an obligation imposed on a particular member by a multilateral agreement;

3. decisions to amend provisions of the multilateral agreements can be adopted through approval either by all members or by a two-thirds majority depending on the nature of the provisions concerned; and

4. a decision to admit a new member is taken by a two-thirds majority in the Ministerial Conference.

BASIC PRINCIPLES OF THE WTO TRADING SYSTEM

Non-Discrimination: The "Final Act" retained the GATT tradition of outlawing discrimination among members and between imported and domestically produced merchandise. Under the famous "most-favored-nation" clause, WTO members are required to grant the products of other members no less favorable treatment than that accorded the product of any other country. Therefore, all members are on an equal basis and share the benefits of any moves toward lower trade barriers.

A second form of non-discrimination known as "national treatment" requires that once goods have entered a market, they must be treated no less favorably than comparable domestically produced products. These non-discrimination provisions are included not only in GATT 1994, but also embodied in other WTO agreements such as the General Agreement on Trade in Services (GATS) and agreements on rules of origin, preshipment inspection, trade-related investment measures, and the application of sanitary and phytosanitary measures.

Mutually Beneficial Tariff Reductions: The existence of predictable and growing access to markets is largely determined by the use and level of tariffs, which are legal in the WTO system. WTO continues GATT's tradition of progressively reducing tariff levels. Tariffs on industrial goods for industrial countries will be slashed an average of 40 percent, from an average of 6.3 percent to 3.8 percent. Also there is a jump from 20 percent to 44 percent in the value of imported industrial product that receive duty-free treatment in developed countries. At the higher end of the tariff structure, the proportion of imports into developed countries from all sources that encounter tariffs above 15 percent will decline from 7 percent to 5 percent and from 9 percent to 5 percent for imports from developing countries.

Tariff reductions made by the members are contained in National Tariff Schedules and for the most part will be phased in over five years. Once the tariff level of a particular product is reduced, it cannot be increased without compensation. This so-called "bound product lines" applies to nearly all products for developed countries, 73 percent for developing countries, and 98 percent for economies in transition. This provides a substantially higher degree of market security for traders and investors.

Transparency: The key to predictable trading conditions is often the "transparency" of domestic laws, regulations, and practices. Many WTO agreements contain transparency provisions that require disclosure at the national level. For instance, this may be through publication in official journals. At the multilateral level, formal notification to the WTO is required. For example, the WTO must be notified about details of any new anti-dumping or countervailing legislation, new technical standards affecting trade, changes to regulations affecting trade in services, and laws or regulations concerning the Trade-Related Intellectual Property agreement. Much of the work of WTO bodies is concerned with reviewing such notifications.

The regular surveillance of national trade policies through the Trade Policy Review Mechanism (TPRM) provides a further means of encouraging transparency both domestically and at the multilateral level. Reviews are conducted on a periodic basis. The four biggest traders—EU, United States, Japan, and Canada—are examined approximately once every two years. The next 16 countries in terms of their share of world trade are reviewed every four years. The remaining countries are reviewed every six years, with the possibility of a longer interim period for the least-developed countries.

Reviews are conducted in the Trade Policy Review Body on the basis of two documents: a policy statement prepared by the government under review, and a detailed report prepared independently by the WTO Secretariat. These two reports, together with the proceedings of the review body are published after the review meeting. In this way member governments are encouraged to follow more closely the WTO rules and disciplines and to fulfil their commitments.

Economic Development: Countries are classified by the levels of economic development. There are the "developed countries" such as the United States. There are "developing countries" such as Mexico and "underdeveloped countries" such as Haiti.

Over three-quarters of WTO members are developing countries and countries in the process of economic reform from non-market systems. The latter include Russia and some of its former satellites. During the Uruguay Round trade talks, developing countries and transition economies took a much more active and influential role than in any previous rounds. With 129 members, and many more wanting to join, WTO is no longer the "rich man's club" existing only for industrialized countries. Although developing countries showed themselves prepared to take on most of the obligations, they were given transition periods to adjust to the more unfamiliar WTO provisions. This was particularly so for the "least-developed" countries.

MAIN SUBSTANTIVE RULES OF WTO TRADING SYSTEM

Rules on Agricultural Products

The agreement on agricultural products addresses three critical issues.

1. Export subsidies: budgetary outlays for export subsidies will be reduced by 36 percent.

2. Market subsidies: all non-tariff barriers must be converted to tariff equivalents, this is known as "tarification."
3. Internal supports: trade distorting farm subsidies must be cut by 20 percent from 1986 base period levels.

Market access in agricultural products is now governed by a "tariffs-only" regime that provides substantially equivalent levels of protection. Tariffs are to be reduced by an average 36 percent in developed countries and 24 percent in developing countries. Tariff reductions will be phased in over six years in developed countries and 10 years in developing countries. Least-developed countries are not required to reduce their tariffs.

In many countries, there is special support given to the producing of agricultural products. Domestic support measures are disciplined through reductions in the Total Aggregate Measurement of Support (Total AMS). This "formula" is a means of quantifying the aggregate value of domestic support or subsidy given to each category of agricultural products. Based on Total AMS measured from the period of 1986 to 1988, developed countries are required to reduce their Total AMS by 20 percent over six years. Developing countries have 10 years to make a 13 percent reduction, and least-developing countries are not required to make any deductions.

Caveat Bene: For purchasing managers engaged in purchasing agricultural products on which there have been high tariffs should be able to see price savings in years to come.

Rules on Trade in Textiles and Clothing

Currently, textiles and clothing trade is largely governed by the Multi-Fibre Arrangement (MFA). The MFA provides the basis on which many industrial countries, through bilateral agreements or unilateral actions, establishes quotas on imports of textiles and clothing from the more competitive developing countries with much cheaper labor and plant costs. The objective of the agreement for textiles and clothing is to secure the eventual integration of the textiles and clothing sector into the WTO free-trade system. Under the agreement, there will be a gradual phase out of quotas over a 10-year period, after which the textile and clothing trade will be fully integrated into the mainstream of WTO disciplines.

The textile and clothing integration program has four stages:

- By January 1, 1995, each party integrated from the specific list in the MFA products accounting for not less than 16 percent of its total volume of textile and clothing imports in 1990.

- By January 1, 1998, products accounting for not less than a further 17 percent of 1990 imports must be integrated.

- By January 1, 2002, products accounting for not less than a further 18 percent of 1990 imports must be integrated.

- By January 1, 2005, all remaining products must be integrated.

At each of the first three stages, products are to be chosen from each of the following categories: tops and yarns, fabrics, made-up textile products, and clothing. For products remaining under restraint, at whatever stage, the agreement lays down a formula for increasing the existing growth rates. Thus, during stage 1, for each restriction under MFA bilateral agreements in force for 1994, the annual growth should be not less than 16 percent higher than the growth rate established for the previous MFA restriction. During stage 2, annual growth rates should be 25 percent higher than stage 1 rates. For stage 3, annual growth rates should be 27 percent higher than the stage 2 rates. Non-MFA restrictions maintained by any WTO member and not justified under GATT 1994 will be brought into conformity with GATT 1994 by 1996 or be phased out progressively before 2005.

Caveat Bene: For the purchasing manager who may have occasion to purchase textile products, there will be greater competition and hopefully lower comparative prices over the years to come. The agreement also includes provisions to cope with possible circumvention of commitments through transshipment, re-routing, false declaration concerning country or place of origin, and falsification of official documents. It also envisions special treatment to certain categories of countries. For example, those countries that have not been MFA members since 1986, new market entrants, small suppliers, and least-developed countries. The Textiles Monitoring Body oversees the detailed implementation of commitments and must prepare reports for the Council on Trade in Goods which reviews the operation of the agreement before the end of the each stage of the integration process.

Rules on Intellectual Property

The Agreement on Trade-Related Aspects of Intellectual Property Rights (TRIPS) will improve standards for the protection of a full range of intellectual property rights and enforcement. TRIPS adds a significant number of new or higher standards where the existing Paris Convention and Berne Convention were silent or thought inadequate. Specifically:

- Computer programs will be protected as literary works under the Berne Convention.

- Authors of computer programs and producers of sound recordings and films have the right to authorize or prohibit the commercial rental of their works to the public and to prevent the reproduction of recordings for a period of 50 years; performers are protected from unauthorized recording, reproduction, and broadcast of live performances for no less than 50 years.

- Trademarks and service marks that have become well known in a particular country enjoy additional protection; requirements that foreign marks be used in conjunction with local marks will generally be prohibited.

- The use of any indication which mislead the consumer as to the origin of goods and any use which would constitute an act of unfair competition are prohibited; higher levels of protection are provided for geographical indications for wines and spirits.

- Industrial designs are protected under the agreement for a period of 10 years.

- 20-year patent protection is available for all inventions, whether of products or processes, in almost all fields of technology.
- Layout designs of integrated circuits are protected for a minimum period of 10 years. However, innocent infringers are allowed to use or sell stock in hand or ordered before learning of the infringement.
- Trade secrets and know-how are protected against breach of confidence and other unfair commercial practices.

Developed countries have a one year (developing countries have five years) transition period to bring their legislation and practice into conformity. Developing countries which do not at present provide product patent protection in an area of technology have up to 10 years to introduce such protection. However, in the case of pharmaceutical and agricultural chemical products, they must accept the filing of patent applications from the beginning of the transitional period, though the patent need not be granted until the end of this period.

Caveat Nota: These provisions primarily protect United States sellers of technology and "high-tech" products to other countries. They stop production in those countries of their technological products by foreign companies initiating these products without permission or license. The effect on most purchasing managers in the United States would seem negligible.

Rules on Anti-Dumping Measures

The practice of "dumping," which is selling in an export market at a lower price than in the exporter's domestic market or at a price less than the cost of production, was addressed during the Uruguay Round. Under the revised Antidumping Code, the remedy for dumping is the imposition of an additional duty on dumped imports, amounting to the equivalent of the price discrimination. Many countries, including the United States, have enacted national antidumping laws to impose duties for dumping.

The new Antidumping Code set up clearer rules under which an antidumping dispute will be resolved. The rules include the following:

- An antidumping petition may be filed "on behalf of" an industry as well as by certified trade unions representing workers in an industry.

- The antidumping case shall be immediately terminated where the authorities determine that the margin of dumping is de minimis, which is defined as a margin of less than 2 percent of the export price. Investigation should also be terminated if the volume of dumped imports from a particular country is less than 3 percent of the importing country's total imports of a like product. However, the authorities need not terminate if countries charged with dumping collectively account for more than 7 percent of the importing country's total imports of the like product, even though such countries individually account for less than 3 percent.

- If more than one country is subject to an antidumping investigation of a product, authorities may cumulatively assess the effects of the imports in question from the countries involved. Cumulation of import may only occur if: the dumping margins are more than de minimis; the volume of imports from each country is not negligible; and a cumulative assessment "is appropriate in light of the conditions of competition between the imported products and the domestic like product."

- An antidumping duty will be terminated five years after its imposition, or five years after the duration of the duties would be likely to lead to the continuation or recurrence of dumping and injury.

- When home-market or third-country prices are inadequate or otherwise inappropriate as a basis for determining the "normal value" against which "export prices" should be compared, constructed value is used in calculating the normal value. Constructed value is a calculation of the fully allocated costs of production—fixed and variable costs of production, selling, general and administrative costs plus profit—of the merchandise in question.

- The dumping margins shall be established on the basis of a comparison of a weighted average normal value with a weighted average of prices of all comparable export transactions, or by a comparison of normal value and export prices on a transaction-to-transaction basis.

- Cost calculations should be adjusted appropriately for start-up operations. The size of dumping duty could potentially be doubled where the importer is related to the exporter.

- In dispute settlement, so long as a national antidumping proceeding establishes the facts properly and evaluates them in an unbiased and objective way, its evaluation cannot be overturned by a WTO panel even though the panel may have reached a different conclusion.

Caveat Nota: Stricter standards and enforcement of antidumping measures may mean higher prices occasionally for purchasing managers who buy imported goods.

Rules on Technical Barriers

The Agreement on Technical Barriers to Trade is designed to ensure that technical negotiations and standards will not create unnecessary obstacles to trade. The prohibited technical barriers may include "packaging, marking and labeling requirements, and procedures for assessment of conformity with technical regulations and standards." Following the principle of national treatment, the agreement essentially restricts attempts to establish purchasing specifications that might be more discriminatory towards foreign suppliers than domestic ones. A more difficult issue concerns regulations based on processes and production methods (PPMs). Such regulations prescribe how a product should be manufactured. Under the terms of the agreement, PPM standards are restricted. In other words, technical (environmental and Occupational Safety and Health)) specifications on imports must be related to the product only and not to its production process. This restriction prevents governments from imposing their particular regulatory standards on foreign suppliers.

Caveat Bene: This could result in some savings for purchasing managers engaged in buying imports.

Rules on Health and Safety Measures

An agreement was reached concerning the application of food safety and animal and plant health regulations. The agreement recognizes governments' rights to take sanitary and phytosanitary measures but stipulates that they must be based on science, and should be applied only to the extent necessary to protect human, animal, or plant life or health. Such governmental regulations should not arbitrarily or unjustifiably discriminate between members under similar conditions. Also, WTO members are encouraged to comply with recommendations where they exist. A Committee on Sanitary and Phytosanitary Measures provides a forum for consultation on matters with potential trade impacts. This agreement complements the agreement on technical barriers to trade.

Rules on Government Procurement

The Agreement on Government Procurement was specified as a "plurilateral" agreement, meaning that only countries choosing to sign the Agreement must comply with it and that signatories to the rest of WTO agreements were not required to adhere to its rules. Currently, only Austria, Canada, the EU, Finland, Israel, Japan, Norway, Sweden, Switzerland, and the United States have signed. Hong Kong and South Korea are covered under transitional agreements. The Agreement has 34 observers that may attend and participate in Agreement meetings even though they are not allowed to vote.

The Agreement forbids offsets, defining them as "measures used to encourage local development or improve the balance-of-payments accounts by means of domestic content, licensing of technology, investment requirements, counter-trade or similar requirements." Offsets are defined broadly to prevent governments from converting an explicit offset program such as a local subcontracting requirement into hidden offsets such project-specific agreements to develop local technology in return for procurement contracts. Thus, government entities are forbidden from pressuring foreign companies into making concessions that are not required in the bidding documents and from favoring those companies that offer such concessions. However, foreign companies may voluntarily structure their business plans to help the procuring country's balance of payments. Nonetheless, a government that rewards such voluntary acts in the bidding process in most likely violating the Agreement.

The Agreement also requires a national treatment. It mandates open and transparent procurement, including prompt publication of all procurement rules and regulations. It also obligates members to provide mechanisms for obtaining bid rejection explanations and for the hearing and review of complaints.

Finally, the Agreement does not apply to all government contracts by parties. Only those government entities listed in a member's annex (that the member has agreed, during the negotiation, to make subject to the Agreement) are covered. Moreover, only contracts above a minimum monetary value or threshold are subject to the Agreement. Thresholds vary slightly from country to country and range from approximately $85,000, or 130,000 Special Drawing Rights (SDRs—a basket of currencies used as an international unit of account) for central government supplies to around $3,263,000 (5,000,000 SDRs) for construction services.

Rules on Dispute Resolution

One significant change expected to improve trade is the system to resolve trade disputes. The GATT 1947 dispute resolution mechanism was based on conciliation, mediation, and arbitration. This has been criticized as ineffective. The new WTO dispute resolution mechanism has largely changed that image.

The WTO can authorize retaliatory measures in case of nonimplementation of its recommendations. Although this mechanism to resolve disputes is designed to be more effective than under GATT, there are some weaknesses. The WTO still cannot legally impose its panel's decision on a member country. Further, the retaliatory measure cannot exceed the damage caused by the offending trade barrier. Thus, Panel decisions must still seek consensus between the disputing parties.

The first stage of settling disputes requires bilateral consultations between the governments concerned. If a solution is not arrived at after 60 days, a three-person "Panel" is selected by the WTO Secretariat to examine the complaint and issue a ruling within six months. A final Panel report or ruling is submitted to the parties. Three weeks later it is circulated to all WTO members. Panel reports are adopted by the DSB within 60 days of issuance, unless one party appeals.

The seven-person Appellate Body can uphold, modify, or reverse the legal findings and conclusions of the DSB. The appeal proceedings are generally not to exceed 60 days (90 days in complicated cases), and the Appellate Body's report is both adopted by the DSB and "unconditionally accepted by the parties to the dispute" or there is a consensus against its adoption.

This system was demonstrated in January 1995, when the WTO acted on a petition by Venezuela and Brazil and ruled that the United States gasoline requirements under the Clean Air Act discriminated against imports. In its first major test, the WTO ruled the United States environmental legislation forced countries exporting gasoline to the United States to meet higher gasoline standards for emissions of aromatics than it required for its own domestic gasoline products. Although the United States argued that Venezuelan-formulated gasoline was higher in smog-producing aromatics such as benzene, the WTO ruling concerned itself only with whether the law favored domestic formulations over foreign ones. The Panel decision was against the United States but was narrowed substantially by the appellate body. The United States was forced to modify its regulations. However, the entire case will become moot by 1998 when regulations regarding emissions for imported and domestically produced gasoline are harmonized.

Critics of the WTO say the WTO ruling against the United States is wrong. In fact, the United States was clearly using a "double standard" and was discriminating against foreign produced gasoline. Its "concern" for the environment should have resulted in equally strict standards for American produced gasoline. It also is argued that this demonstrates the sacrifice of national sovereignty to the WTO. In fact, the WTO has no power to force United States adoption of its recommendations. WTO remedies are flexible. The United States could, if she wishes, cut other tariffs for Venezuelan goods and not remove the emissions regulation for environmental reasons. One more thing, individuals cannot sue to change GATT rules or decisions, only national governments can.

THE URUGUAY ROUND IMPACT

The conclusion of the Uruguay Round and the establishment of the WTO should pave the way for further substantial reductions in trade barriers around the world. That development will in turn open up new opportunities for U.S. businesses, particularly multinational businesses, to expand their global sourcing of supplies and worldwide exporting of products.

Caveat Bene: For purchasing managers looking to goods produced throughout the world, this is most beneficial. In order to take advantage of such additional opportunities, purchasing managers need to be able to react quickly and to know the various markets around the globe. In a sense, the purchasing manager's job requires more skill and expertise than ever before.

Congress has enacted legislation to implement the Uruguay Round. The legislation includes an extensive set of notification and consultation procedures and reports to address cases where the WTO activities could substantially affect United States interests or law. Consultations and annual reports will provide Congress and the public with better means to monitor the WTO activities. In the event of a vote in the WTO that would affect United States interests, the United States Trade Representative (USTR) will consult with Congress. Each year,

USTR is required to report on: (1) the consequences for the United States of WTO votes, including rights and obligations; and (2) any action that the administration intends to take in response to the vote. In addition, USTR will issue an annual report addressing the WTO's major activities, work programs, administrative issues, dispute settlement panel reports, the status of recent cases affecting United States federal or state law, and progress in achieving openness in WTO procedures. If as a result of a dispute settlement proceeding, the Panel recommends a change in United States law or regulatory practice, advice must be sought from private sector advisory committees and the public. For all cases in which the United States is a party, public comments will be solicited through a Federal Register notice, and United States submissions to the dispute panel will be made available to the public.

The legislation requires that USTR establish an expanded consultative process with individual states to provide information. A WTO Coordinator for State Matters will be designated to serve as liaison between states and federal agencies for WTO-related matters. The Department of Commerce will provide support for this coordination effort with the states.

The Uruguay Round will affect the world economy positively. It is estimated that the world as a whole will gain substantially from the reforms agreed on under the Uruguay Round: about $96 billion annually in the short run and $171 billion in the long run. However, the short-run gains are concentrated in developed countries, especially in Japan, EU, and the United States which gain $39 billion, $17 billion, and $13 billion annually, respectively. Some smaller countries also gain significantly: Malaysia gains 3.3 percent of GDP, Singapore and Thailand about 2.1 percent of GDP each, and South Korea and the Philippines about 1.6 percent of GDP each.

Although the developing countries as a whole gain from the Uruguay Round, a few developing regions are estimated to lose, on balance, in the short run. Countries in sub-Saharan Africa would lose about 0.2 percent of GDP annually, while for countries in the Middle East and North Africa, the effect would be slightly negative (a loss of 0.1 percent of GDP). While developing countries gain less overall than industrial countries, the opposite would be true if only the reduction of protection in manufactured goods is considered since industrial countries have relatively lower protection, on average, in this area.

However, the Uruguay Round left a list of "unfinished business," especially in the service trade area such as financial services, information service, and shipping. The free-trade commitment of WTO members will also be tested by several challenges. First is continuing liberalization in trade in goods and services. Negotiation on further liberalization of agricultural trade is due to begin in 1999 and a fresh round of talks on services is due to start in 2000. Second, how and on what terms to admit China into the WTO. Various hard negotiations can be anticipated in the near future. Third, whether and how should WTO extend its rules into other trade policy issues such as labor standards and environment. The Uruguay Round failed to reach agreement on these issues. The potentially dramatic expansion in these areas is sure to await the next millennium and the next round of trade talks. Fourth, the spread and challenge of regional trade arrangements, especially the EU, NAFTA, and the potential APEC free trade area.

Fortunately, WTO passed the first test. In its first ministerial meeting in Singapore, WTO members reached the Information Technology Agreement on December 12, 1996. The agreement will eliminate by the year 2000 all tariffs on computers, semiconductors, and telecommunications equipment. It is a $5 billion cut in tariffs on the American products exported to other nations. Global trade in information technology was valued at $500 billion a year in 1996 and is projected to reach $800 billion by 2000. However, the agreement will bind only those countries that accede to it.

BENEFITS TO THE UNITED STATES ECONOMY

Foreign trade has been a particularly important source of the United States economic growth since World War II. It now accounts for about a quarter of the value the United States produces. The United States economy has now become more woven into the global economy than ever before. However, United States companies exporting goods and services are often limited by trade barriers, tariff or non-tariff, set by other countries to protect the local industries. The reduction of trade barriers will benefit the United States economy in substantial ways.

The Uruguay Round will ultimately reduce by more than one-third tariffs on United States trade with WTO partners. Tariffs will be entirely eliminated in several industries in which the United States is highly competitive. Many non-tariff trade barriers will also be eliminated or reduced. Moreover, WTO rules will be expanded into areas of services trade, certain investment measures, and intellectual property protection. The reduction in trade barriers and the resulting expansion of trade will have a dynamic effect on the United States economy and stimulate long-term economic growth.

Trade liberalization has a minimal impact on total United States employment over time. One should not expect any sudden surge or fall in levels of employment in the United States in the short run. Increased export opportunities arising from the Round should support rather than undermine the growth-led increases in higher-value-added employment now apparent in the economy. On average, every billion dollar increase of merchandise exports results in 16 to 17 thousand new jobs here in the United States.

The lowering of trade barriers will also result in lower prices and greater variety of imported products, which will benefit the consumers. In addition, greater global competition will force domestic producers to become more efficient and to lower their prices. This will benefit not only individual consumers buying clothing or food, but also businesses buying parts. That, in turn, will make those companies more competitive and help protect United States jobs.

The WTO will have much stronger trade rules than the GATT, thus enabling United States businesses to compete with their foreign counterparts on more equal terms and on a level playing field. The new trade rules will strengthen United States ability to combat unfair trading practices by allowing "cross retaliation" when a country fails to modify its laws or regulations in response to a dispute settlement decision. However, the WTO dispute settlement mechanism will also have impact on the United States. As a practical matter, United States procedures and substantive rules will, by and large, be modified to accommodate decisions made in Geneva. Only in the few explosive cases in which a panel departs fundamentally from its rightful duties, the United States might refuse to implement the decision. Interestingly, the accretion of cases that reject and alter national laws of WTO member countries may create a new body of international trade common law in areas and of a context beyond original anticipation.

NORTH AMERICAN FREE TRADE AGREEMENT

What Is NAFTA?

When the idea for a free trade area encompassing the three North American countries—Canada, United States, and Mexico—was first seriously introduced by Mexican President Carlos Salinas in early 1990, it was considered to have little chance of success. The differences between the three countries are huge. Canada and the United States are highly developed countries while Mexico is a developing country, with a civil law legal system as opposed to a common law system like its northern neighbors. However, the growing interdependence of the world at the end of the twentieth century, and the seemingly unending negotiation in the Uruguay Round talks, made the alternative of a North American regional trade arrangements more attractive.

Accordingly, in June of 1990, United States and Mexico announced their intention to negotiate a bilateral free trade agreement. Canada was originally the least enthusiastic of the NAFTA partners. Canadian-Mexican trade had averaged only about US $2 billion a year during that period of time. The 1988 Canada-United States Free Trade Agreement (CFTA), under which the tariff phase-out between the two countries was already under way, had been blamed for many of the economic woes Canada had experienced in the early 1990s. However, faced with the choice of remaining on the sidelines or participating in the talks, Canada chose to participate in late 1990. The official text of NAFTA was signed by President George Bush, Canadian Prime Minister Brian Mulroney, and Mexican President Carlos Salinas on December 17, 1992. After respective domestic approval procedures, NAFTA went into effect on January 1, 1994.

The objectives of NAFTA are to:

(a) eliminate barriers to trade in goods and services between the territories of the parties;

(b) to promote fair competition in the free trade area ("leveling playground");

(c) to increase the investment opportunities throughout the parties;

(d) to protect adequately intellectual property rights of each party;

(e) to create effective procedures for joint administration of the agreement and joint resolution of related disputes; and

(f) to establish a framework to further "trilateral, regional and multilateral cooperation to expand and enhance the benefits" of the Agreement.

However, each country has different national objectives. A primary objective of the United States and Canada was to open up the many highly protected sectors of the Mexican economy. Prime examples include the protected automobile, telecommunications, agriculture, textiles, and financial services sectors. United States and Canada also aimed to eliminate Mexico's import restrictions on a variety of products and consolidate and expand Mexico's intellectual property rights protections. Political objectives also played a significant role in the United States' decision. Institutionalizing the Mexican reforms was as attractive to the United States as to Mexico. A stable and increasingly prosperous and democratic southern neighbor would mean reduced friction and fewer problems for the United States, for example, less illegal immigration at the border.

From the Mexican perspective, general objectives include guarding against resurgent United States protectionism by securing market access and continuing domestic reforms that have been occurring since Mexico joined GATT. The Mexican economy would benefit from the guaranteed preferential access to United States and Canadian markets under NAFTA. Also, Mexico would be able to re-attract foreign capital that left when the banks were nationalized in the early 1980s.

NAFTA establishes a Free Trade Commission (Commission) composed of cabinet level representatives of the Parties (Countries) or their designees. The Commission generally acts by consensus, but may agree, by consensus, to act otherwise than by consensus. The functions of the Commission are generally to supervise the implementation, oversee the elaboration, and assist in the resolution of disputes under the agreement, as well as to supervise the work of the various committees and working groups established under the agreement. The Commission shall "consider any other matter that may affect the operation of this Agreement" and "take such other action in the exercise of its functions as the Parties may agree." The accession by third countries will be negotiated by the Commission, too. But the accession agreements still must be approved in accordance with the applicable legal procedures of each Party or country. The Commission does not have authority to bind the Parties by legislative or regulatory measures.

The Commission undertakes to establish and oversee a Secretariat, the functions of which are to provide assistance to the Commission and provide administrative assistance to dispute settlement panels, committees and working groups. The Secretariat is comprised of national sections (National Administrative Office), each with its own nationally appointed Secretary. There is no single Secretary-General or comparable official. Each Party funds the operations of its national Secretariat section.

NAFTA establishes a number of working groups and committees to assist in monitoring and facilitating the cooperative implementation of various sectors of the agreement. The NAFTA dispute settlement mechanism involves the appointment of arbitrators on a case-by-case basis. There is no permanent juridical organ comparable to the European Court of Justice. The NAFTA establishes no parliamentary assembly.

NAFTA members are also party to two Supplemental Agreements: the North American Agreement on Environmental Cooperation (NAAEC) and North American Agreement on Labor Cooperation (NAALC). These two agreements sought by President Clinton were agreed upon on August 12, 1993. The NAAEC establishes a Commission composed of a Council, Secretariat, and Joint Public Advisory Committee. The role of the NAAEC Council is to promote cooperation on environmental issues, make recommendations regarding environmental matters, and oversee the activities of the NAAEC Secretariat. Montreal, Canada, hosts the Environmental Secretariat. The NAALC establishes a Commission for Labor Cooperation composed of a Council and Secretariat, with a role comparable to that of the NAAEC organs. Dallas, Texas, was chosen to host the Labor Secretariat.

In connection with, but not technically part of, NAFTA, the United States and Mexico entered into an Agreement Concerning the Establishment of a Border Environment Commission and a North American Development Bank, which will provide funding for border environmental projects and worker adjustment assistance programs in the United States and Mexico. The Bank is situated in San Antonio, Texas.

Caveat Nota: NAFTA does not provide for the formulation and conduct of a coordinated external policy. Each Party is free to conduct its own external trade policy as long as it is consistent with its obligations under the agreement. Nevertheless, the Parties can, if they wish, formulate and implement a common external commercial policy. For example, NAFTA parties may choose to coordinate their activities with respect to the WTO or EU.

In Article 103 of NAFTA, the Parties affirm their existing rights and obligations to each other under GATT(WTO), but provide that NAFTA prevails over GATT(WTO) to the extent that it also prevails over agreements between the Parties, which means NAFTA supersedes the Canada-United States Free Trade Agreement, too.

KEY NAFTA PROVISIONS

The essence of NAFTA is a phase-out of most tariffs and nontariff barriers immediately or within 5 or 10 years and their final elimination within 15 years.

Caveat Bene: This should allow purchasing managers to obtain better prices on products imported from Canada or Mexico in the years to come. The process of trade barrier phase-out is as follows:

- *Manufactured goods*—tariffs on some 65 percent of goods traded among the three countries were eliminated immediately when the agreement took effect, 15 percent will be eliminated over five years, most of the remaining tariffs over 10 years, and for a limited number of products in 15 years.
- *Agricultural products*—tariffs will be gradually eliminated likewise. The distinction is that Mexico will have separate bilateral agreements with the United States and Canada since the parties were unable to agree on a single document.
- *Autos*—Mexico will phase out its restrictions on imports of autos and parts. To qualify for duty-free treatment autos must contain a minimum level of North American parts and labor of 50 percent for the first 4 years, 56 percent for the second 4 years, and 62.5 percent after 8 years.
- *Computers*—Mexico will phase out its 20 percent tariff for United States and Canada and lower tariff to the 3.9 percent level vis-a-vis all other countries. Local content rules will apply with regard to computer motherboards.
- *Energy*—Mexico preserves most of Mexico's restrictions on foreign investment and private participation in its petroleum industry. The Mexican government will retain its monopoly in gasoline, fuel oil, and electricity sales. United States natural gas deliveries will have to be channeled through the state-owned Petroleos Mexicanos. Mexico refused to commit itself to specific volumes of oil deliveries to the United States.

- *Environment*—numerous environmental provisions insuring that increased trade does not harm the ecology of the border region between United States and Mexico or undermine United States environmental laws.

- *Financial services*—Mexico agreed to phase out restrictions on foreign ownership of its banks and insurance companies within 7 years and securities firms within 10 years. United States promised to grant special waivers that would allow a limited number of Canadian and Mexican banks to underwrite securities in the United States.

- *Government procurement*—opening of bidding to supply goods and services to the Mexican government by United States and Canadian companies. Free access for 50 percent of procurement upon implementation of NAFTA, rising to 70 percent over 8 years, and lifting all restrictions after 10 years.

- *Investment*—Mexico will liberalize its restrictions on foreign investment. Canada and United States will retain their respective systems of screening foreign investment.

- *Textiles*—Mexico will phase out its tariffs for United States and Canadian-made textiles and apparel over five to six years. Under the local content rule, to qualify for duty-free entry, apparel would have to be made from yarn spun in North America and fabric would have to be made from North American fibers. Mexico and Canada will be allowed for 5 years to ship to the United States specific amounts of clothing and textiles made from foreign materials under a rising quota.

- *Duty drawbacks*—A very important component of NAFTA from the standpoint of third country exporters to the region are changes mandated with respect to duty drawback and remission rules. Duty drawbacks and remission refer to refunds or remissions of duties generally contingent on the reexportation of the goods as to which the duty was paid or was otherwise due upon importation. In order to limit the use of Mexico by third countries as an export platform for the NAFTA region, NAFTA establishes significant limitations on duty drawback and remission programs.

Under NAFTA, goods must pay the higher of the two possible customs duties to which they may have been subject either upon importation into the first NAFTA country or upon export to a second NAFTA country. Thus, assuming that Mexico's duties are higher than those of the United States, a third country exporter to Mexico must have effectively paid the Mexican rate of tariff when its goods enter the United States. Since goods which originate in NAFTA will not be subject to duty, the limitations on the drawback or remission program do not disadvantage NAFTA-origin products, but operate only to disadvantage third country originating products. Under NAFTA, duty drawback programs will be eliminated on Mexican-related trade by 2001. Duty drawback in United States-Canada trade was phased out by 1996.

Moreover, customs user fees charged by Mexico (0.8% of the value of the goods) and the United States (0.17% of the import value, up to a specified ceiling) will be eliminated by mid-1999. Much of bilateral United States-Mexico trade is conducted under a duty remission program known as the Maquiladora system under which United States manufacturers are able to ship components to Mexico for assembly and re-exported to the United States without payment of Mexican duties and with generally favorable tariff treatment by the United States. However, Mexican duty drawback and remission programs are not limited to United States exporters. Therefore, they could be used to establish an export platform in Mexico for large Asian manufacturers. Such manufacturers will be able to recoup the import duties paid to Mexico on Asian components imported for incorporation into products to be produced for the United States or Canadian market. The NAFTA provision in effect puts United States manufacturers in a better position vis-a-vis third country manufacturers. Unfortunately, the Mexican Maquiladora industry will be adversely affected and will retain few advantages over other locations in Mexico.

Dispute Resolution

NAFTA employs a number of dispute settlement models, most of which are accessible only to the governmental Parties, but some provide direct or indirect access to private parties. Disputes between the Parties arising under both NAFTA and GATT may be resolved at the discretion of the complaining Party. If a third NAFTA Party requests dispute settlement under NAFTA, a dispute will ordinarily be settled pursuant to NAFTA. Following a consultation and conciliation period, at the request of a Party, an arbitral panel is established. Five panelists are selected by the disputing Parties. The panel receives written and oral testimony from the Parties, and may request the input of outside experts. The panel renders a majority decision to the Parties that recommends actions to be taken by a Party whose measures have been found inconsistent with NAFTA. Such a decision is not subject to appeal. A Party is expected to comply with the decision of an arbitral panel, preferably by reforming or removing an offending measure. A panel cannot compel compliance with its recommendations.

A separate dispute settlement mechanism is established for anti-dumping and countervailing duty matters. Under this procedure, decisions of arbitral panels with respect to appeals of anti-dumping and countervailing final determinations are binding on the Parties as to the matter at issue. In addition, the Parties agree to submit disputes with investors of the Parties to bringing in third-party arbitration. Thus, private party investors may have recourse against the NAFTA governments under the third-party arbitration provisions. Also, the investment arbitration process should be open to third-country-owned enterprises established in the NAFTA territory.

NAFTA RULES OF ORIGIN

One of the major issues and areas of concern is that of Rules of Origin and how the NAFTA process and procedures of Rules of Origin, as well as its Customs Administration, will affect United States business. These rules are the most important area of NAFTA for they determine when goods qualify as NAFTA—goods-which allows the system to work. The rules are very long and complex and are designed to benefit only NAFTA members' products and are used to determine when products receive the benefits of lower tariffs under the Agreement. Most important, and an area of much concern during the drafting of the agreement, was the designing of rules to determine the origin when material and goods from non-NAFTA member countries are incorporated into an otherwise NAFTA product. Special rules, requiring enhanced percentage of North American components, have been designed to protect certain industries like textiles and apparel and automobiles.

To achieve the benefits of NAFTA, the objectives of the Rules of Origin must therefore be strict so that these benefits will go to NAFTA countries and not to products of non-member countries that are only part of NAFTA products. This ensures that Mexico will not become a platform for third countries' exports. It is for this reason that restrictive rules are important. However, they must not be too restrictive or they would require products to use materials solely of NAFTA countries; this would violate WTO rules. Only when fair and workable rules are in place can products that use non-member materials but which have been substantially transformed by significant processing operations be allowed to qualify as NAFTA goods. This prevents non-members from using NAFTA member countries as a drop off or "pass-through" of their materials.

The process and procedure of Rules of Origin and Customs Administration affect United States business because they are the first steps that must be taken for a business to qualify for benefits under NAFTA. For businesses to plan properly, they must be intimately familiar with the rules so that the products they plan to manufacture, to export, to compete against, or to import can be assessed to determine whether they qualify for the benefit of reduced tariffs. The reduced costs can also be taken into account, which may affect price or the potential and profitability of a product in a specific industry.

Under NAFTA, a product is a product of North American origin if it meets one of several tests:

1. If the product is wholly obtained or produced in the territory of one or more of the Parties, it is a product of North American origin. NAFTA defines this by examples, which include agricultural goods (e.g., fruits or vegetables grown and harvested in North America, fish, extracted mineral goods, even waste or trash if produced in North America). Products that contain non-member components or ingredients do not qualify.

2. An extension of the above is, if the product is produced entirely in the territory of one or more of the Parties or exclusively from originating materials, it qualifies for preferential treatment under NAFTA. A good, for example, that is made of part Canadian, part Mexican, and part American material qualifies. However, like the first test, if any component or ingredient from non-member countries is included, it does not qualify.

3. Another test is a change in tariff classification test, which replaces the "substantial transformation," the standard previously used by the United States. It works in the following way: if a product contains materials that do not originate in North America, but the final product is so changed that it now would be classified under a different tariff scheme under the HTS, then it is still classified as a North American good and qualifies for preferential treatment. However, the change in tariff classification must occur by production that occurs entirely within the three NAFTA member countries. For example, a steak produced in North America from a cow imported from France would qualify—it changes from a tariff classification of live animal to a tariff classification of edible meat.

4. If the parts of a product are not considered independent of the whole product, according to the tariff classification test and the tariff heading, the product still may be able to qualify under the regional value content test. In other words, if the unassembled parts are in the same tariff classification as the final product then there is no change in tariff classification. A good example is a bicycle, because each component part (e.g., the

tires, handle bar, chain, and seat) is classified under the same tariff heading; therefore, there is no change in classification. To overcome this determination, the regional value content test could be applied. If the goods include a specified percentage of North American content added, they may qualify.

The Regional Content test, which requires that a product's regional content be calculated to determine if it should receive preferential treatment under NAFTA, has two methods. One is the transaction method, which is based on the price paid or payable for a good. The calculation requires taking the transaction value, minus the value of non-NAFTA member materials used in the production of the products, divided by the transaction value, times 100, and this equals the regional value content as a percentage. Usually, the regional content must be 60 percent of the good under this calculation. Transaction value cannot be used if not acceptable under the GATT Custom Valuation Code.

The second method is the net cost method, which is based on the total cost of a good. Here the regional value content percentage equals the net cost of the goods, minus the value of non-NAFTA member materials used in the production of the product, divided by the net cost, times 100. Usually the regional content must be 50 percent if calculated this way. Either method can be used, except for certain products (e.g., automotive goods and footwear), which specify which calculation is necessary.

Some products that qualify under the change in tariff classification test may also have to qualify under the regional value content test. An example is shoes made in North America from Brazilian leather. Not only does there need to be a tariff classification change from leather to footwear, but the shoes must also add 55 percent of their cost from North American materials.

5. A final test is the De Minimis test where a good that fails the above tests could qualify for preferential treatment if its non-NAFTA material content is less than 7 percent of transaction value price or the total cost of the goods. There are, however,

many exceptions to this test—certain products do not qualify for this test, and some not only require the less than 7 percent De Minimis requirement, but also add the tariff classification change test as well.

These tests, however, do not all apply to certain specific industries. The Rules of Origin for textiles and apparel and automobiles are stricter. The test for textiles and apparel is a "yarn forward rule," which requires that yarn used in the manufacture of the product is produced in a NAFTA member country. The rules therefore require that for textiles and apparel "the yarn be produced, the fabric made, and the clothing sewn in the NAFTA area." There are certain exceptions, such as materials that are not produced in abundance in the United States, or if a material is in short supply.

Automobiles also require very restrictive Rules of Origin and a higher regional value content than other North American products. They use a net cost method in calculating regional value content, which requires tracing the value of inputs of component parts for automobiles from countries where they came, in order to determine a correct regional value content. This tracing and net cost method is very complex and hence costly to perform. Automobile parts require 62.5 percent North American content to receive beneficial treatment.

The restrictiveness of automobiles Rules of Origin shows the influence the industry was able to exert during NAFTA negotiations to protect their industry. This discriminates against foreign manufacturers and forces domestic companies to manufacture automobile parts within the free trade area. This may not be more efficient, but costs some manufacturers more and hence consumers pay more.

After having determined that a business's product qualifies for the benefit of NAFTA's lower tariff, one must then look to the tariff schedules to determine exactly what lower tariff the product will receive; or for Canada the tariff schedules of the

CFTA need to be looked at. There are three schedules: agricultural goods, textiles and apparel, and manufactured goods. A business's product will fit into one of these categories.

With many component parts being assembled in various nations, somewhat restrictive rules are needed. Even with uniform tariff and preferential treatment on the base level, if the implementation of the process is too complex or costly in the interpretation and determination of whether the goods comply at the borders, no one will benefit. Whether very restrictive specific rules really promote free trade is of course questionable, because the more limitations you impose, the more you move away from free trade. Thus, despite possibly lowering tariffs, you may be increasing other non-tariff barriers to trade. There is of course a danger to using Rules of Origin as a protectionist device, but of course the goal of totally free trade with no quotas or tariffs worldwide encounters political resistance. The goals should be to make Rules of Origin as transparent as possible so that they are not hidden barriers to trade. Making them easy to apply, although restrictive, will mean greater business certainty and predictability.

Caveat Nota: The importance of Rules of Origin is in the fact that they define which goods are eligible for this preferential treatment.

Note Bene: One of the major things that purchasers should be ascertaining in considering a purchase from a NAFTA seller is the basic origin of the goods.

NAFTA CUSTOMS ADMINISTRATION AND PROCEDURES

The next major step, after determining that the product qualifies under NAFTA is that the business must document in a Certificate of Origin that the requirements of NAFTA for this product have been met. This is where the process and procedures of customs administration become very important because the goods will not qualify if not documented properly and prove they qualify. Under NAFTA, the United States, Mexico, and Canada have agreed to many uniform customs procedures and regulations. Their purposes are to promote transparency and predictability in the exporting process, to make the process work more efficiently and smoothly, so that the process will not have to be repeated at each border, to help companies understand and deal with sometimes complex procedures and, finally, to promote certainty in the process.

Both importers and exporters must be intimately familiar with the Certificate of Origin and what it requires as far as information proving the product's qualifications. The Certificate of Origin may have to be put in the language of the area into which the product is being imported. The certificate is good for 12 months from the initial importation and covers a single importation, or many of the same product. The certificate is effective up to 4 years from the time it is signed by the exporter or producer and the certificate is not required for an importation below the value of $1,000. Exporters or producers are required to complete and sign the certificate for exporting treatment. The exporter or producer's signature signifies or warrants their knowledge that the product qualifies.

The certificate is extremely important for an importer because to get the reduced tariff they need to have possession of the certificate and be able to show it to a customs officer. If the product's lower tariff treatment was not claimed, although it would have qualified, the importer can file for a refund of the duties paid within one year of the importation if they have the certificate as proof.

To receive this treatment, the certificate must be signed by the exporter or producer. However, nowhere in NAFTA does it require the certificate to be signed or even provided by the producer. It is completely voluntary. If the producer of the goods does not sign but another party is the exporter, the exporter must produce and sign the certificate or else the importer cannot claim the benefit of the lower tariff. The exporter, who is not the producer of the product, signs that to the best of its knowledge, or upon reasonable reliance on the producer's statement, the good qualifies. So the question remains as to who is at fault, if in fact the product does not comply, although it was represented by either the producer or the exporter in the certificate to qualify. It is extremely important to keep records to prove what basis you relied upon to find if the goods qualified.

A violation of the customs regulations will enable a NAFTA member country's Customs to impose penalties. Article 508 of the treaty states that each country shall maintain measures imposing criminal, civil, or administrative penalties for violations of its laws and regulations relating to this chapter. Not knowing the law is not a defense for violation.

The penalties can include fines or even jail or the products can be seized by Customs officials if not documented properly, and each country can conduct an investigation to verify the origin. Each member obtains an advance ruling through its Customs service, including the process and information required. They must provide this to any importer within their own country or an exporter or producer in another NAFTA member country who plans to import into their country. Therefore, an importer needs to obtain an advance ruling from the country it produces in, and an exporter or producer must get a ruling from the country it plans to export to. For United States exporters, this requires rulings from Mexican and Canadian Customs. This shows how important it is for United States business to know these customs systems.

There will still be Customs clearance procedures at each border. But the process and much of the procedure and the law to this point and some beyond will be uniform, which will make the system easier to perform. There is, however, going to be inevitable controversy and argument over interpreting tariff classifications, especially if the product being imported hurts a domestic industry. But this process's impact and its consequences on the state of Customs law, and the benefits of NAFTA, will remain to be seen because it will be a slow process. This is especially so because there is a phase-out period for most tariff duties and quotas that will last several years. Furthermore, so that the process is not undermined, there will need to be much enforcement and investigation, or verification of the origin of products, and increased penalties, to safeguard United States trade. But there will also have to be cooperation in the verification and enforcement process between the countries to keep third world countries' products from benefiting. Much of the procedure has yet to be established but the probable effect is clear. It will be very important for businesses to clearly know the process or else be penalized, because the Customs services, of the United States especially, are sure to increase their efforts to protect trade and make sure that it is fair, as well as try to safeguard against non-NAFTA products benefiting. The danger, of course, is that too much enforcement against other NAFTA member countries will again be a barrier to trade. Hopefully the NAFTA rules and custom's procedures clarity will eliminate this danger.

Caveat Nota: For a business, a better way to handle the whole process, and one that is highly recommended, is to get an advance ruling, especially if a business is uncertain whether a product will qualify under NAFTA.

NAFTA'S IMPACT

NAFTA affects not only NAFTA members but also other countries. Within the NAFTA countries, exporters and importers are not the only ones affected. NAFTA's implications are far reaching: The Rules of Origin and Customs process affects foreign and domestic manufacturers or producers, exporters, as well as importers the same way. Both producers and exporters will be limited in what kinds of products they will be able to produce and export. They must look closer at the makeup of their products and estimate their costs through tariffs. As a business, the goals are to reduce costs and take advantage of opportunities to export or to import at the lowest possible duty rate. This will affect the types of goods offered. It will also affect importers because they may not be able to import the goods they want.

NAFTA also affects consumers in that ultimately, increased jobs and lower prices will result for consumers. The most intriguing effect, however, is the effect NAFTA has on countries outside NAFTA. Clearly the rules make it more difficult for other trading partners in Europe and the Far East to benefit, because NAFTA requires that significant changes or significant value be added in one of the NAFTA countries, especially with regard to automotive products and textiles and apparel.

Third-party countries will not be excluded from trading with NAFTA countries; they just won't be able to receive the better and reduced tariff treatment. Since each country will maintain its own tariffs on imports from non-NAFTA countries, these products will cost more. Therefore, third-party countries will not be adversely affected, neither will they be able to take advantage of the benefits of the reduced trade tariffs between NAFTA countries. NAFTA Rules of Origin prevent circumvention through minor changes and transshipment, thus creating incentives for using North American parts and labor. The result is that businesses from third-party countries may have to locate operations in NAFTA countries, no matter what the costs, if they want to compete.

Caveat Bene: For the purchasing manager, the prices of similar goods may be lower if they come from one of the other NAFTA countries because of the savings on tariffs, as compared with goods produced elsewhere in the world. Of course, labor costs and other efficiencies also must be taken into account, so comparative pricing of goods produced throughout the world is necessary. Legally, a Certificate of Origin is a necessary requirement, and in any case of doubt an advanced ruling is advantageous.

THE EUROPEAN UNION

Another major regional economic integration development is the European Union (EU), which has been expanding quickly. The purchasing managers should be generally aware that EU as a free marketplace without customs and tariffs is not available to U.S. businesses. It would seem at first that such a closed region might make prices higher for goods being purchased by United States businesses, since customs and tariffs are still applicable. However, the purchasing manager should keep in mind the fact that the overall effect of the EU may be to create within it more efficiencies and thereby make prices for goods lower than previously. So U.S. purchasers may still come out ahead on price despite the fact that this country is not a member and goods are still subject to the normal customs.

WHAT IS THE EUROPEAN UNION?

European integration began in the aftermath of World War II. This Union has evolved out of many different treaties and agreements some of which were originally formed to serve as military alliances. Founding members of the Community first pooled their heavy industries. The European Coal and Steel community was established by the Treaty of Paris in 1951. The Treaty of Rome of 1957 created the European Economic Community (EEC) and the European Atomic Energy Community (EUROTOM). These two entities were eventually merged in 1967 into a single institution referred to as the European Communities (EC). The European Communities changed its name and became the European Union (EU) after the Maastricht Treaty on European Union took effect on November 1, 1993. The European Coal and Steel Community will become part of EU in 2004.

The present day European Union consists of fifteen member countries that are part of an economic pact to achieve greater success both on the continent of Europe and abroad. The six founding members were Belgium, France, Germany, Denmark, Italy, Luxembourg, and the Netherlands. The 15 members in existence today are: Austria, Benelux nations of Belgium, The Netherlands and Luxee, Germany, Greece, Ireland, Italy, Portugal, Spain, and Sweden. With the exception of Cyprus and Malta, which have applied for membership, Liechtenstein, Iceland, Switzerland, and Norway, whose people have rejected membership in the Union (six countries with a population of just under 12 million people), every country in Western Europe has now chosen to join in the same shared venture.

The European Union is a mix of rich and poor. Its richest regions—Hamburg in Germany or the Paris region of France—have living standards five times higher than the poorest areas. The least wealthy member states— Spain, Portugal, Greece, Ireland, and the former East Germany—receive considerable financial support from the European Union to help narrow the gap between the rich and the poor.

The next great stage in the integration of Europe is the involvement of the neighbors in Central and Eastern Europe. Public opinion in the existing member states strongly support bringing in Central and Eastern Europe. A study for the European Commission published in January 1995 found majorities of more than 60 percent for bringing Hungary, Poland, and the Czech Republic into the Union. Support was only marginally less strong (55%–58%) for the memberships of Bulgaria, Slovak, Romania, and Slovenia. The above countries plus the three Baltic States are in the associated category eligible for membership. So far, only Poland and Hungary have formally applied for membership in the Union. The Union has launched a gradual process of rapprochement to enable these countries to meet the economic and political conditions necessary for membership. Programs have been set up to aid development and stimulate investment in Central and Eastern Europe. Meetings at heads of government and ministerial level were regularly held to discuss pan-European issues, such as energy, environment, transport, telecommunications, research, science and technology, as well as home affairs, justice and education. By the end of the century the Union may well be enlarged to 20 or 25 members.

EU has as its fundamental aim to create a harmonious single internal market free of internal trading barriers and to bring the economics of its various members closer together. More specifically, EU aims:

- To lay the foundation of an ever-closer union among the peoples of Europe.
- To promote balanced and sustainable economic and social progress by creating an area without internal frontiers, by strengthening economic and social cohesion, and by establishing economic and

monetary union, ultimately including a central bank and a single currency.

- To project the Union to the rest of the world, through a Common foreign and security policy, and eventually, a common defense policy.
- To strengthen the protection of the rights and interests of the nationals of its member states through the introduction of a citizenship of the Union.
- To develop close cooperation on justice and home affairs.

Caveat Nota: Certain non-commercial factors may be important in deciding where to purchase or market in EU. Each EU member retains its own national characteristics and cultures and technical preferences. The cultural diversity of Europe is well known and it is as well to be aware of the differences in advance. Linguistic barriers still exist within Europe, although these are becoming increasingly eroded with the growth of English as the international language of trade. Business practices also differ widely between different parts of the Union. England offers a culture more familiar to Americans and London's position as one of the leading financial centers and the ready access to competitive financing may also assist.

HOW THE EUROPEAN UNION WORKS

Just as the United States has its government structured in a manner that allows for an executive branch to carry out the laws that are passed, a legislative branch that actually makes the laws, and a judicial branch that interprets what the laws mean, the EU system is devised somewhat similarly.

The European Commission, the executive branch, is a body composed of twenty members, two from each of the larger states (France, Germany, Spain, Italy, and the United Kingdom) and one from each of the other states. Each commissioner is appointed by mutual agreement of the 15 governments of the member states. However, once appointed the commissioners may not take directions from their own national governments. They are to act in the interests of the community separate from their own nationalistic concerns.

The Commission has generally four main tasks: to carry out detailed implementation of decisions reached by its political master, the Council of Ministers; to exercise its own powers of decision, which include managing various important funds (the European Agricultural Guidance and Guarantee Fund, the European Social Fund, and the European Regional Development Fund) as well as carrying out investigations under the EU competition policy; to serve as the initiator of EU policies by making policy proposals to the Council of Ministers; to act as guardian of the EU treaties by investigating breaches and by summoning offenders before the European Court of Justice.

A Commissioner has a term of five years. This coincides with the terms of the European Parliament, which exercises supervisory power over the Commission. The President of the Commission is chosen from the list of nominated Commissioners.

Just as the European Commission is known as the initiator and executive of the European Union, the Council of Ministers are known as "the decision makers of the European Union." Their role consists mostly of providing broad guidelines of policy, representing the interests of the member states, making decisions about the adoption of the legislation and performing the preeminent role in the context of the intergovernmental pillars of the EU.

The Council is made up of the representatives of the governments of the member states. Each member state has a seat on the Council of Ministers. The Council meets in closed sessions and the frequency of the meetings vary. There are no set times, but there are usually meetings once a month depending on the subject being discussed. Each of the member states of the EU holds the Presidency of the Council in turn for six-month periods, which are determined by the alphabetical spelling of the state's name.

The Council is assisted by a Permanent Representative Committee, which comprises the Permanent Representatives (ambassadors) of the member states to the Union. Its main task is to prepare the ground for Council meetings. The European Parliament (EP) is an advisory body, which may be viewed as also a part of the legislative branch. It debates proposals of the Commission and advises both the Commission and the Council. It has veto power, based on the Maastricht treaty, over legislation in certain areas, such as consumer protection, health, education, culture, environment, and the single market. A large part of the European Parliament's legislative work is done by 20 specialized committees. Each member belongs to at least one of these committees.

The Single European Act of 1987, which amended the original Treaties, was influential in shifting more of the power towards the European Parliament and the Commission and away from the Council of Ministers. The new EP powers include more involvement in the enactment of legislation and the right of prior approval of the appointment of the Commission President and the Commissioners. The EP's powers to amend the legislation have been increased to include the EU's policies on transport, social action, research, environmental protection, and overseas development. Treaties with non-EU states have become subject to the approval of the European Parliament before they are ratified.

The judicial branch of the EU is the European Court of Justice. Its decisions take precedence over the laws of member states. The Court is outside the decision-making process of the EU and the role of the Court in interpreting the EU agreed law makes the decision-making process effective. The member states have agreed to be bound by the rulings of the Court.

In performing its two main functions, that of directly applying the laws of the Union and that of interpreting the provisions of the Union law, the Court must ensure that the application of the law by the member states is consistent for the whole of the EU. The Court, which is based in Luxembourg, has 15 judges. Most of the work of the Court is done by groups or chambers of judges. There are four chambers of three judges and two chambers of 5 judges. The judges are assisted by 9 advocate-generals.

All 15 states of the EU appoint a judge. The 9 advocate-generals are appointed from Germany, France, Italy, and the United Kingdom, with the remaining four coming from other member states. The work of the judges is guaranteed to be independent. This comes from the Treaties themselves and is ensured by the member states through their ratification of the Treaties. Enforcement of the Court decisions was given a pillar of strength when the Treaty on the European Union (art. 171 TUE) gave the Court the right to fine member states that did not comply with earlier judgments of the Court.

To assist with the growing workload of the Court, the Court of First Instance was established in 1989 under the Single European Act. It has 15 members appointed for renewable terms of six years, one judge coming from each member state. Under this method, all proceedings brought by individuals and corporations are dealt with by the Court of First Instance. The European Court of Justice deals with proceedings brought by the member states and the EU institution and with appeals from decisions of the Court of First Instance.

This arrangement reinforces the European Court of Justice's focus on ensuring uniform application of Union law by member states' courts and on safeguarding the balance of power among the EU institutions. There is a European Court of Human Rights which is a specialized part of the "judicial branch." It was created under the 1950 European Convention for the Protection of Human Rights and Fundamental Freedoms along with the Commission on Human Rights. When an individual is injured because one of his/her human rights has been violated, he has the recourse of formulating an independent claim before the Commission and then the Court. The Court will render decisions on the issue of whether or not there was a violation of the convention and how the applicant is to be compensated or to exercise his/her rights.

Other EU institutions are more "executive branch" or mixed in nature. These include the Court of Auditors (monitors the management of Union Community finance), the Economic and Social Committee (an advisory body consisting of 222 representatives of the various economic and social groups), the Committee of the Regions (an advisory committee consisting of 222 representatives of local and regional authorities), the European Investment Bank (finances investment projects, particularly in the less-developed regions, together with the Community Structural Funds), European Police Office (Europe, the cross-border police intelligence agency).

It is inevitable to ask what is the balance of power between EU and member states? In fact, the Union can only act on the basis of powers freely granted to it by member states in its founding treaties. In areas involving trade, agriculture, industry, competition, environment, regional development, transport, energy and monetary affairs, member states can be said to be "pooling" at least a part of their sovereignty. Policies in other areas are the responsibility of national governments. Under the principle of "subsidiary," EU action is limited to areas where it is better placed to act than the individual member states. Also, the cultural heritage of member states is to be encouraged as long as it does not interfere with any EU policies or laws.

Caveat Nota: Although the basic dichotomy between common law and civil law jurisdiction remains, there is increasing harmonization of the legal framework. EU legislation has created a level playing field. It ensures that member states give effect to their EU obligations. However, under EU's approach of harmonization of laws, some only lay down minimum legal principles that have to be observed by member states in their national legislation. Some businesses might find an advantage in establishing in a country with lessor legal requirements and therefore lower compliance costs. Nevertheless, the choice of business location should be primarily a commercial and not a legal one.

EU COMMERCIAL RULES

The new Union contains provisions in its treaty which create European Union citizenship, establish a common foreign and security policy, and set the goal of economic and monetary union. This includes a central bank and a single currency. According to the Treaty, "Every person holding the nationality of a member state shall be a citizen of the Union." The Treaty describes rights held by Union citizens: freedom to move and reside freely within the Union; right to vote and stand as a candidate in the European Parliament and local elections; diplomatic protection from any member state embassy; the right to petition the European Parliament; and the right to seek redress from an ombudsman's office concerning possible misconduct by any EU organ in the execution of its duties.

Currency fluctuations can cause distortions in the price of goods traded internationally. This creates uncertainty for buyer and seller. Currency fluctuations can block trade just as effectively as the barriers that the nations of Europe have gradually eliminated over the years. In 1979, the European Monetary System (OEMs) was created. It is based on the European Currency Unit (ECU). At present time the ECU is the form of payment used to operate the organs of the European Union. For example, anyone who works at the Court of Justice in Luxembourg will receive their pay in ECU's and then will have it transferred to the currency of their choice. A single currency removes the need for travelers to change money when traveling within the Union. The ordinary citizen also gets a strong and stable currency backed by the combined economic power of the EU and its member states. However, while traveling to Europe, an American visitor need not worry about exchanging dollars for ECUs yet. Also American based credit cards are readily accepted in Europe and make the currency conversion with a high degree of precision.

A single currency will be introduced in most member states of EU on January 1, 1999. The Maastricht treaty obliges all countries that meet the convergence criteria to lock their exchange rates irrevocably on the first day of 1999, in preparation for the adoption of a common currency, the Euro, in 2002. The convergence criteria are to be tested on figures for 1997, available in the spring of 1998, and are as follows:

- Inflation—no more than one-and-a half percentage points higher than the average of the three best-performing states.
- Long-term interest rates—no more than two points above the same benchmark.

- Budget deficit—3 percent of GDP or less.
- Public debt—no more than 60 percent of GDP.
- Exchange rate—observe the "normal margins" of the exchange-rate mechanism (EM) for two years.

There will be a three-year transition period from January 1, 1999, to December 31, 2001. There will be fixed and irrevocable conversion rates between National Currency Units and the Euro. Euro bank notes and coins will be introduced on January 1, 2002, and national bank notes and coins will cease to be legal tender by no later than June 30, 2002. A single monetary policy will operate across the Eurozone. That policy will be controlled centrally by a fully independent European Central Bank, which will be responsible for maintaining price stability and for setting interest rates.

EU established a common commercial policy covering the external trade relations of all the member states. There is a common system of customs and tariffs applicable wherever goods are imported into the Union from outside. There also is a common set of rules for valuation and tariff classification and for determining the origin of goods. In addition, well-developed antidumping legislation is based on the relevant provisions of the GATT.

EU members are prohibited from introducing or maintaining any direct or indirect barriers to trade within the Union. This rule has its main impact on product specifications, packaging and labeling, health and safety and product registration requirements for food products, pharmaceuticals and agro-chemicals and other industrial products. Under the principles of "non-discrimination" and "mutual recognition," a product authorized for sale in one member state must be free to be sold in all other member states. member states cannot impose quantitative restrictions on imports or measures having equivalent effect unless such measures are used to protect a general public interest, such as consumer protection and protection against unfair competition and environmental protection. Even then they are not to be more restrictive than necessary.

Under the principle of "exhaustion of rights" applicable to intellectual property rights, once the owner of an intellectual property right has allowed his product to be sold in one member state, he cannot generally rely on intellectual property rights subsisting in that product elsewhere in the Union to prevent that product from being sold on through licensees, wholesalers, or other traders in other markets. The owner will, therefore, be unable to enforce those rights by obtaining an injunction against import or damages for infringement. In certain cases, intellectual property rights can be enforced against imported goods. In particular, this is so where these goods are infringing products manufactured and sold without the right owner's consent and without the consent of any associated company or licensee. Any provision of national law that is discriminatory as between domestic and imported goods is unenforceable. This applies to all trading rules.

Companies involved in service industries can provide services across frontiers in the other member states on an equal footing with service companies already established there. However, in order to benefit from the rules, one must have a basic establishment (branches or subsidiaries) in one member state. For this reason, many American companies or firms have founded branches or subsidiaries in Europe in recent years. Similar rights apply to self-employed persons.

As for financial services, the Union has introduced the concept of the single "Union passport," avoiding the need for companies to comply with authorization requirements in more than one member state. Any non-EU company wanting to take advantage of the rules, however, needs first to establish a subsidiary and obtain relevant authorizations in at least one member state. Branches of non-EU entities still require separate authorization in each state.

The rules on free movement of workers allow recruitment and transfer of personnel within the Union. Work permits are not necessary, although certain registration requirements may remain. For some professionals, certification may be required, but slowly the market is moving towards mutual recognition of "equivalent" qualifications for a number of professions.

The EU anti-competition rules prohibit both horizontal and vertical agreements that, directly or indirectly, have adverse affects on competition. These include agreements which fix purchase or selling prices or any other trading conditions; limit or control production, markets, technical development, or investment; share markets or sources of supply; apply dissimilar conditions to equivalent transactions with other trading parties, thereby placing them at a competitive disadvantage; make the conclusion of contracts subject to the acceptance of supplementary obligations which has no connection with the subject of such contracts. Any violating agreements are automatically void.

Once a company has acquired a high market share in the Union as a whole or in one of its constituent markets, there is a risk that it could be treated as dominant. Dominance may also arise where a company has strong patent or trademark protection giving it a significant market advantage over its competitors. Dominant companies are prohibited from abusing their privileged market position through abusive behavior. Abusive behavior may be exploitative, such as charging disproportionately high prices, or refusing to supply a product for which there is consumer demand, or exclusionary, such as predatory pricing, discriminatory discounts, tie-ins, exclusive purchasing or distribution, discriminatory conditions of sale or purchase.

The enforcement of competition rules lies with the Commission, which may act at the request of a third party or on its own initiative. The Commission has a limited discretion in deciding how to prioritize its cases and has indicated that it will tend to give priority to cases raising important issues of principle or a novel point of law. The Commission has wide-ranging power to seek out suspected infringements, to search premises with or without prior notice, to demand information and to take copies of any documents relevant to its inquiries, to impose fines with respect to breaches of the procedural regulations, to issue cease and desist orders requiring parties to put an end to infringements, to impose periodic penalty payments for non-implementation, and to require parties to submit periodic reports to ensure future compliance.

There are various ways of dealing with EU competition rules depending on the type of agreement, the market positions of the parties, and their relevant size and commercial objectives. Block exemptions, in the form of regulations issued by the Commission, automatically authorize a given category of agreement, such as distribution, patent licensing, know-how licensing, and cooperation agreements. Individual parties may also formally notify the Commission of the agreement and be granted individual exemptions. From the moment of notification the parties can no longer be fined. An individual party may choose to notify of the agreement if there is a reasonable chance that the agreement would benefit from individual exemption if notified and fines would be highly unlikely.

On December 21, 1989, the Council of the European Community, the European Community's decision-making body, adopted a mergers control that will have a very significant effect on corporate reorganization, not only within the EU but also with non-EU businesses. The Commission under this ruling has the exclusive power to oppose large-scale mergers likely to impact on the EU market. The Commission will have jurisdiction over deals of a certain nature and size: mergers that have a "European Community dimension" having significant contact with the EEC will be subject to these regulations.

What does this mean to corporations planning large-scale mergers within the European Union? Experts in international trade law view this as a victory for the corporations that will no longer face double investigations by the Commission and member states' authorities. This will provide a one-stop control for faster and easier clearance to the markets in the EU.

Another form of regulation that U.S. businesses must be aware of is in the area of employee participation in management. This comes from the example of Germany that has emphasized this innovation. In 1976 the Codetermination Act was passed. This Act mandates the formation of a supervisory board composed of 50 percent shareholders and 50 percent employees' representatives. It applies to all business organizations regularly employing more than 2,000 employees. Exemptions are allowed for mutual insurance companies and all partnerships. In addition, the press, television, radio, churches, educational, and charitable institutions are exempted.

In 1989, the Charter of Fundamental Social Rights of Workers was passed. It is a non-binding political declaration intended to harmonize worker rights and is not a legal basis for European Community law. Nonetheless it is still important because it is a separate agreement among the member states. The Social Charter is a means of consolidating social policy concepts in a single document. The scope of this document is the working environment including such issues as working conditions, workers health and safety, disclosure of information, sex discrimination, and worker consultation. The Charter allows for member states to opt out if they so desire. England has done this because it disagrees with the comprehensive social program being forced on the member states. These examples are just a few of the many laws, regulations, restrictions, and codes that any American business will have to understand and deal with as it tries to break into the competitive market of the European Union.

Caveat Nota: U.S. plaintiffs seeking to enforce a contract or intellectual property rights in EU, may frequently face a Euro-defense, a legal defense based on one of the EU treaty provisions, or a regulation or directive. The most common Euro-defenses are that the contract is void and unenforceable or that the plaintiff is abusing its dominant position, or that the action in question is in breach of the free movement rules.

Caveat Nota: There is still the possibility of regional grants and tax breaks. Under a limited number of circumstances, member states may grant direct or indirect state aids or subsidies, particularly when designed to promote the economic development of an area where the standard of living is abnormally low or where there is serious under-employment. Thus, it is worthwhile for American investors to check which country offers financial incentives or tax breaks to companies setting up in that country or particular region.

Caveat Nota: During the transition period, businesses will be free to transact business in Euros if they wish, although they cannot be compelled by law to do so. However, businesses outside the Euro-zone may find themselves under pressure from their European and multinational trading partners to transact business in Euros from as early as January 1, 1999. Those that are able to meet their trading partners' Euro requirements will secure a competitive advantage. But a company's ability to do so will depend heavily on whether its systems are able to cope with the new currency.

UNITED STATES—EU RELATIONS

EU is the largest global market of the United States. The EU is the largest market for more than 20 of the 50 United States. Trade and investment balance between the United States and EU has over the past 25 years or so netted out to just about zero. The EU market is among the most open to the United States, at least in terms of manufactured goods. The United States market, too, is among the most open to the EU countries. After the Uruguay Round tariff cuts, tariffs on each other's industrial products averaged about 3 percent.

EU is also America's largest global competitor. The EU has about 40 percent of the Middle Eastern market, while United States has 13 percent. The EU has about 16 percent of China's market, compared to America's 12 percent share. EU exporters are supported with a broad array of government backing, including export promotion support, strong government advocacy, and abundant export credits. The United States spends far less than EU competitors on export promotion.

The United States has maintained diplomatic relations with the European Community and its forerunners since 1953. The United States Mission to the ECSC formally opened in Luxembourg in 1956. In 1961 the United States Mission to the European Communities was established in Brussels. The United States has a strong tradition in supporting the development of the European Communities. It holds a strong conviction that European unity is good for Europe, good for the Atlantic partnership, and good for the world. A strengthened EU has a vital role to play in assuring a stable and prosperous Europe and a humane world order.

In November 1990, the United States and the European Community issued the Transatlantic Declaration, which provides for biannual meetings among presidents of the United States, the EU Council and the EU Commission. Also there are bi-annual consultations between the Secretary of State and the EU Foreign Ministers. On December 3, 1995, a United States-EU Summit meeting held in Madrid, Spain, included the United States President, European Commission President and European Council President. They agreed on a "New Transatlantic Agenda" that sets the course in the entirety of the United States-EU political and economic relationship. This includes an Action Plan and the creation of a "New Transatlantic Marketplace," a program that will implement steps to remove the remaining obstacles to trade and investment across the Atlantic. It is only through these forms of official contact that a strong and lasting relationship can be achieved to further the goals of both the EU and the United States. These relationships will hopefully foster long-standing agreements on international business relations.

In the effort to create a New Transatlantic Marketplace, United States and EU agreed to take actions in the following areas:

- Further reduce or eliminate tariff and nontariff barriers to facilitate trade in goods and services.
- Resolve bilateral trade issues and disputes to build confidence.
- Mutual recognition of conformity assessment, including certification and testing procedures, for certain sectors; cooperate to set up international standards or procedures in various areas; harmonize regulatory measures on safety and environmental protection requirements such as vehicle safety and pollution regulations.
- Customs cooperation: simplification of customs procedures, computerization (information, data exchange, common access to database, etc.), and consultation within international organizations, methods of work.
- A commitment to combat corruption and bribery by implementing antibribery legislation.

- Improve intellectual property rights protection throughout the world and intensify efforts in the WTO.
- Negotiation of a multilateral investment agreement, which will stress right of establishment and full national treatment.
- Improve access to information services through information technology and telecommunications.
- Cooperate to improve air and maritime transport safety and management.
- Cooperation on energy-related issues such as environmental protections and energy technology.
- Exchange of information on issues affecting health and safety.

The optimistic hope is that there will eventually be a Trans-Atlantic Free Trade Area (TAFTA). A study completed by the Economic Strategy Institute (ESI) in 1995 estimated that eliminating barriers to trade across the Atlantic could boost economic output in the United States by $142–$239 billion (or between 1.6% and 2.8% of GDP) and in the EU by $94–$184 billion (or between 1.0% and 1.9% of total EU output) by the year 2000. Two-way trade between the United States and EU could increase between $70 and $100 billion annually between 20 percent and 30 percent by the century's end, with each region enjoying about the same amount of increased exports.

REGIONAL ECONOMIC COOPERATIONS IN ASIA

The progress of the EU, the successful implementation of NAFTA, the symbolic implications of regionalism with both North America and Europe in regions, and their modest discrimination against Asia added pressure to the Asian economics. There is a growing concern that the highly trade-dependent economies of East Asia have been left without a bloc of their own. An East Asian trading bloc has now come under serious consideration in many capitals in the region.

An East Asian trading bloc is an idea with considerable appeal. It will remove much or all of the intra-regional trade barriers, erected especially against other East Asian countries for the purpose of protecting domestic industries from the competing industries of other regional countries in order to pursue industrial policy objectives or to pursue "dynamic" comparative advantages. Such a market-led integration of the East Asian regional economies will mitigate the acute adjustment pressure that East Asia has been imposing on the rest of the world and will ease the balance-of-payment problem between East Asia and Europe and North America. An East Asian trading bloc could also enhance the East Asian economies' bargaining leverage vis-a-vis the other blocs. The division of the world into large trading blocs may be conducive to global trade liberalization because it would help eliminate the free-rider problem and also because the interbloc trade negotiation may be an efficient way of reorganizing otherwise complex multilateral trade negotiations.

However, an East Asian trading bloc is likely to weaken the trade linkage between East Asia and North America because of its trade-diverting effect. Hence comes the idea of an Asia-Pacific trading bloc, which will encompass East Asia, North America, and Australia, with a possible extension to Latin America. The Asia Pacific Economic Cooperation (APEC) forum is a step toward this direction.

Another major regional trade bloc in East Asia is the ASEAN Free Trade Area (AFTA). Notably, there are many subregional growth polygons in East Asia. For example, the East ASEAN Growth Area has total population of 24 million; the greater Mekong subregion, with a population of 220 million; the Southern China Growth triangle, with a population of 120 million; the Tumen River development zone in Northeast Asia, involving China, North and South Korea, Russia, and Japan. However, East Asia has not created the same super-national structure as the EU, although the market-driven regional economic integration has gone far ahead.

ASIA PACIFIC ECONOMIC COOPERATION

The APEC concept was initiated by Australian Prime Minister Bob Hawke and the first APEC meeting was held in Canberra, Australia, in 1989. This 12-nation meeting pledged to promote open regional cooperation without the characteristics of an exclusive regional trading bloc. The second meeting was held in Singapore in July 1990, with members agreeing to work for a successful conclusion of the Uruguay Round of multilateral trade negotiations. The Seoul meeting in November 1991 extended membership to China, Hong Kong, and Taiwan. The 1992 APEC meeting in Bangkok agreed to establish an APEC Secretariat in Singapore as well as to form an independent advisory panel known as the Eminent Persons Group (each member to appoint one person as representative). The group would present annual reports and make policy recommendations on request.

The 1993 Seattle meeting proved a major turning point for APEC. The meeting was elevated through the attendance by presidents and prime ministers for the first time for all members but Hong Kong, Taiwan, and Malaysia. However, this meeting produced no concrete results and rejected United States initiative of transforming the Asian Pacific area into a free trade zone. Nevertheless, the meeting set as APEC's goal "the progressive development of a community of Asia-Pacific economies with free and open trade and investment." The leaders charged the Eminent Persons Group "to present further more specific proposals on how the recommended long-term vision might be realized." In response, the Eminent Persons Group issued a report on August 30, 1994, calling for an APEC-wide free trade and investment area.

This challenge was taken by the November 1994 summit in Bogor, Indonesia. In the Bogor Declaration of Common Resolve, the APEC heads of government agreed to create a "free trade and investment area in the Asia-Pacific." Under this plan, the industrialized economies will achieve free and open trade and investment no later than the year 2010 and developing economies no later than the year 2020. As an initial step, member economies also announced their intention to accelerate the implementation of Uruguay Round commitments. The meeting also announced a commitment to achieve an open investment regime early in the 21st century.

The November 1995 Osaka, Japan, meeting endorsed the Osaka Action Agenda. The agenda includes 15 broad areas targeted for liberalization through a combination of concerted unilateralism and collective actions, a list of principles to guide member economies as they moved toward fulfilling their Bogor pledges, and 13 areas of economic and technical cooperation to be pursued by APEC participants.

The 15 areas of liberalization are: Tariffs, nontariff border measures, services, investment, standards and conformance, customs procedures, intellectual property rights, competition policy, government procurement, deregulation, rules of origin, dispute mediation, mobility of business people, information gathering and analysis, and implementation of Uruguay Round commitments.

APEC's general principles are:

- *Comprehensiveness*—the APEC liberalization and facilitation process will be comprehensive, addressing all impediments to achieving the long-term goals of free and open trade and investment.

- *WTO-Consistency*—the liberalization and facilitation measures undertaken in the context of the APEC Action Agenda will be WTO-consistent.

- *Comparability*—APEC economies will endeavor to ensure the overall comparability of their trade and investment liberalization and facilitation, taking into account the general level of liberalization and facilitation already achieved by each APEC economy.

- *Nondiscrimination*—APEC economies will apply or endeavor to apply the principle of nondiscrimination between and among them in the process of liberalization and facilitation of trade and investment. The outcome of trade and investment liberalization in the Asia-Pacific region will be the actual reduction of barriers not only among APEC economies but also between APEC and non-APEC economies.

- *Transparency*—each APEC economy will ensure transparency of its respective laws, regulations, and administrative procedures which affect the flow of goods, services, and capital among APEC economies in order to create and maintain an open and predictable trade and investment environment in the Asia-Pacific region.

- *Standstill*—each APEC economy will endeavor to refrain from using measures which would have the effect of increasing levels of protection, thereby ensuring a steady and progressive trade and investment liberalization and facilitation process.

- *Simultaneous Start, Continuous Process, and Differentiated Timetables*—APEC economies will begin simultaneously and without delay the process of liberalization, facilitation, and cooperation, with each member economy contributing continuously and significantly to achieve the long-term goal of free and open trade and investment.

- *Flexibility*—considering the different levels of economic development among the APEC economies and the diverse circumstances in each economy, flexibility will be available in dealing with issues arising from such circumstances in the liberalization and facilitation process.

- *Cooperation*—economic and technical cooperation contributing to liberalization and facilitation will be actively pursued.

The 13 areas of cooperation are: human resources development, industrial science and technology, small and medium enterprises, economic infrastructure, energy, transportation, telecommunications and information, tourism, trade and investment data, trade promotion, marine resources conservation, fisheries and agricultural technology. More than 300 projects are underway carried out by APEC's various working groups in the 13 areas of cooperation designated by the Osaka Action Agenda.

The concerted unilateralism ("modality"), adopted at the Osaka meeting, charged each forum member with developing individual action plans that lay out the liberalization steps each would take in the 15 areas of liberalization described in the Osaka Action Agenda. These plans were to include specific and concrete details, with time frames, for the near to medium term, while outlining the basic direction of liberalization through to the target dates of 2010 or 2020. These plans will be subject to peer review to help assure compliance in achieving the ultimate goal. Concerted unilateralism allows APEC members to take small but concrete steps each year and to gain confidence in each other.

The collective action plans are developed through close consultations among APEC members in the forum's working-level committee's focus on detailed, often highly technical issues. Examples include the harmonization of customs procedures, the development of mutual recognition agreements covering product standards and the introduction of business visas to expedite travel throughout the region, as well as organized efforts to collect and disseminate information. These efforts are invaluable contributions to improving the Asian Pacific's business environment.

The November 1996 APEC summit in Subic, Philippines, concentrated on the development of these plans. A number of the individual plans included market-opening measures of substance, especially in the area of tariff reductions. Several members announced tariff-cutting packages that go beyond their Uruguay Round obligations. In fact, half of APEC members have unveiled plans to cut tariffs to levels that exceed their Uruguay Round obligations. The following are highlights of selected individual action plans:

- *China*—By 2000, it will reduce the simple average tariff rate to about 15 percent, down from the current rate of 23 percent; will make further reductions in the medium and long term; will reduce or relax nontariff measures in 384 areas; will improve transparency of investment regime and open more sectors to foreign investment.

- *Indonesia*—Tariffs of 20 percent or less in 1995 will be reduced in stages to 5 percent or less by 2000; tariffs of more than 20 percent in 1995 will be reduced in stages to 20 percent and under by 1998 and to 10 percent or less by 2003; will eliminate 98 nontariff barriers by 2004; it will continue to align national standards with international standards.

- *Philippines*—Applied tariffs will be reduced to 5 percent by 2004 from a current simple average of 16 percent; 40 percent of local standards will be aligned with international standards within 10 years, 100 percent by 2020; it will progressively privatize government telecommunications facilities and will review restrictions on foreign equity participation in the financial services sector.

- *Chile*—This country intends to eliminate tariffs on most items, some agricultural products being the main exceptions by 2010, fully 10 years before developing economies' deadline for achieving free trade.

- *Malaysia*—It will continue to reduce tariffs unilaterally; nontariff measures will be reviewed and reduced where appropriate; will gradually liberalize the financial services sector, allowing higher levels of foreign investment; will place high priority on aligning domestic standards with international standards.

- *Japan*—It will align industrial and agricultural standards more closely with international standards; will expedite import inspections by strengthening animal and plant quarantine systems; will end prior notification requirements for foreign investment in the mining sector; will introduce by June 1997 Pest Risk Analysis to implement appropriate phytosanitary measures; will ease restrictions in the telecommunications sector.

- *United States*—The government expressed support for zero tariffs by 2000 for information technology products as well as wood products, oilseed products, white distilled spirits, and nonferrous metals.

Like the individual action plans, the collective action plans include a long-term work program in each of the 15 targeted areas. Some efforts are designed to achieve practical outcomes, with many scheduled to be realized over the short term. However, not all of these cooperative efforts are geared toward concrete goals reached under specific timetables.

The following is a list of examples of collective action plans:

Tariffs and Nontariff Measures

- In 1997, establish a data base covering customs information and the applied tariffs of member economies. Information will be available on CD-ROM or over the Internet.
- In 1998, release an expanded APEC database containing information and data on customs, tariffs, trade flows, and nontariff measures.
- In 1998, produce a list of measures recognized as nontariff impediments to trade among APEC economies and a list of products affected by them.

Standards and Conformance

- In 1996, undertake alignment (by 2000 or 2005) of member economies' standards with international standards on appliances, rubber products, and food labeling.
- In 1996, complete an APEC Mutual Recognition Arrangement covering conformity assessments of food products.

Customs Procedures

- In 1996, harmonize tariff nomenclature among APEC members to be six-digit level.
- In 1998, adopt the principles of the Kyoto Convention, simplifying and harmonizing customs procedures.

- By 2000, introduce an advance tariff classification ruling system providing greater certainty and transparency for exporters.

Intellectual Property Rights

- In 1996, perform a survey of domestic intellectual property rights legislation.
- In 1997, conduct a survey of enforcement mechanisms to develop principles for enforcement.

Government Procurement

- In 1997, complete a survey of the government procurement systems of APEC members and make arrangements to publish APEC information on government procurement.

Mobility of Business People

- In 1996, publish an APEC business travel handbook providing information on the short-term entry and visa arrangements of the forum's members.

APEC has 18 members, including Australia, Brunei, Canada, Chile, China, Hong Kong, Indonesia, Japan, South Korea, Malaysia, Mexico, New Zealand, Papua, New Guinea, the Philippines, Singapore, Taiwan, Thailand, and the United States. By the end of 1996, there were 11 other countries or regions that wanted to join this popular club: Columbia, Ecuador, India, Macau, Mongolia, Pakistan, Panama, Peru, Sri Lanka, Vietnam, and Russia. After three years moratorium, APEC will begin accepting new members in 1998. The most hopeful candidates would be Vietnam, Russia, Peru, and India.

APEC is unique in many aspects. Its members include several of the world's wealthiest nations as well as some of its poorest. Political systems represented include open, democratic governments, military dictatorships, and communist one-party states. APEC populations have primarily Judeo-Christian, Buddhism, and Islam backgrounds. Serious territorial and political disputes also widely exist among its members. Despite the various differences among Asia-Pacific nations, a common desire for freer trade and investment has attracted these nations together. Furthermore, new members could be considered in the future.

Currently, the 18 APEC members have a gross domestic product exceeding $13 trillion, or about one-half of the world's total output. APEC members account for 46 percent of the world's total merchandise trade.

The United States preferred a conventional model of regional free trade areas like the NAFTA for Asia Pacific economic cooperation. Under such a model, APEC members would lower trade barriers in a preferential way only for themselves, not for non-members. The forum would then have free trade for members, but relative protection against non-members. However, the Asian members of APEC have enunciated a policy that trade liberalization be done by APEC members on a most-favored-nation (MFN) basis. That means such liberalization is automatically extended to non-members of the forum.

The APEC forum serves its strategic objectives. The forum can exert pressure to keep the WTO trading system unrestricted through open regionalism. The emergence of APEC as a regional trade organization in 1993 is widely credited with bringing the Uruguay Round to a successful conclusion. APEC also greatly facilitated the conclusion of the Information Technology Agreement in the first WTO Ministerial Meeting in 1996. APEC can help United States maintain its interest in the region and help stabilize United States-Japan economic relations. APEC prevents the emergence of an Asia-only trading bloc as advocated by Malaysia. APEC provides a vehicle for China, as well as Taiwan, to be involved in the region. APEC offers a new model of North-South relations in a regional text.

The APEC economies are important to the United States. In 1995, total United States two-way merchandise trade with APEC members was $872.4 billion or 65.7 percent of America's total two-way merchandise trade. Exports of goods to APEC members provide paychecks to approximately 7.3 million American workers. Moreover, citizens of the United States and other APEC members are large investors in each other's economies. In 1995, United States direct investment in other APEC members was $225.4 billion or 31.7 percent of United States direct investment worldwide. Direct investment by other APEC members in the United States was $172.5 billion or 30.7 percent of total foreign direct investment in the United States.

ASEAN FREE TRADE AREA (AFTA)

ASEAN members include Brunei, Indonesia, Malaysia, Philippines, Singapore, Thailand, and Vietnam. ASEAN has now a combined population of more than 400 million. ASEAN is also expanding ties with the three non-ASEAN countries in Southeast Asia, namely, Cambodia, Laos, and Myanmar. Hopefully, ASEAN will draw these three countries into the regional development mainstream.

In 1992, ASEAN heads of governments agreed to establish an ASEAN Free Trade Area (AFTA) by the year 2008. The ASEAN countries committed to lowering tariffs on wide categories of intra-ASEAN trade beginning in January 1993, with the final goal of 0–5 percent (ad valorem) tariffs by 2008. Based on the existing ASEAN Common Effective Preferential Tariff Scheme, the AFTA tariff reductions will go through two stages. During the first phase of implementation (5–8 years), tariffs on goods currently subject to tariffs of more than 20 percent will be reduced to a maximum of 20 percent. The rate at which the decease is implemented will be decided by individual members. The second stage, lasting an additional 7–10 years, would bring tariffs to 0–5 percent. However, fifteen product categories, including cement, chemicals, pharmaceuticals, fertilizers, vegetable oils, and plastics, were subject to accelerated reduction, lowering tariff level to 0–5 percent in 10 years.

By the middle of 1994, only two ASEAN countries had implemented AFTA to any significant degree. Therefore, late that year, ASEAN decided to accelerate the implementation of AFTA. The "normal track" reduction of tariffs moved forward to 2003, five years earlier than originally scheduled. Likewise, tariffs on fast track items would be lowered to 0–5 percent by 1998. In addition, ASEAN countries agreed to broaden the scope of products covered by AFTA. For example, unprocessed agricultural products and other primary commodities—a large portion of ASEAN's exports—will now be included in AFTA. ASEAN members have also begun considering the possibility of liberalizing intraregional trade in services, including financial services, insurance, and other areas. Liberalizing trade in services means the elimination of numerous non-tariff barriers. More important, ASEAN will consider on an on-going basis whether to include additional products for tariff reductions. It is possible that tariffs on some products currently considered sensitive will eventually be lowered.

The way ASEAN members seek to implement AFTA is unique. In a departure from ASEAN's usual requirement for unanimity, ASEAN members agreed on a "six minus x" formula to facilitate the implementation of AFTA. Under this formula, ASEAN members wanting to lower tariffs on various products can do so without waiting for similar commitments from other ASEAN countries. Also, members may unilaterally exclude "sensitive" products like automobiles from tariff reductions. For example, as several ASEAN countries are attempting to develop national automobile industries, it is unlikely that tariffs on imported automobiles will be affected by AFTA.

Businesses play an important role in the selection of products for tariff reductions. The respective local industries are often consulted in the course of deciding on the products to be included or excluded from AFTA treatment. In fact, during 1993–1994, the implementation of AFTA in several countries was delayed due to the desire of many local industries to be excluded from AFTA tariff reductions.

To qualify for preferential tariffs under AFTA, traders will have to meet the AFTA rules of origin requirements, which generally requires an ASEAN content or value of only 40 percent. This is lower than that of many other preferential trading arrangements, e.g., NAFTA.

The implementation of AFTA will present numerous business opportunities for United States businesses. Collectively, ASEAN is the world's fourth largest trade group after the United States, the EU, and Japan. Beginning in 1975, ASEAN has averaged a GDP growth rate of around 6 percent. No doubt, AFTA will encourage faster economic growth and integration in the expanding regional market of Southeast Asia. A bigger market will make ASEAN more attractive to investment from sources outside Southeast Asia.

The United States and ASEAN have established several consultative forums to increase cooperation and to address several areas of common concern. These include the ASEAN Economic Ministers meeting, the United States-ASEAN Dialogue, the Trade Investment Coordinating Committee, and Economic Cooperation Committee in Washington. In November 1993, United States and ASEAN agreed to establish the United States-ASEAN Alliance for Mutual growth, a program to promote increased commercial engagement between the two sides. Collectively, ASEAN is the fourth largest trading partner of United States. ASEAN ranks third in Asia as a destination for United States investment. American investment in ASEAN is dominant in petroleum, insurance, and electronics manufacturing. A significant portion of products manufactured by United States companies in ASEAN are reexported back to the United States or to third countries.

United States companies with existing manufacturing facilities in any of the ASEAN countries will be able to export their products to the other member countries at reduced tariffs if they meet the local content requirements. Companies without manufacturing facilities in ASEAN can also benefit from AFTA. Products originated in United States can be re-exported through an ASEAN joint venture partner after obtaining a 40 percent ASEAN content. With AFTA, United States companies contemplating investing in or purchasing from ASEAN will have further incentives to do so.

Caveat Nota: American businesses are advised to inquire whether their products will qualify for AFTA treatment before making

AFTA the basis of their business decisions. Businesses should make use of various trade promotion agencies or government units in ascertaining the inclusion and exclusion of their products and the respective tariff schedules.

CONCLUSIONS

As the world grows ever closer together through the advent of sophisticated technology and science, the hope that the many peoples of the world will become closer economically, socially, and culturally remains alive. As the next millennium approaches a whole new world will open for those willing to expand their horizons. All of this provides opportunity for the informed businessperson. Sellers will find new markets and purchasers and new bargains within the expanding European Union, NAFTA, East Asia, and Latin America. Purchasing managers must have a large base of knowledge and contacts. But they will find a greatly expanded base of opportunities. So far, these regional trade arrangements have not demonstrated significant discriminatory tendencies that might be cause for serious concern among third world countries that are not parties to these arrangements. Yet some of the countries left out of some of these regional arrangements are seeking inclusion.

The established laws, rules, and customs under WTO and various trade arrangements should not be feared by the American businessperson who wishes to open these markets. It should instead be studied and understood as a way to further strengthen the ties of international trade. On the whole, various trade arrangements, in which the United States is not a participant, remain open to United States traders and investors. Of course, the United States government should work with other governments to harmonize the existing free-trade agreements or customs unions within Europe, North America, Latin America, and the Asia-Pacific region.

SELECTED BIBLIOGRAPHY ON WORLD TRADE AND REGIONALISM

Books

Abbott, Frederick M., *Law and Policy of Regional Integration: The NAFTA and Western Hemispheric Integration in the World Trade Organization System,* Martinus Nijhoff Publishers, 1995.

Bergsten, C. Fred & Noland, Marcus, (Eds.) *Pacific Dynamism and the International Economic System,* Institute for International Economics, 1993.

Dijck, Pitou van and Gerrit Faber, (Eds.) *Challenges to the New World Trade Organization,* Kluwer Law International, The Hague, Netherland, 1996.

Gutterman, Alan S., (Ed.) *Counseling Emerging Companies in Going International,* American Bar Association Section of International Law and Practice, 1994.

Schott, Jeffrey J., *The Uruguay Round: An Assessment,* Institute for International Economics, Washington, D.C., 1994.

Shaw, J. O. & Gillian More, *New Legal Dynamics of European Union,* Clarendon Press, Oxford, 1995.

Stewart, Terence P., (Ed.) *The World Trade Organization: Multilateral Trade Framework for the 21st Century and United States Implementing Legislation,* American Bar Association, Section of International Law and Practice, 1996.

Weintraub, Sidney, *NAFTA: What Comes Next?* The Center for Strategic and International Studies, Washington, D.C. 1994.

Periodicals

Asia Week, December 13, 1996.

Business America, Jan. 1995, Vol. 116, No. 1, pp. 4-7.

Chemical Marketing Reporter, Feb. 19, 1996, Vol. 249, No.8, pp. SR8-9.

China Business Review, January/February, March/April, September/October, 1995 issues.

East Asian Executive Reports, March 15, 1994, Vol. 16, No. 3, pp. 6, 15.

The Economist, Various issues.

Europe, Nov. 1994, Vol. 233, No. 22, pp. 26-27.

International Labor Review, 1995, Vol. 134, No. 4-5, pp. 497-519.

Purchasing & Supply Management, March 1995, pp. 24-25.

World Trade, Jan. 1996, Vol. 9, No..1, pp. 28-33.

Finance & Development, Dec. 1995, Vol. 32, No. 4, pp. 38-41.

Supplement to Chapter XXXIII

Cultural-Legal Problems in Foreign Purchasing

BUSINESS FENG SHUI

Feng Shui—literally "wind water"—is the traditional Chinese art of cultivating spiritual power in buildings by augmenting their design—for example, placing a goldfish bowl here, or a potted plant there. Feng shui is a blend of astrology, design, and Eastern philosophy aimed at harmonizing the placement of manmade structures in nature. The millennia-old craft of feng shui has begun to exert a subtle influence on the hard-edged world of real estate in the United States, especially in areas with large concentration of Asian population. Many businessman are willing to accommodate this traditional custom when dealing with Chinese businesses.

Appendix A

Additional Information

A purchasing manager may wish to obtain even more specific information about discrimination in employment by contacting:

Equal Employment Opportunity Commission
1801 L Street, NW
Washington, DC 20507
(800) 669-4000 (Voice), (800) 669-6820 (TDD)
(202) 663-4900 (Voice—for 202 Area Code)
(202) 663-4494 (TDD—for 202 Area Code)

If the purchasing agent needs more specific information about the Americans with Disabilities Act requirements affecting *public accommodations and state and local government services* contact:

Department of Justice
Office on the Americans with Disabilities Act
Civil Rights Division
P.O. Box 66118
Washington, DC 20035-6118
(202) 514-0301 (Voice)
(202) 514-0381 (TDD)
(202) 514-0383 (TDD)

For more specific information about requirements for *accessible design in new construction and alterations,* contact:

Architectural and Transportation Barriers
Compliance Board
1111 18th Street, NW
Suite 501
Washington, DC 20036
800-USA-ABLE

For more specific information about ADA requirements affecting *transportation,* contact:

Department of Transportation
400 7th Street, SW
Washington, DC 20590
(202) 366-9305
(202) 755-7687 (TDD)

For more specific information about ADA requirements for *telecommunications,* the Federal Communications Commission may be contacted: 1919 M Street, NW, Washington, DC 20554, (202) 634-1837, (202) 632-1836 (TDD)

Purchasing agents may obtain a special booklet on employment discrimination generally and on disabilities in alternate formats upon request by dialing 800-669-3362 or 800-800-3302.

Appendix B

United Nations Convention on Contracts for the International Sale of Goods: Official English Text

The following is the official English text of the United Nations Convention on Contracts for the International Sale of Goods. For a detailed legal analysis of the provisions, see Appendix C.

[Public Notice 1004]

**U.S. Ratification of 1980 United Nations Convention
on Contracts for the International Sale of Goods:
Official English Text**

On December 11, 1986 the United States deposited at United Nations Headquarters in New York its instrument of ratification of the 1980 U.N. Convention on Contracts for the International Sale of Goods. The United States did so jointly with China and Italy. The Convention will enter into force on January 1, 1988 between the United States and the following countries: Argentina, China, Egypt, France, Hungary, Lesotho, Syria, Yugoslavia and Zambia.

The Convention sets out substantive provisions of law to govern the formation of international sales contracts and the rights and obligations of the buyer and seller. It will apply to sales contracts between parties with their places of business in different countries bound by Convention, provided the parties have left their contracts silent as to applicable law. Parties are free to specify applicable law and to derogate from or vary the effect of provisions of the Convention. Certain types of sales and sales of certain types of goods are excluded from the Convention's scope, and the Convention is not concerned with the validity of the contract. Part I of the Convention sets out its sphere of application and general provisions. For the Convention to be applicable the contract of sale need not be concluded in or evidenced by writing unless one of the parties has its place of business in a country that has made a reservation in this regard. The United States did not make this reservation. Article 100 deals with the Convention's applicability to sales contract formation and sales contracts themselves in relation to its entry into force.

United States ratification was coupled with a declaration that the United States would not be bound by Article 1(1)(b), which will have a narrowing effect on the sphere of application of the Convention.

Traders and their counsel are advised to study the Convention carefully in light of international sales and purchases involving parties in the above-mentioned countries and additional countries for which the Convention will eventually be entering into force.

The legal analysis that accompanied the Convention to the Senate and that relates its provisions to the corresponding provisions of the Sales Article of the Uniform Commercial Code may be found in 22 *International Legal Materials* 1368–80 (1984) (a bi-monthly publication of the American Society of International Law). A complete bibliography with citations to publications that reproduce the Convention text and legislative materials concerning the Convention, as well as secondary literature including books, symposia and law review articles, is to be published by Professor Peter Winship, Southern Methodist University School of Law, in the Spring 1987 issue of *The International Lawyer,* the law review published by the Section of International Law and Practice of the American Bar Association.

For the most current information about countries that have ratified or acceded to the Convention, write or phone the United Nations, which was designated as the depositor for the Convention: United Nations, Treaty Section, New York, N.Y. 10017 (212) 754 or 958/5048.

The Office of Treaty Affairs, Department of State, maintains records on multilateral treaties such as the 1980 Sales Convention that are based, in part, on information provided it by the United Nations. It updates that information and, on a monthly basis, publishes information in the *State Department Bulletin* about developments concerning treaties and conventions to which the United States is a party. The Department of State publication "Treaties in Force" annually lists all states parties to treaties and conventions to which the United States is a party, with the status as of January 1 of any given year, noting also whether a state may have made reservations when becoming a party.

The Department understands that a number of legal publications will be printing the text of the Convention and materials that accompanied it to the Senate, some

Additional Information **159**

listing countries becoming parties and any reservations or declarations to which their ratification may have been subject. These include: United States Code Annotated, 1987 pocket part to 15 U.S.C.A. Appendix; Uniform Laws Annotated, Appendix to Uniform Commercial Code, with a reference to the Convention in connection with Article 2; United States Code Service in an Appendix at the end of Title 15; Martindale-Hubbell Law Directory in Volume VIII, Part VII: Selected International Conventions to which the United States is a party.

There is reproduced below a photocopy of the United Nations-certified English text of the Convention which traders and their counsel are encouraged to use, as typographical errors may be contained in any other published version of the text. It should be noted that the Arabic, Chinese, French, Russian and Spanish Convention texts have equal authenticity with the English text.

Peter H. Pfund,

Assistant Legal Adviser for Private International Law

UNITED NATIONS CONVENTION ON CONTRACTS FOR THE INTERNATIONAL SALE OF GOODS

The states parties to this Convention:

Bearing in mind the broad objectives in the resolutions adopted by the sixth special session of the General Assembly of the United Nations on the establishment of a New International Economic Order,

Considering that the development of international trade on the basis of equality and mutual benefit is an important element in promoting friendly relations among States,

Being of the Opinion that the adoption of uniform rules which govern contracts for the international sale of goods and take into account the different social, economic and legal systems would contribute to the removal of legal barriers in international trade and promote the development of international trade,

Have agreed as follows:

PART I—SPHERE OF APPLICATION AND GENERAL PROVISIONS

CHAPTER I—SPHERE OF APPLICATION

Article 1

(1) This Convention applies to contracts of sale of goods between parties whose places of business are in different States:

(a) When the States are Contracting States; or

(b) When the rules of private international law lead to the application of the law of a Contracting State.

(2) The fact that the parties have their places of business in different States is to be disregarded whenever this fact does not appear either from the contract or from any dealings between, or from information disclosed by, the parties at any time before or at the conclusion of the contract.

(3) Neither the nationality of the parties nor the civil or commercial character of the parties or of the contract is to be taken into consideration in determining the application of this Convention.

Article 2

This Convention does not apply to sales:

(a) Of goods bought for personal, family or household use, unless the seller, at any time before or at the conclusion of the contract, neither knew nor ought to have known that the goods were bought for any such use;

(b) By auction;

(c) On execution or otherwise by authority of law;

(d) Of stocks, shares, investment securities, negotiable instruments or money;

(e) Of ships, vessels, hovercraft or aircraft;

(f) Of electricity.

Article 3

(1) Contracts for the supply of goods to be manufactured or produced are to be considered sales unless the party who orders the goods undertakes to supply a substantial part of the materials necessary for such manufacture or production.

(2) This Convention does not apply to contracts in which the preponderant part of the obligations of the party who furnishes the goods consists in the supply of labour or other services.

Article 4

This Convention governs only the formation of the contract of sale and the rights and obligations of the seller and the buyer arising from such a contract. In particular, except as otherwise expressly provided in this Convention, it is not concerned with:

(a) the validity of the contract or of any of its provisions or of any usage;

(b) the effect which the contract may have on the property in the goods sold.

Article 5

This Convention does not apply to the liability of the seller for death or personal injury caused by the goods to any person.

Article 6

The parties may exclude the application of this Convention or, subject to article 12, derogate from or vary the effect of any of its provisions.

CHAPTER II—GENERAL PROVISIONS

Article 7

(1) In the interpretation of this Convention, regard is to be had to its international character and to the need to promote uniformity in its application and the observance of good faith in international trade.

(2) Questions concerning matters governed by this Convention which are not expressly settled in it are to be settled in conformity with the general principles on which it is based or, in the absence of such principles, in conformity with the law applicable by virtue of the rules of private international law.

Article 8

(1) For the purposes of this Convention statements made by and other conduct of a party are to be interpreted according to his intent where the other party knew or could not have been unaware what that intent was.

(2) If the preceding paragraph is not applicable, statements made by and other conduct of a party are to be interpreted according to the understanding that a reasonable person of the same kind as the other party would have had in the same circumstances.

(3) In determining the intent of a party or the understanding a reasonable person would have had, due consideration is to be given to all relevant circumstances of the case including the negotiations, any practices which the parties have established between themselves, usages and any subsequent conduct of the parties.

Article 9

(1) The parties are bound by any usage to which they have agreed and by any practices which they have established between themselves.

(2) The parties are considered, unless otherwise agreed, to have impliedly made applicable to their contract or its formation a usage of which the parties knew or ought to have known and which in international trade is widely known to, and regularly observed by, parties to contracts of the type involved in the particular trade concerned.

Article 10

For the purposes of this Convention:

(a) If a party has more than one place of business, the place of business is that which has the closest relationship to the contract and its performance, having regard to the circumstances known to or contemplated by the parties at any time before or at the conclusion of the contract;

(b) If a party does not have a place of business, references are to be made to his habitual residence.

Article 11

A contract of sale need not be concluded in or evidenced by writing and is not subject to any other requirement as to form. It may be proved by any means, including witnesses.

Article 12

Any provision of article 11, article 29 or Part II of this Convention that allows a contract of sale or its modification or termination by agreement or any offer, acceptance or other indication of intention to be made in any form other than in writing does not apply where any party has his place of business in a Contracting State which has made a declaration under article 96 of this Convention. The parties may not derogate from or vary the effect of this article.

Article 13

For the purposes of this Convention "writing" includes telegram and telex.

PART II—FORMATION OF THE CONTRACT

Article 14

(1) A proposal for concluding a contract addressed to one or more specific persons constitutes an offer if it is sufficiently definite and indicates the intention of the offeror to be bound in case of acceptance. A proposal is sufficiently definite if it indicates the goods and expressly or implicitly fixes or makes provision for determining the quantity and the price.

(2) A proposal other than one addressed to one or more specific persons is to be considered merely as an invitation to make offers, unless the contrary is clearly indicated by the person making the proposal.

Article 15

(1) An offer becomes effective when it reaches the offeree.

(2) An offer, even if it is irrevocable, may be withdrawn if the withdrawal reaches the offeree before or at the same time as the offer.

Article 16

(1) Until a contract is concluded an offer may be revoked if the revocation reaches the offeree before he has dispatched an acceptance.

(2) However, an offer cannot be revoked:

(a) If it indicates, whether by stating a fixed time for acceptance or otherwise, that it is irrevocable; or

(b) If it was reasonable for the offeree to rely on the offer as being irrevocable and the offeree has acted in reliance on the offer.

Article 17

An offer, even if it is irrevocable, is terminated when a rejection reaches the offeror.

Article 18

(1) A statement made by or other conduct of the offeree indicating assent to an offer is an acceptance. Silence or inactivity does not in itself amount to acceptance.

(2) An acceptance of an offer becomes effective at the moment the indication of assent reaches the offeror. An acceptance is not effective if the indication of assent does not reach the offeror within the time he has fixed or, if no time is fixed, within a reasonable time, due account being taken of the circumstances of the transaction, including the rapidity of the means of communication employed by the offeror. An oral offer must be accepted immediately unless the circumstances indicate otherwise.

(3) However, if, by virtue of the offer or as a result of practices which the parties have established between themselves or of usage, the offeree may indicate assent by performing an act, such as one relating to the dispatch of the goods or payment of the price, without notice to the offeror, the acceptance is effective at the moment the act is performed, provided that the act is performed within the period of time laid down in the preceding paragraph.

Article 19

(1) A reply to an offer which purports to be an acceptance but contains additions, limitations or other modifications is a rejection of the offer and constitutes a counter-offer.

(2) However, a reply to an offer which purports to be an acceptance but contains additional or different terms which do not materially alter the terms of the offer constitutes an acceptance, unless the offeror, without undue delay, objects orally to the discrepancy or dispatches a notice to that effect. If he does not so object, the terms of the contract are the terms of the offer with the modifications contained in the acceptance.

(3) Additional or different terms relating, among other things, to the price, payment, quality and quantity of the goods, place and time of delivery, extent of one

party's liability to the other or the settlement of disputes are considered to alter the terms of the offer materially.

Article 20

(1) A period of time for acceptance fixed by the offeror in a telegram or a letter begins to run from the moment the telegram is handed in for dispatch or from the date shown on the letter or, if no such date is shown, from the date shown on the envelope. A period of time for acceptance fixed by the offeror by telephone, telex or other means of instantaneous communication, begins to run from the moment that the offer reaches the offeree.

(2) Official holidays or non-business days occurring during the period for acceptance are included in calculating the period. However, if a notice of acceptance cannot be delivered at the address of the offeror on the last day of the period because that day falls on an official holiday or a non-business day at the place of business of the offeror, the period is extended until the first business day which follows.

Article 21

(1) A late acceptance is nevertheless effective as an acceptance if without delay the offeror orally so informs the offeree or dispatches a notice to that effect.

(2) If a letter or other writing containing a late acceptance shows that it has been sent in such circumstances that if its transmission had been normal it would have reached the offeror in due time, the late acceptance is effective as an acceptance unless, without delay, the offeror orally informs the offeree that he considers his offer as having lapsed or dispatches a notice to that effect.

Article 22

An acceptance may be withdrawn if the withdrawal reaches the offeror before or at the same time as the acceptance would have become effective.

Article 23

A contract is concluded at the moment when an acceptance of an offer becomes effective in accordance with the provisions of this Convention.

Article 24

For the purposes of this Part of the Convention, an offer, declaration of acceptance or any other indication of intention "reaches" the addressee when it is made orally to him or delivered by any other means to him personally, to his place of business or mailing address, or if he does not have a place of business or mailing address, to his habitual residence.

PART III—SALE OF GOODS

CHAPTER I—GENERAL PROVISIONS

Article 25

A breach of contract committed by one of the parties is fundamental if it results in such detriment to the other party as substantially to deprive him of what he is entitled to expect under the contract, unless the party in breach did not foresee and a reasonable person of the same kind in the same circumstances would not have foreseen such a result.

Article 26

A declaration of avoidance of the contract is effective only if made by notice to the other party.

Article 27

Unless otherwise expressly provided in this Part of the Convention, if any notice, request or other communication is given or made by a party in accordance with this Part and by means appropriate in the circumstances, a delay or error in the transmission of the communication or its failure to arrive does not deprive that party of the right to rely on the communication.

Article 28

If, in accordance with the provisions of this Convention, one party is entitled to require performance of any obligation by the other party, a court is not bound to enter a judgment for specific performance unless the court would do so under its own law in respect of similar contracts of sale not governed by this Convention.

Article 29

(1) A contract may be modified or terminated by the mere agreement of the parties.

(2) A contract in writing which contains a provision requiring any modification or termination by agreement to be in writing may not be otherwise modified or terminated by agreement. However, a party may be precluded by his conduct from asserting such a provision to the extent that the other party has relied on that conduct.

CHAPTER II—OBLIGATIONS OF THE SELLER

Article 30

The seller must deliver the goods, hand over any documents relating to them and transfer the property in the goods, as required by the contract and this Convention.

Section I. Delivery of the Goods and Handing Over of Documents

Article 31

If the seller is not bound to deliver the goods at any other particular place, his obligation to deliver consists:

(a) If the contract of sale involves carriage of the goods—in handing the goods over to the first carrier for transmission to the buyer;

(b) If, in cases not within the preceding subparagraph, the contract relates to specific goods, or unidentified goods to be drawn from a specific stock or to be manufactured or produced, and at the time of the conclusion of the contract the parties knew that the goods were at, or were to be manufactured or produced at, a particular place—in placing the goods at the buyer's disposal at that place;

(c) In other cases—in placing the goods at the buyer's disposal at the place where the seller had his place of business at the time of the conclusion of the contract.

Article 32

(1) If the seller, in accordance with the contract or his Convention, hands the goods over to a carrier and if the goods are not clearly identified to the contract by markings on the goods, by shipping documents or otherwise, the seller must give the buyer notice of the consignment specifying the goods.

(2) If the seller is bound to arrange for carriage of the goods, he must make such contracts as are necessary for carriage to the place fixed by means of transportation appropriate in the circumstances and according to the usual terms for such transportation.

(3) If the seller is not bound to affect insurance in respect of the carriage of the goods, he must, at the buyer's request, provide him with all available information necessary to enable him to affect such insurance.

Article 33

The seller must deliver the goods:

(a) If a date is fixed by or determinable from the contract, on that date;

(b) If a period of time is fixed by or determinable from the contract, at any time within that period unless circumstances indicate that the buyer is to choose a date; or

(c) In any other case, within a reasonable time after the conclusion of the contract.

Article 34

If the seller is bound to hand over documents relating to the goods, he must hand them over at the time and place and in the form required by the contract. If the seller has handed over documents before that time, he may, up to that time, cure any lack of conformity in the documents, if the exercise of this right does not cause the buyer unreasonable inconvenience or unreasonable expense. However, the buyer retains any right to claim damages as provided for in this Convention.

Section II. Conformity of the Goods and Third Party Claims

Article 35

(1) The seller must deliver goods which are of the quantity, quality and description required by the contract and which are contained or packaged in the manner required by the contract.

(2) Except where the parties have agreed otherwise, the goods do not conform with the contract unless they:

(a) Are fit for the purposes for which goods of the same description would ordinarily be used;

(b) Are fit for any particular purpose expressly or impliedly made known to the seller at the time of the conclusion of the contract, except where the circumstances show that the buyer did not rely, or that it was unreasonable for him to rely, on the seller's skill and judgment;

(c) Possess the qualities of goods which the seller has held out to the buyer as a sample or model;

(d) Are contained or packaged in the manner usual for such goods or, where there is no such manner, in a manner adequate to preserve and protect the goods.

(3) The seller is not liable under subparagraphs (a) to (d) of the preceding paragraph for any lack of conformity of the goods if at the time of the conclusion of the contract the buyer knew or could not have been unaware of such lack of conformity.

Article 36

(1) The seller is liable in accordance with the contract and this Convention for any lack of conformity which exists at the time when the risk passes to the buyer, even though the lack of conformity becomes only after that time.

(2) The seller is also liable for any lack of conformity which occurs after the time indicated in the preceding paragraph and which is due to a breach of any of his obligations, including a breach of any guarantee that for a period of time the goods will remain fit for their ordinary purpose or for some particular purpose or will retain specified qualities or characteristics.

Article 37

If the seller has delivered goods before the date for delivery, he may, up to that date, deliver any missing part or make up any deficiency in the quantity of the goods delivered, or deliver goods in replacement of any non-conforming goods delivered or remedy any lack of conformity in the goods delivered, provided that the exercise of this right does not cause the buyer unreasonable inconvenience or unreasonable expense. However, the buyer retains any right to claim damages as provided for in this Convention.

Article 38

(1) The buyer must examine the goods, or cause them to be examined, within as short a period as is practicable in the circumstances.

(2) If the contract involves carriage of the goods, examination may be deferred until after the goods have arrived at their destination.

(3) If the goods are redirected in transit or redispatched by the buyer without a reasonable opportunity for examination by him and at the time of the conclusion of the contract the seller knew or ought to have known of the possibility of such redirection or redispatch, examination may be deferred until after the goods have arrived at the new destination.

Article 39

(1) The buyer loses the right to rely on a lack of conformity of the goods if he does not give notice to the seller specifying the nature of the lack of conformity within a reasonable time after he has discovered it or ought to have discovered it.

(2) In any event, the buyer loses the right to rely on a lack of conformity of the goods if he does not give the seller notice thereof at the latest within a period of two years from the date on which the goods were actually handed over to the buyer, unless this time-limit is inconsistent with a contractual period of guarantee.

Article 40

The seller is not entitled to rely on the provisions of articles 38 and 39 if the lack of conformity relates to facts of which he knew or could not have been unaware and which he did not disclose to the buyer.

Article 41

The seller must deliver goods which are free from any right or claim of a third party, unless the buyer agreed to take the goods subject to that right or claim. However, if such right or claim is based on industrial property or other intellectual property, the seller's obligation is governed by article 42.

Article 42

(1) The seller must deliver goods which are free from any right or claim of a third party based on industrial property or other intellectual property, of which at the time of the conclusion of the contract the seller knew or could not have been

unaware, provided that the right or claim is based on industrial property or other intellectual property:

(a) Under the law of the State where the goods will be resold or otherwise used, if it was contemplated by the parties at the time of the conclusion of the contract that the goods would be resold or otherwise used in that State; or

(b) In any other case, under the law of the State where the buyer has his place of business.

(2) The obligation of the seller under the preceding paragraph does not extend to cases where:

(a) At the time of the conclusion of the contract the buyer knew or could not have been unaware of the right or claim; or

(b) The right or claim results from the seller's compliance with technical drawings, designs, formulae or other such specifications furnished by the buyer.

Article 43

(1) The buyer loses the right to rely on the provisions of article 41 or article 42 if he does not give notice to the seller specifying the nature of the right or claim of the third party within a reasonable time after he has become aware or ought to have become aware of the right or claim.

(2) The seller is not entitled to rely on the provisions of the preceding paragraph if he knew of the right or claim of the third party and the nature of it.

Article 44

Notwithstanding the provisions of paragraph (1) of article 39 and paragraph (1) of article 43, the buyer may reduce the price in accordance with article 50 or claim damages except for loss of profit, if he has a reasonable excuse for his failure to give the required notice.

Section III. Remedies for Breach of Contract by the Seller

Article 45

(1) If the seller fails to perform any of his obligations under the contract or this Convention, the buyer may:

(a) Exercise the rights provided in articles 46 to 52;

(b) Claim damages as provided in articles 74 to 77.

(2) The buyer is not deprived of any right he may have to claim damages by exercising his right to other remedies.

(3) No period of grace may be granted to the seller by a court or arbitral tribunal when the buyer resorts to a remedy for breach of contract.

Article 46

(1) The buyer may require performance by the seller of his obligations unless the buyer has resorted to a remedy which is inconsistent with this requirement.

(2) If the goods do not conform with the contract, the buyer may require delivery of substitute goods only if the lack of conformity constitutes a fundamental breach of contract and a request for substitute goods is made either in conjunction with notice given under article 39 or within a reasonable time thereafter.

(3) If the goods do not conform with the contract, the buyer may require the seller to remedy the lack of conformity by repair, unless this is unreasonable having regard to all the circumstances. A request for repair must be made either in conjunction with notice given under article 39 or within a reasonable time thereafter.

Article 47

(1) The buyer may fix an additional period of time of reasonable length for performance by the seller of his obligations.

(2) Unless the buyer has received notice from the seller that he will not perform within the period so fixed, the buyer may not, during that period, resort to any remedy for breach of contract. However, the buyer is not deprived thereby of any right he may have to claim damages for delay in performance.

Article 48

(1) Subject to article 49, the seller may, even after the date for delivery, remedy at his own expense any failure to perform his obligations, if he can do so without unreasonable delay and without causing the buyer unreasonable inconvenience or uncertainty of reimbursement by the seller of expenses advanced by the buyer. However, the buyer retains any right to claim damages as provided for in this Convention.

(2) If the seller requests the buyer to make known whether he will accept performance and the buyer does not comply with the request within a reasonable time, the seller may perform within the time indicated in his request. The buyer may not, during that period of time, resort to any remedy which is inconsistent with performance by the seller.

(3) A notice by the seller that he will perform within a specified period of time is assumed to include a request, under the preceding paragraph, that the buyer make known his decision.

(4) A request or notice by the seller under paragraph (2) or (3) of this article is not effective unless received by the buyer.

Article 49

(1) The buyer may declare the contract avoided:

(a) If the failure by the seller to perform any of his obligations under the contract or this Convention amounts to a fundamental breach of contract; or

(b) In case of non-delivery, if the seller does not deliver the goods within the additional period of time fixed by the buyer in accordance with paragraph (1) of article 47 or declares that he will not deliver within the period so fixed.

(2) However, in cases where the seller has delivered the goods, the buyer loses the right to declare the contract avoided unless he does so:

(a) In respect of late delivery, within a reasonable time after he has become aware that delivery has been made;

(b) In respect of any breach other than late delivery, within a reasonable time:

(i) After he knew or ought to have known of the breach;

(ii) After the expiration of any additional period of time fixed by the buyer in accordance with paragraph (1) of article 47, or after the seller has declared that he will not perform his obligations within such an additional period; or

(iii) After the expiration of any additional period of time indicated by the seller in accordance with paragraph (2) of article 48, or after the buyer has declared that he will not accept performance.

Article 50

If the goods do not conform with the contract and whether or not the price has already been paid, the buyer may reduce the price in the same proportion as the value that the goods actually delivered had at the time of the delivery bears to the value that conforming goods would have had at that time. However, if the seller remedies any failure to perform his obligations in accordance with article 37 or article 48 or if the buyer refuses to accept performance by the seller in accordance with those articles, the buyer may not reduce the price.

Article 51

(1) If the seller delivers only a part of the goods or if only a part of the goods delivered is in conformity with the contract, articles 46 to 50 apply in respect of the part which is missing or which does not conform.

(2) The buyer may declare the contract avoided in its entirety only if the failure to make delivery completely or in conformity with the contract amounts to a fundamental breach of the contract.

Article 52

(1) If the seller delivers the goods before the date fixed, the buyer may take delivery or refuse to take delivery.

(2) If the seller delivers a quantity of goods greater than that provided for in the contract, the buyer may take delivery or refuse to take delivery of the excess quantity. If the buyer takes delivery of all or part of the excess quantity, he must pay for it at the contract rate.

CHAPTER III—OBLIGATIONS OF THE BUYER

Article 53

The buyer must pay the price for the goods and take delivery of them as required by the contract and this Convention.

Section I. Payment of the Price

Article 54

The buyer's obligation to pay the price includes taking such steps and complying with such formalities as may be required under the contract or any laws and regulations to enable payment to be made.

Article 55

Where a contract has been validly concluded but does not expressly or implicitly fix or make provision for determining the price, the parties are considered, in the absence of any indication to the contrary, to have impliedly made reference to the price generally charged at the time of the conclusion of the contract for such goods sold under comparable circumstances in the trade concerned.

Article 56

If the price is fixed according to the weight of the goods, in case of doubt it is to be determined by the net weight.

Article 57

(1) If the buyer is not bound to pay the price at any other particular place, he must pay it to the seller:

(a) At the seller's place of business; or

(b) If the payment is to be made against the handing over of the goods or of documents, at the place where the handing over takes place.

(2) The seller must bear any increase in the expenses incidental to payment which is caused by a change in his place of business subsequent to the conclusion of the contract.

Article 58

(1) If the buyer is not bound to pay the price at any other specific time, he must pay it when the seller places either the goods or documents controlling their disposition at the buyer's disposal in accordance with the contract and this Convention. The seller may make such payment a condition for handing over the goods or documents.

(2) If the contract involves carriage of the goods, the seller may dispatch the goods on terms whereby the goods, or documents controlling their disposition, will not be handed over to the buyer except against payment of the price.

(3) The buyer is not bound to pay the price until he has had an opportunity to examine the goods, unless the procedures for delivery or payment agreed upon by the parties are inconsistent with his having such an opportunity.

Article 59

The buyer must pay the price on the date fixed by or determinable from the contract and this Convention without the need for any request or compliance with any formality on the part of the seller.

Section II. Taking Delivery

Article 60

The buyer's obligation to take delivery consists:

(a) In doing all the acts which could reasonably be expected of him in order to enable the seller to make delivery; and

(b) In taking over the goods.

Section III. Remedies for Breach of Contract by the Buyer

Article 61

(1) If the buyer fails to perform any of his obligations under the contract or this Convention, the seller may:

(a) Exercise the rights provided in articles 62 to 65;

(b) Claim damages as provided in articles 74 to 77.

(2) The seller is not deprived of any right he may have to claim damages by exercising his right to other remedies.

(3) No period of grace may be granted to the buyer by a court or arbitral tribunal when the seller resorts to a remedy for breach of contract.

Article 62

The seller may require the buyer to pay the price, take delivery or perform his other obligations, unless the seller has resorted to a remedy which is inconsistent with this requirement.

Article 63

(1) The seller may fix an additional period of time of reasonable length for performance by the buyer of his obligations.

(2) Unless the seller has received notice from the buyer that he will not perform within the period so fixed, the seller may not, during that period, resort to any remedy for breach of contract. However, the seller is not deprived thereby of any right he may have to claim damages for delay in performance.

Article 64

(1) The seller may declare the contract avoided:

(a) If the failure by the buyer to perform any of his obligations under the contract or this Convention amounts to a fundamental breach of contract; or

(b) If the buyer does not, within the additional period of time fixed by the seller in accordance with paragraph (1) of article 63, perform his obligation to pay the price or take delivery of the goods, or if he declares that he will not do so within the period so fixed.

(2) However, in cases where the buyer has paid the price, the seller loses the right to declare the contract avoided unless he does so:

(a) In respect of late performance by the buyer, before the seller has become aware that performance has been rendered; or

(b) In respect of any breach other than late performance by the buyer, within a reasonable time:

(i) After the seller knew or ought to have known of the breach; or

(ii) After the expiration of any additional period of time fixed by the seller in accordance with paragraph (1) of article 63, or after the buyer has declared that he will not perform his obligations within such an additional period.

Article 65

(1) If under the contract the buyer is to specify the form, measurement or other features of the goods and he fails to make such specification either on the date agreed upon or within a reasonable time after receipt of a request from the seller,

the seller may, without prejudice to any other rights he may have, make the specification himself in accordance with the requirements of the buyer that may be known to him.

(2) If the seller makes the specification himself, he must inform the buyer of the details thereof and must fix a reasonable time within which the buyer may make a different specification. If, after receipt of such a communication, the buyer fails to do so within the time so fixed, the specification made by the seller is binding.

CHAPTER IV—PASSING OF RISK

Article 66

Loss of or damage to the goods after the risk has passed to the buyer does not discharge him from his obligation to pay the price, unless the loss or damage is due to an act or omission of the seller.

Article 67

(1) If the contract of sale involves carriage of the goods and the seller is not bound to hand them over at a particular place, the risk passes to the buyer when the goods are handed over to the first carrier for transmission to the buyer in accordance with the contract of sale. If the seller is bound to hand the goods over to a carrier at a particular place, the risk does not pass to the buyer until the goods are handed over to the carrier at that place. The fact that the seller is authorized to retain documents controlling the disposition of the goods does not affect the passage of the risk.

(2) Nevertheless, the risk does not pass to the buyer until the goods are clearly identified to the contract, whether by markings on the goods, by shipping documents, by notice given to the buyer or otherwise.

Article 68

The risk in respect of goods sold in transit passes to the buyer from the time of the conclusion of the contract. However, if the circumstances so indicate, the risk is assumed by the buyer from the time the goods were handed over to the carrier who issued the documents embodying the contract of carriage. Nevertheless, if at the time of the conclusion of the contract of sale the seller knew or ought to have known that the goods had been lost or damaged and did not disclose this to the buyer, the loss or damage is at the risk of the seller.

Article 69

(1) In cases not within articles 67 and 68, the risk passes to the buyer when he takes over the goods, or if he does not do so in due time, from the time when the goods are placed at his disposal and he commits a breach of contract by failing to take delivery.

(2) However, if the buyer is bound to take over the goods at a place other than a place of business of the seller, the risk passes when delivery is due and the buyer is aware of the fact that the goods are placed at his disposal at that place.

(3) If the contract relates to goods not then identified, the goods are considered not to be placed at the disposal of the buyer until they are clearly identified to the contract.

Article 70

If the seller has committed a fundamental breach of contract, articles 67, 68 and 69 do not impair the remedies available to the buyer on account of the breach.

CHAPTER V—PROVISIONS COMMON TO THE OBLIGATIONS OF THE SELLER AND OF THE BUYER

Section I. Anticipatory Breach and Installment Contracts

Article 71

(1) A party may suspend the performance of his obligations if, after the conclusion of the contract, it becomes apparent that the other party will not perform a substantial part of his obligations as a result of:

(a) A serious deficiency in his ability to perform or in his creditworthiness; or

(b) His conduct in preparing to perform or in performing the contract.

(2) If the seller has already dispatched the goods before the grounds described in the preceding paragraph become evident, he may prevent the handing over of the goods to the buyer even though the buyer holds a document which entitles him to obtain them. The present paragraph relates only to the rights in the goods as between the buyer and the seller.

(3) A party suspending performance, whether before or after dispatch of the goods, must immediately give notice of the suspension to the other party and must continue with performance if the other party provides adequate assurance of his performance.

Article 72

(1) If prior to the date for performance of the contract it is clear that one of the parties will commit a fundamental breach of contract, the other party may declare the contract avoided.

(2) If time allows, the party intending to declare the contract avoided must give reasonable notice to the other party in order to permit him to provide adequate assurance of his performance.

Additional Information **177**

(3) The requirements of the preceding paragraph do not apply if the other party has declared that he will not perform his obligations.

Article 73

(1) In the case of a contract for delivery of goods by installments, if the failure of one party to perform any of his obligations in respect of any installment constitutes a fundamental breach of contract with respect to that installment, the other party may declare the contract avoided with respect to that installment.

(2) If one party's failure to perform any of his obligations in respect of any installment gives the other party good grounds to conclude that a fundamental breach of contract will occur with respect to future installments, he may declare the contract avoided for the future, provided that he does so within a reasonable time.

(3) A buyer who declares the contract avoided in respect of any delivery may, at the same time, declare it avoided in respect of deliveries already made or of future deliveries if, by reason of their interdependence, those deliveries could not be used for the purpose contemplated by the parties at the time of the conclusion of the contract.

Section II. Damages

Article 74

Damages for breach of contract by one party consist of a sum equal to the loss, including loss of profit, suffered by the other party as a consequence of the breach. Such damages may not exceed the loss which the party in breach foresaw or ought to have foreseen at the time of the conclusion of the contract, in the light of the facts and matters of which he then knew or ought to have known, as a possible consequence of the breach of contract.

Article 75

If the contract is avoided and if, in a reasonable manner and within a reasonable time after avoidance, the buyer has bought goods in replacement or the seller has resold the goods, the party claiming damages may recover the difference between the contract price and the price in the substitute transaction as well as any further damages recoverable under article 74.

Article 76

(1) If the contract is avoided and there is a current price for the goods, the party claiming damages may, if he has not made a purchase or resale under article 75, recover the difference between the price fixed by the contract and the current price at the time of avoidance as well as any further damages recoverable under article 74. If, however, the party claiming damages has avoided the contract after

taking over the goods, the current price at the time of such taking over shall be applied instead of the current price at the time of avoidance.

(2) For the purposes of the preceding paragraph, the current price is the price prevailing at the place where delivery of the goods should have been made or, if there is no current price at that place, the price at such other place as serves as a reasonable substitute, making due allowance for differences in the cost of transporting the goods.

Article 77

A party who relies on a breach of contract must take such measures as are reasonable in the circumstances to mitigate the loss, including loss of profit, resulting from the breach. If he fails to take such measures, the party in breach may claim a reduction in the damages in the amount by which the loss should have been mitigated,

Section III. Interest

Article 78

If a party fails to pay the price or any other sum that is in arrears, the other party is entitled to interest on it, without prejudice to any claim for damages recoverable under article 74.

Section IV. Exemptions

Article 79

(1) A party is not liable for a failure to perform any of his obligations if he proves that the failure was due to an impediment beyond his control and that he could not reasonably be expected to have taken the impediment into account at the time of the conclusion of the contract or to have avoided or overcome it, or its consequences.

(2) If the party's failure is due to the failure by a third person whom he has engaged to perform the whole or a part of the contract, that party is exempt from liability only if:

(a) He is exempt under the preceding paragraph; and

(b) The person whom he has so engaged would be so exempt if the provisions of that paragraph were applied to him.

(3) The exemption provided by this article has effect for the period during which the impediment exists.

(4) The party who fails to perform must give notice to the other party of the impediment and its effect on his ability to perform. If the notice is not received

by the other party within a reasonable time after the party who fails to perform knew or ought to have known of the impediment, he is liable for damages resulting from such non-receipt.

(5) Nothing in this article prevents either party from exercising any right other than to claim damages under this Convention.

Article 80

A party may not rely on a failure of the other party to perform, to the extent that such failure was caused by the first party's act or omission.

Section V. Effects of Avoidance

Article 81

(1) Avoidance of the contract releases both parties from their obligations under it, subject to any damages which may be due. Avoidance does not affect any provision of the contract for the settlement of disputes or any other provision of the contract governing the rights and obligations of the parties consequent upon the avoidance of the contract.

(2) A party who has performed the contract either wholly or in party may claim restitution from the other party of whatever the first party has supplied or paid under the contract. If both parties are bound to make restitution, they must do so concurrently.

Article 82

(1) The buyer loses the right to declare the contract avoided or to require the seller to deliver substitute goods if it is impossible for him to make restitution of the goods substantially in the condition in which he received them.

(2) The preceding paragraph does not apply:

(a) If the impossibility of making restitution of the goods or of making restitution of the goods substantially in the condition in which the buyer received them is not due to his act or omission;

(b) If the goods or part of the goods have perished or deteriorated as a result of the examination provided for in article 38; or

(c) If the goods or part of the goods have been sold in the normal course of business or have been consumed or transformed by the buyer in the course of normal use before he discovered or ought to have discovered the lack of conformity.

Article 83

A buyer who has lost the right to declare the contract avoided or to require the seller to deliver substitute goods in accordance with article 82 retains all other remedies under the contract and this Convention.

Article 84

(1) If the seller is bound to refund the price, he must also pay interest on it, from the date on which the price was paid.

(2) The buyer must account to the seller for all benefits which he has derived from the goods or part of them:

(a) If he must make restitution of the goods or part of them; or

(b) If it is impossible for him to make restitution of all or part of the goods or to make restitution of all or part of the goods substantially in the condition in which he received them, but he has nevertheless declared the contract avoided or required the seller to deliver substitute goods.

Section VI. Preservation of the Goods

Article 85

If the buyer is in delay in taking delivery of the goods, or where payment of the price and delivery of the goods are to be made concurrently, if he fails to pay the price, and the seller is either in possession of the goods or otherwise able to control their disposition, the seller must take such steps as are reasonable in the circumstances to preserve them. He is entitled to retain them until he has been reimbursed his reasonable expenses by the buyer.

Article 86

(1) If the buyer has received the goods and intends to exercise any right under the contract or this Convention to reject them, he must take such steps to preserve them as are reasonable in the circumstances. He is entitled to retain them until he has been reimbursed his reasonable expenses by the seller.

(2) If goods dispatched to the buyer have been placed at his disposal at their destination and he exercises the right to reject them, he must take possession of them on behalf of the seller, provided that this can be done without payment of the price and without unreasonable inconvenience or unreasonable expense. This provision does not apply if the seller or a person authorized to take charge of the goods on his behalf is present at the destination. If the buyer takes possession of the goods under this paragraph, his rights and obligations are governed by the preceding paragraph.

Article 87

A party who is bound to take steps to preserve the goods may deposit them in a warehouse of a third person at the expense of the other party provided that the expense incurred is not unreasonable.

Article 88

(1) A party who is bound to preserve the goods in accordance with article 85 or 86 may sell them by any appropriate means if there has been an unreasonable delay by the other party in taking possession of the goods or in taking them back or in paying the price or the cost of preservation, provided that reasonable notice of the intention to sell has been given to the other party.

(2) If the goods are subject to rapid deterioration or their preservation would involve unreasonable expense, a party who is bound to preserve the goods in accordance with article 85 or 86 must take reasonable measures to sell them. To the extent possible he must give notice to the other party of his intention to sell.

(3) A party selling the goods has the right to retain out of the proceeds of sale an amount equal to the reasonable expenses of preserving the goods and of selling them. He must account to the other party for the balance.

PART IV—FINAL PROVISIONS

Article 89

The Secretary-General of the United Nations is hereby designated as the depositary for this Convention.

Article 90

This Convention does not prevail over any international agreement which has already been or may be entered into and which contains provisions concerning the matters governed by this Convention, provided that the parties have their places of business in States parties to such agreement.

Article 91

(1) This Convention is open for signature at the concluding meeting of the United Nations Conference of Contracts for the International Sale of Goods and will remain open for signature by all States at the Headquarters of the United Nations, New York until 30 September 1981.

(2) This Convention is subject to ratification, acceptance or approval by the signatory States.

(3) This Convention is open for accession by all States which are not signatory States as from the date it is open for signature.

(4) Instruments of ratification, acceptance, approval and accession are to be deposited with the Secretary-General of the United Nations.

Article 92

(1) A Contracting State may declare at the time of signature, ratification, acceptance, approval or accession that it will not be bound by Part II of this Convention or that it will not be bound by Part III of this Convention.

(2) A Contracting State which makes a declaration in accordance with the preceding paragraph in respect of Part II or Part III of this Convention is not to be considered a Contracting State within paragraph (1) of article 1 of this Convention in respect of matters governed by the Part to which the declaration applies.

Article 93

(1) If a Contracting State has two or more territorial units in which, according to its constitution, different systems of law are applicable in relation to the matters dealt with in this Convention, it may, at the time of signature, ratification, acceptance, approval or accession, declare that this Convention is to extend to all its territorial units or only to one or more of them, and may amend its declaration by submitting another declaration at any time.

(2) These declarations are to be notified to the depositary and are to state expressly the territorial units to which the Convention extends.

(3) If, by virtue of a declaration under this article, this Convention extends to one or more but not all of the territorial units of a Contracting State, and if the place of business of a party is located in that State, this place of business, for the purposes of this Convention, is considered not to be in a Contracting State, unless it is in a territorial unit to which the Convention extends.

(4) If a Contracting State makes no declaration under paragraph (1) of this article, the Convention is to extend to all territorial units of that State.

Article 94

(1) Two or more Contracting States which may have the same or closely related legal rules on matters governed by this Convention may at any time declare that the Convention is not to apply to contracts of sale or to their formation where the parties have their places of business in those States. Such declarations may be made jointly or by reciprocal unilateral declarations.

(2) A Contracting State which has the same or closely related legal rules on matters governed by this Convention as one or more non-Contracting States may at any time declare that the Convention is not to apply to contracts of sale or to their formation where the parties have their places of business in those States.

(3) If a State which is the object of a declaration under the preceding paragraph subsequently becomes a Contracting State, the declaration made will, as from the date on which the Convention enters into force in respect of the new Contracting State, have the effect of a declaration made under paragraph (1), provided that the new Contracting State joins in such declaration or makes a reciprocal unilateral declaration.

Article 95

Any State may declare at the time of the deposit of its instrument of ratification, acceptance, approval or accession that it will not be bound by subparagraph (1)(b) of article 1 of this Convention.

Article 96

A Contracting State whose legislation requires contracts of sale to be concluded in or evidenced by writing may at any time make a declaration in accordance with article 12 that any provision of article 11, article 29, or Part II of this Convention, that allows a contract of sale or its modification or termination by agreement or any offer, acceptance, or other indication of intention to be made in any form other than in writing, does not apply where any party has his place of business in that State.

Article 97

(1) Declarations made under this Convention at the time of signature are subject to confirmation upon ratification, acceptance or approval.

(2) Declarations and confirmations of declarations are to be in writing and be formally notified to the depositary.

(3) A declaration takes effect simultaneously with the entry into force of this Convention in respect of the State concerned. However, a declaration of which the depositary receives formal notification after such entry into force takes effect on the first day of the month following the expiration of six months after the date of its receipt by the depositary. Reciprocal unilateral declarations under article 94 take effect on the first day of the month following the expiration of six months after the receipt of the latest declaration by the depositary.

(4) Any State which makes a declaration under this Convention may withdraw it at any time by a formal notification in writing addressed to the depositary. Such withdrawal is to take effect on the first day of the month following the expiration of six months after the date of the receipt of the notification by the depositary.

(5) A withdrawal of a declaration made under article 94 renders inoperative, as from the date on which the withdrawal takes effect, any reciprocal declaration made by another State under that article.

Article 98

No reservations are permitted except those expressly authorized in this Convention.

Article 99

(1) This Convention enters into force, subject to the provisions of paragraph (6) of this article, on the first day of the month following the expiration of twelve months after the date of deposit of the tenth instrument of ratification, acceptance, approval or accession, including an instrument which contains a declaration made under article 92.

(2) When a State ratifies, accepts, approves or accedes to this Convention after the deposit of the tenth instrument of ratification, acceptance, approval or accession, this Convention, with the exception of the Part excluded, enters into force in respect of that State, subject to the provisions of paragraph (6) of this article, on the first day of the month following the expiration of twelve months after the date of the deposit of its instrument of ratification, acceptance, approval or accession.

(3) A State which ratifies, accepts, approves or accedes to this Convention and is a party to either or both the Convention relating to a Uniform Law on the Formation of Contracts for the International Sale of Goods done at The Hague on 1 July 1964 (1964 Hague Formation Convention) and the Convention relating to a Uniform Law on the International Sale of Goods done at The Hague on 1 July 1964 (1964 Hague Sales Convention) shall at the same time denounce, as the case may be, either or both the 1964 Hague Sales Convention and the 1964 Hague Formation Convention by notifying the Government of the Netherlands to that effect.

(4) A State party to the 1964 Hague Sales Convention which ratifies, accepts, approves or accedes to the present Convention and declares or has declared under article 92 that it will not be bound by Part II of this Convention shall at the time of ratification, acceptance, approval or accession denounce the 1964 Hague Sales Convention by notifying the Government of the Netherlands to that effect.

(5) A State party to the 1964 Hague Formation Convention which ratifies, accepts, approves or accedes to the present Convention and declares or has declared under article 92 that it will not be bound by Part III of this Convention shall at the time of ratification, acceptance, approval or accession denounce the 1964 Hague Formation Convention by notifying the Government of the Netherlands to that effect.

(6) For the purpose of this article, ratifications, acceptances, approvals and accessions in respect of this Convention by States parties to the 1964 Hague Formation Convention or to the 1964 Hague Sales Convention shall not be effective until such denunciations as may be required on the part of those States in respect of the latter two Conventions have themselves become effective. The depositary of this

Additional Information

Convention shall consult with the Government of the Netherlands, as the depositary of the 1964 Conventions, so as to ensure necessary co-ordination in this respect.

Article 100

(1) This Convention applies to the formation of a contract only when the proposal for concluding the contract is made on or after the date when the Convention enters into force in respect of the Contracting States referred to in subparagraph (1)(a) or the Contracting State referred to in subparagraph (1)(b) of article 1.

(2) This Convention applies only to contracts concluded on or after the date when the Convention enters into force in respect of the Contracting States referred to in subparagraph (1)(a) or the Contracting State referred to in subparagraph (1)(b) of article 1.

Article 101

(1) A Contracting State may denounce this Convention, or Part II or Part III of the Convention, by a formal notification in writing addressed to the depositary.

(2) The denunciation takes effect on the first day of the month following the expiration of twelve months after the notification is received by the depositary. Where a longer period for the denunciation to take effect is specified in the notification, the denunciation takes effect upon the expiration of such longer period after the notification is received by the depositary.

Done at Vienna, this eleventh day of April, one thousand nine hundred and eighty, in a single original, of which the Arabic, Chinese, English, French, Russian and Spanish texts are equally authentic.

In witness whereof the undersigned plenipotentiaries, being duly authorized by their respective Governments, have signed this Convention.

PARTIES TO THE CONVENTION

United Nations convention on contracts for the international sale of goods. Done at Vienna April 11, 1980; entry into force for the United States January 1, 1988.

States which are parties:

Argentina[1]
Australia[2]
Austria
Belarus[3]
Bulgaria
Canada[4]
Chile[5]
China[6]

Czechoslovakia[7]
Denmark[8]
Ecuador[9]
Egypt
Finland[10]
France
Germany, Fed.Rep. of[11]
Guinea[12]
Hungary[13]
Iraq
Italy
Lesotho
Mexico
Netherlands
Norway[14]
Romania
Russian Federation[15]
Spain
Sweden[16]
Switzerland
Syrian Arab Republic
Uganda[17]
Ukraine[18]
United States[19]
Yugoslavia
Zambia

MESSAGE ACCOMPANYING TRANSMITTAL

When the Convention was transmitted to the Senate by the President on September 21, 1983, the following message accompanied it (Treaty Document No. 98–9):

LETTER OF TRANSMITTAL

THE WHITE HOUSE, *September 21, 1983.*

To the Senate of the United States:

With a view to receiving the advice and consent of the Senate to ratification, I transmit herewith the United Nations Convention on Contracts for the International Sale of Goods. This Convention was adopted on April 11, 1980, by the United Nations Conference on Contracts for the International Sale of Goods and was signed on behalf of the United States at United Nations Headquarters on August 31, 1981.

The Convention would unify the law for international sales, as our Uniform Commercial Code in Article 2 unifies the law for domestic sales.

The Convention was prepared, with the active participation of representatives of the United States, by the United Nations Commission on International Trade Law (UNCITRAL) and received the unanimous approval of this worldwide body; the Convention was then adopted, without dissent, by the United Nations Conference of sixty-two States. This unanimity attests to the broadly perceived need for the Convention and the value of its provisions.

The House of Delegates of the American Bar Association recommended in 1981 that the United States ratify the Convention, subject to a declaration permitted under Article 95 as to the grounds for applicability. I concur fully in this recommendation for the reasons set forth in the enclosed report of the Department of State.

The report of the Department of State provides a summary of the Convention and describes its approach. Worthy of emphasis is the international deference that the Convention accords to the contract made by the parties to an international sale. The parties may agree that domestic law rather than the Convention will apply, and their contract may modify or supplant the Convention's rules. The uniform international rules play their significant role when, as often occurs, a problem arises that the parties did not anticipate and solve by contract.

International trade now is subject to serious legal uncertainties. Questions often arise as to whether our law or foreign law governs the transaction, and our traders and their counsel find it difficult to evaluate and answer claims based on one or another of the many unfamiliar foreign legal systems. The Convention's uniform rules offer effective answers to these problems.

Enhancing legal certainty for international sales contracts will serve the interests of all parties engaged in commerce by facilitating international trade. I recommend that the Senate of the United States promptly give its advice and consent to the ratification of this Convention.

RONALD REAGAN.

LETTER OF SUBMITTAL

DEPARTMENT OF STATE,
Washington, August 30, 1983.

THE PRESIDENT.
The White House.

THE PRESIDENT: I have the honor to submit to you the United Nations Convention on Contracts for the International Sale of Goods with the recommendation that it be transmitted to the Senate for its advice and consent to ratification. This Convention, adopted without dissent on April 11, 1980, by a United Nations conference of sixty-two States, culminated a half-century of work to prepare uniform law for the international sale of goods.

Sales transactions that cross international boundaries are subject to legal uncertainty—doubt as to which legal system will apply and the difficulty of coping with unfamiliar foreign law. The sales contract may specify which law will apply, but our sellers and buyers cannot expect that foreign trading partners will always agree on the applicability of United States law. Insistence by both parties on this sensitive point can prolong and jeopardize the making of the contract.

The Convention's approach provides an effective solution for this difficult problem. When a contract for an international sale of goods does not make clear what rule of law applies, the Convention provides uniform rules to govern the questions that arise in the making and performance of the contract.

The Convention does not restrict the parties' freedom to settle by contract the full range of their rights and obligations. Instead it provides that its rules yield to the terms of the international sales contract. A major need for the Convention's uniform law arises from the fact that the buyer and the seller do not anticipate every question that might arise or consider it essential to deal with every problem, and it is often inexpedient to hold up the transaction until the parties find a solution for all foreseeable contingencies. In short, the Convention (like modern national systems of commercial law) serves the significant function of providing solutions for problems that the parties have failed to resolve by contract.

The usefulness of the Convention is enhanced by the fact that its rules were specially fashioned to meet the problems and needs of international trade. Our sellers and buyers now must cope with foreign statutes and code that were prepared a century or more ago, and were designed for domestic sales that bear little resemblance to current international transactions. Even when these problems have been ameliorated by case-law, such developments are often unknown or inaccessible to our lawyers.

The present Convention was adopted in six languages; English, of course, is one. The legislative history of the Convention is readily available in English, and most of the explanatory writing about the Convention is in English. Under the Convention our traders will not be forced to rely on foreign advice concerning the implications of the rules of a wide variety of foreign legal systems and often inadequate translations of such advice or rules.

This Convention replaces the Hague Sales Convention of 1964 which, because of defects, has not been widely accepted. (The United States has neither signed nor become a party to these Conventions.) These defects were discussed and resolved during a decade of preparatory work by the United Nations Commission on International Trade Law (UNCITRAL). The thirty-six member States of UNCITRAL provided representation for all major legal systems and regions of the world. United States representatives played an active and influential part in this preparatory work and in the 1980 Conference. UNCITRAL unanimously approved the draft Convention, and the 1980 Plenipotentiary conference of sixty-two States, again without dissent, adopted the final text.

During the eighteen-month period for signing the Convention after the 1980 Conference the following became Signatory States: Austria; Chile; Czechoslovakia; Denmark; Finland; France; German Democratic Republic; Germany, Federal Republic of; Ghana; Hungary; Italy; Lesotho; Netherlands; Norway; People's Republic of China; Poland; Singapore; Sweden; United States of America; Venezuela; and Yugoslavia. Steps for both Signatory and non-Signatory States to become parties to the Convention are now under way. Argentina, Egypt, France, Hungary, Lesotho and Syria have already ratified or acceded to the Convention, which will come into force approximately one year after four more countries have submitted their ratifications or accessions (Article 99(1)). Signature and ratification by the United States were recommended by the House of Delegates of the American Bar Association in 1981.

For the reasons set forth in Appendix B of the Legal Analysis, I recommend that United States ratification be made subject to the declaration permitted under Article 95 that the United States will not be bound by Article 1(1)(b) of the Convention. As a result of this reservation, the Convention will be applicable only when the seller and the buyer have their places of business in different Contracting States. This limitation, also approved by the American Bar Association, provides a clear, fair and adequate basis for the applicability of the Convention.

Enclosed is a Legal Analysis comparing the Convention's provisions with those of the Sales Article of the Uniform Commercial Code (UCC), which has been enacted by every State of the United States except Louisiana. It will be noted that the Convention embodies the substance of many of the important provisions of the UCC and is generally consistent with its approach and outlook.

The Convention is subject to ratification by signatory states (Article 91(2)), but is self-executing and thus requires no federal implementing legislation to come into force throughout the United States. As already indicated, the Convention's effect is limited to foreign commerce of the United States and it will not affect purely domestic contracts of sale.

The Convention is a notable example of world-wide legal cooperation. It provides practical help for sellers and buyers, in our country and abroad, and by adding certainty to law it will facilitate international trade.

The Department of Commerce supports this recommendation and the Department of Justice has no objection to it.

It is hoped that the Senate will promptly give favorable consideration to this Convention and approve ratification by the United States.

Respectfully submitted.

GEORGE P. SHULTZ.

Appendix C

Legal Analysis of the Convention on Contracts for the International Sale of Goods

Although the Convention on Contracts for the International Sale of Goods (see Appendix E) has been discussed both in the main volume and this supplement, it may be helpful for the reader to have the State Department notes interpreting the various provisions. These are set forth herein.

Legal Analysis of the United Nations Convention on Contracts for the International Sale of Goods (1980)

The Convention provides uniform rules to resolve questions that have not been answered by the contracts made by the seller and the buyer in an international sale. The salient features of the Convention were summarized in the Letter of Submittal to the President. To assist in a closer study of these rules, the present statement provides a brief synopsis of the 101 articles of the Convention.

It is not feasible in this brief analysis to provide a thorough commentary on the Convention's uniform rules of law for the sale of goods. Such a commentary calls for a substantial book; detailed studies are provided by books and articles.

The present document is designed to spot-light the most significant provisions of the Convention, and to indicate the relationship between these provisions and United States law as set forth in Article 2 on Sale of Goods of the Uniform Commercial Code, which has been enacted by virtually all States of the United States.

STRUCTURE OF THE CONVENTION

The uniform rules for sales transactions appear in Parts I–III of the Convention. Part I (Arts. 1–13) defines the Convention's field of application and includes other general provisions. Part II (Arts. 14–24) governs formation of the contract. Part III (Arts. 25–88) governs the rights and obligations of the parties to the contract of sale. Part IV ("Final Provisions": Arts. 89–101) establishes procedures for implementing the Convention and sets out the reservations that a State may make.

PART I: SPHERE OF APPLICATION AND GENERAL PROVISIONS

(Articles 1–13)

INTRODUCTION TO PART OF THE CONVENTION

Part I sets forth rules that apply throughout the Convention. Chapter I defines the Convention's field of application. Chapter II addresses other general questions, notably interpretation of the Convention and the sales contract.

A. The Convention's Field of Application: Chapter I

Article 1 addresses two issues that control the applicability of the Convention: (1) When is a sale "international"? and (2) What contact between the sales transaction and a Contracting State will invoke the Convention? (A "Contracting State" is a country that has become a party to the Convention.) Articles 2 and 3 exclude specified types of *commodities and transactions.* Articles 4 and 5 draw the line between *issues* that are regulated and those that are excluded; the excluded issues include the validity of the contract, the effect of the contract on the ownership rights of third persons (Art. 4) and liability for death or personal injury (Art. 5). The chapter closes with a brief but important provision (Art. 6) yielding overriding effect to the contract made by the parties.

CHAPTER I. SPHERE OF APPLICATION

(Articles 1–6)

Article 1. Basic Rules on Applicability

Under Article 1 the Convention will apply only if two requirements are met: (1) the seller and the buyer have their "places of business in different States," and (2) both of these States are Contracting States (i.e. States that have adopted the Convention). This simplified basis for applicability reflects a recommendation that the United States ratify subject to a declaration authorized by Article 95; the reasons for making this declaration and its effect are set forth in Appendix B. Thus, an American court would apply the Convention only to sales with an international character between parties in whose countries the Convention is in force.

Article 2. Exclusions from the Convention

Article 2 provides for six exclusions from the Convention. Three (paragraphs (a)–(c)) are based on the nature of the transaction and three (paragraphs (d)–(f)) are based on the nature of the goods.

Paragraph (a) excludes substantially all consumer purchases by language based on the Uniform Commercial Code (UCC 9–109(1)). The principal impact of the Convention is thus on commercial sales between persons in business.

The remaining five exclusions do not call for discussion in this analysis.

Article 3. Goods to Be Manufactured: Services

Paragraph (1) makes it clear that a sale is not excluded from the scope of the Convention merely because it calls for the manufacture or production of goods. On the other hand, it also makes it clear that the Convention does not extend to transactions in which the party receiving a finished product supplies "a substantial part" of the necessary materials.

Paragraph (2) excludes "service" contracts, in which the "supply of labour or other services" comprises the preponderant part of the transaction.

Article 4. Issues Covered and Excluded; Validity; Effect on Property Interests of Third Persons

While Articles 1–3 identify the *contracts* that are subject to the Convention, Article 4 defines the *issues* to which the Convention applies. Article 4 states that the Convention "governs only" the following: (1) "the formation of the contract" (Part II of the Convention) and (2) "the rights and obligations of the seller and the buyer arising from such a contract" (Part III of the Convention). In addition it excludes from the Convention issues with respect to "the validity of the contract or of any of its provisions or of any usage." One example is a rule of national law that prohibits the sale of specified products, such as heroin, and invalidates contracts relating to such illegal sales.

Article 4 also provides that the Convention "is not concerned with . . . the effect which the contract may have on the property in the goods sold." Whether the sale to the buyer cuts off outstanding property interests of third persons is not dealt with by the Convention. This specific provision illustrates the general rule of

Article 4 that the Convention is concerned only with the "rights and obligations of *the seller and the buyer*" arising from the sales contract. For the buyer's right, *as against the seller,* to receive goods title, see Articles 41–43, *infra*.

Article 5. Exclusion of Liability for Death or Personal Injury; "Product Liability"

Article 5 makes the Convention inapplicable to the liability of the seller for death or personal injury caused by the goods. This was done lest the Convention collide with rules of national law on product liability.

Article 6. The Contract and the Convention

The dominant theme of the Convention is the primacy of the contract. See, *e.g.,* Arts. 4 and 35. Of the many provisions that develop this theme, Article 6 is the most important. Thus, the parties may exclude the Convention or "vary the effect" of any of its provisions. The breadth of the parties' freedom to contract is emphasized by the one exception stated in Article 6—the privilege of an adhering State under Articles 12 and 96 to preserve its domestic rules that require a writing. (See Art. 12, *infra*).

CHAPTER II. GENERAL PROVISIONS

(Articles 7–13)

Article 7. Interpretation of the Convention

A. International Character; Uniformity; Good Faith

Paragraph (1) provides that in interpreting the Convention there shall be regard for two closely-related principles—(a) the Convention's "international character" and (b) "the need to promote uniformity in its application." The latter provision is usual in uniform legislation in the United States. *See* UCC 1–102(2)(c). Paragraph (1) also provides that in interpreting the Convention there shall be regard for promoting "the observance of good faith in international trade." The Uniform Commercial Code states a "good faith" requirement that is broader than the principle of interpretation stated in the Convention. *See* UCC 1–203: "Every contract or duty within this Act imposes a duty of good faith in its performance or enforcement." See also: UCC 2–103(1)(b).

B. "General Principles"

Paragraph (2) provides that, where possible, questions "are to be settled in conformity with the general principles on which [the Convention] is based"—an approach that was designed to strengthen uniform international interpretation of the

Convention. A somewhat similar principle is expressed in the Uniform Commercial Code. For example, section 1–102(1) states that the UCC is to be "liberally construed and applied to promote its *underlying purposes and policies.*"

Article 8. Interpretation of Statements or Other Conduct of a Party

While Article 7 deals with interpretation of the *Convention,* the present Article deals with the interpretation of the statements and conduct of the *parties,* including the provisions of the contract of sale. When there is no common "intent" of the parties, Article 8(2) applies the objective standard familiar to the common law.

Article 8(3) authorizes "due consideration" of conduct subsequent to the agreement as this may shed light on the intentions and expectations of the parties. Similarly, the Uniform Commercial Code states that in some circumstances a "course of performance accepted or acquiesced in without objection shall be relevant to determine the meaning of the agreement" (UCC 2–208). See also UCC 2–207(3) under which "conduct by both parties which recognizes the existence of a contract is sufficient to establish a contract for sale . . ."

Article 9. Practices of the Parties; Trade Usages

One of the important features of the Convention is the legal effect it gives to practices of the parties and to commercial usages.

(1) Practices Established Between the Two Parties

Expectations that have the force of contract can be established by the parties' patterns of behavior. Under Article 9(1) the parties are bound by the "practices which they have established between themselves." The Uniform Commercial Code also gives contractual effect to the "course of dealing between parties"—defined as "a sequence of previous conduct between the parties to a particular transaction which is fairly to be regarded as establishing a common basis of understanding for interpreting their expressions and other conduct." (UCC 1–205)

(2) Usages of Trade

Article 9(2) provides that the agreement embrace a party's expectation that the other party will observe the usages of their trade. Unless the parties have agreed otherwise, effect is given to a trade usage "of which the parties knew or ought to have known" and which "in international trade is widely known to, and regularly observed by, parties to contracts of the type involved in the particular trade concerned." The Uniform Commercial Code also gives contractual effect to a "usage of trade"—defined as "any practice or method of dealing having such regularity of observance in a place, vocation or trade as to justify an expectation that it will be observed with respect to the transaction in question." (UCC 1–205)

Under Article 6, "The parties may . . . derogate from or vary the effect" of the provisions of the Convention, and applicable usage has the same effect as a provision of a sales contract. In short, the provisions of the Convention yield to the expectations of the parties, whether derived from express contract terms, from their established practices or from applicable trade usage.

Article 10. Definition of "Place of Business"

The Convention refers to a party's "place of business" in several articles: 1, 12, 20(2), 24, 31(c), 42(1)(b), 57(1)(a), 69(2) and 96. If a commercial enterprise maintains a central office and one or more branch offices, Article 10 makes applicable the place of business "which has the closest relationship to the contract and its performance. . . ."

Article 11. Inapplicability of Domestic Requirement that Contract Be in Writing

A. Domestic Rules: "Statute of Frauds"

In 1677 the English Parliament (29 Car. II, c.3) enacted a Statute of Frauds which required a signed writing for the enforcement of a wide variety of transactions, including the sale of goods. This requirement was embodied in the United Kingdom's Sale of Goods Act (1893), was closely followed in the (U.S.A.) Uniform Sales Act (1896), and formed the basis for an elaborate statute of frauds included in the Uniform Commercial Code (§ 2–201). In recent decades, however, the tide has been running against such formal requirements. In 1954 Britain repealed this part of the Sale of Goods Act—a step that has been followed by many of the other countries that had adopted this Act. Most civil law countries do not impose such formal requirements for the making of commercial contracts. Formal requirements have generated litigation and uncertainty, and are generally regarded to be of doubtful value for international trade.

B. The Convention

The 1980 Convention rejects such formal requirements (Article 11). This does not, however, bar the parties from imposing formal requirements. An offeror may require that an acceptance be in writing; an oral "acceptance" is not an "assent" to the offer. (See Arts. 18 and 19, *infra.*) In addition, pursuant to Article 29, *infra,* the parties by a contract in writing may require "any modification or termination by agreement" to be in writing.

A Contracting State may protect its formal requirements from Article 11 by making a reservation under Article 96. *See* Article 12, *infra.*

Article 12. Declaration by Contracting State Preserving Its Domestic Requirements as to Form

Laws of the U.S.S.R. impose strict formal requirements for the making of foreign trade contracts. In the UNCITRAL proceedings, delegates of the U.S.S.R. indicated that preserving these requirements was of great importance to protect its established patterns for the making of foreign trade contracts. Most delegates, however, including the United States, concluded that formal requirements were inconsistent with modern commercial practice—particularly in view of the speed and informality that characterized many transactions in a market economy.

The result was a compromise. In Part IV (Final Provisions), Article 96 authorizes a Contracting State "whose legislation requires contracts of sale to be concluded in or evidenced by writing" to make a "declaration" that Article 11 (and certain other provisions of the Convention affecting formal requirements) "does not apply where any party has his place of business in that State." Article 12 articulates the effect of a declaration under Article 96. A declaration (reservation) under Article 96 would not ensure that the formal requirements of the declaring State would apply to transactions involving its buyers and sellers. Such applicability would result only when conflicts rules point to the formal requirements of the declaring State. However, conflicts rules may point to foreign law, which may have no formal requirements or may impose formal requirements that are unfamiliar to traders in the declaring State. These considerations explain why it is not recommended that the United States make a declaration pursuant to Article 96.

Article 13. Telegram and Telex as a "Writing"

This provision does not call for discussion.

PART II: FORMATION OF THE CONTRACT
(Articles 14–24)
INTRODUCTION TO PART II OF THE CONVENTION

A. Relation Between Part II and other Parts of the Convention

Part II of the Convention, Formation of the Contract, is subject to the rules of Part I (Arts. 1–13) on the scope and interpretation of the Convention, but is independent of Part III (Arts. 25–88) which deals with the obligations of the parties to the contract. Article 92 (Part IV) permits a Contracting State to declare that it will not be bound either by Part II or by Part III.

B. Structure of Part II

The first four articles (14–17) deal with the offer—the minimum criteria for an offer (Art. 14), and the withdrawal (Art. 15), revocation (Art. 16) or termination (Art. 17) of an offer. The next five articles (18–22) deal with acceptance—"acceptances" that do not match the offer (Art. 19), the period allowed for acceptance (Arts. 20 and 21), and withdrawal of an acceptance (Art. 22). The two final articles (Arts. 23 and 24) relate to the time when a contract is concluded.

Article 14. Criteria for an Offer

(1) "Public Offers"

Article 14 incorporates the generally accepted premise that a person may make an offer to as large a group as he wishes. However, a communication addressed to a large group, if construed as an offer, can involve practical difficulties and hazards. These practical considerations are reflected in Article 14(2): If a proposal is not "addressed to *one or more specific persons,*" it is not an offer "unless the contrary is clearly indicated by the person making the proposal." See Restatement Second of Contracts § 29.

(2) Definiteness: Unstated Price

Difficult problems arise when the parties neither fix the price, expressly or implicitly, nor agree on a method for fixing the price. The Convention's solution calls for construing Article 14(1) in the light of Article 55, which states that in the above circumstances the parties are considered, in the absence of any indication to the contrary, to have impliedly made reference to the price generally charged for such goods at the time of the conclusion of the contract. The Uniform Commercial Code (§ 2–305) similarly provides that the parties "if they so intend can conclude a contract for sale even though the price is not settled."

Article 15. When Offer Becomes Effective; Prior Withdrawal

Under Article 15 an offeror may withdraw an offer by a communication that reaches the offeree ahead of the offer. The reason supporting Article 15 is that the enforcement of contracts is designed to protect expectations; none can arise until the offer reaches the offeree. *Cf.* Article 18(2), *infra.*

Article 16. Revocability of Offer

Article 16 limits the powers of an offeror to revoke an offer which the offeror has stated or indicated will be "firm" or irrevocable, or on which the offeree has reasonably relied. Compare the provisions giving effect to "firm" offers in the Uniform Commercial Code (UCC 2–205). See Restatement Second of Contracts § 87 and Illustration 6.

Article 17. Rejection of Offer Followed by Acceptance

Under Article 17, an offeree may not accept an offer which he has rejected. The same rule is applied in the United States. See Restatement Second of Contracts § 38.

Article 18. Acceptance: Time and Manner for Indicating Assent

Article 18 states how an offer may be accepted. Its most significant provision is in paragraph (3): under some circumstances, an offeree may accept an offer by performing an act requested by the offeror, such as dispatch of the goods. For a similar rule see Section 2–206(1)(b) of the Uniform Commercial Code.

Article 19. "Acceptance" with Modifications

Article 19 faces the situation in which a reply to an offer purports to be an acceptance but contains modifications of the offer. This situation most commonly results from the routine exchange of the buyer's printed purchase order and the seller's printed acknowledgment of sale form. Under the Convention, no contract results from such an exchange if the purported acceptance contains additional or different terms that materially alter the offer. A list of examples of material alterations makes it clear that most alterations are material. However, an acceptance with an immaterial modification will be effective unless the offeror objects.

The Convention's approach to this difficult problem differs from that of the Uniform Commercial Code, under which even a material alteration may not prevent the purported acceptance from creating a contract (UCC 2–207). The Convention would thus avoid many of the problems that have arisen under and resulted in criticism of the Code provision.

Articles 20–24

The following articles dealing with various aspects of acceptance do not call for discussion:

Article 20. Interpretation of Offeror's Time-Limits for Acceptance

Article 21. Late Acceptances: Response by Offeror

Article 22. Withdrawal of Acceptance

Article 23. Effect of Acceptance; Time of Conclusion of Contracts

Article 24. When Communication "Reaches" the Addressee

These articles complete Part II: Formation of Contract.

PART III: SALE OF GOODS

(Articles 25–88)

INTRODUCTION TO PART III OF THE CONVENTION

When an enforceable international sales contract has been formed, Part III governs the rights and obligations of the seller and buyer.

Part III has five chapters. Chapter I (Arts. 25–29) contains general provisions that are applicable throughout Part III of the Convention. Chapter II (Arts. 30–52) deals with the obligations of the seller (Secs. I & II) and remedies for the seller's breach (Sec. III). Chapter III (Arts. 53–65), paralleling the structure of Chapter II, states the obligations of the buyer (Secs. I and II) and remedies for the buyer's breach (Sec. III). Chapter IV (Arts. 66–70) is devoted to risk of loss. Chapter V (Arts. 71–88) addresses anticipatory breach (Sec. I), damage measurement and interest (Secs. II & III), excuses ("exemptions") based on serious impediments (Sec. IV), effects of avoidance (Sec. V), and duties to preserve goods that face loss or deterioration (Sec. VI).

CHAPTER I. GENERAL PROVISIONS

(Articles 25–29)

Article 25. Definition of "Fundamental Breach"

A. Introduction

The breach of a sales contract by one party gives the other party a right to recover damages, but Article 25 relates to other remedies—the buyer's right to reject goods and the seller's right to refuse to deliver. In domestic law these remedies may be called "rejection," "revocation of acceptance," "avoidance," "termination" or "cancellation." In the Convention (Arts. 49 and 64) a party's privilege not to perform the contract because of the other party's breach is called "avoidance of the contract."

In the Convention, as in our legal system, "avoidance" is not available for every breach. Under Articles 49(1)(a) and 64(1)(a), *infra,* a party may avoid the contract when the other party commits a "fundamental breach"—a term that is defined in Article 25.

The role played by "fundamental breach" under the Convention is similar to that played by Section 2–608 of the Uniform Commercial Code, under which a buyer who has accepted goods that turn out to be defective may revoke his acceptance if the non-conformity *"substantially* impairs" the value of the goods to him (UCC 2–612, but *cf.* 2–601). The UCC does not attempt to define "substantial" impairment.

The Convention's definition of "fundamental breach" also allows leeway to consider whether avoidance is needed to assure full protection for the aggrieved party.

Article 26. Notice of Avoidance

Article 26 provides that a "declaration of avoidance of the contract is effective only if made by notice to the other party." This is one of the significant advances of the 1980 Convention over the 1968 Hague Convention on Sales (ULIS).

At various points ULIS gave an injured party a remedy called "*ipso facto* avoidance." This type of avoidance occurred automatically with no need to notify the other party (ULIS 25, 26(1)). Consequently, the other party might be led to perform in ignorance of the injured party's decision to refuse performance. At the 1964 Hague Conference the delegations of the United States and other states attempted unsuccessfully to eliminate *ipso facto* avoidance.

In the UNCITRAL proceedings, the delegations of the United States and other countries were able to remove the doctrine of *ipso facto* avoidance, resulting in the simple rule of Article 26. Requiring that notice be given of a remedy as drastic as avoidance is consistent with the Uniform Commercial Code. See UCC 2–602(1) (notice of rejection), 2–608(2) (notice of revocation of acceptance).

Article 27. Delay or Error in Communications

Under Article 26, *supra,* avoidance of a contract is effected "by notice" and in other settings communications have important consequences. *E.g.* Arts 39(1) (notice of lack of conformity) and 43 (notice of right or claim of third party). Article 27 addresses the problems that arise when a notice is sent but, because of a mishap in transmission, is delayed, garbled or lost. Article 27 lays down the general rule that a party satisfies his duty to notify if he dispatches the communication "by means appropriate in the circumstances."

This general rule is subject to exceptions in Articles 47(2), 48(4), 63(2), 65(1) & (2) and 79(4). Nearly all of these exceptions involve a communication by a party who is in breach of contract; the "receipt" principle was used so that a mishap in transmission would not add to the burdens of the aggrieved party.

The Uniform Commercial Code similarly requires the buyer to "notify" the seller of breach or "be barred from any remedy," and provides that one "notifies" another "*by taking such steps* as may be reasonably required to inform the other in ordinary course whether or not such other actually comes to know of it" (UCC 2–607(3) and 1–201(26)). The UCC, like the Convention, states exceptions from this general rule (*e.g.* § 2–616).

Article 28. Specific Performance and the Rules of the Forum

The Convention's system of remedies for breach of contract is based on the premise that a party in breach may be compelled to perform his obligations. On the other hand, restrictions on the right to specific performance appear in Articles 46(2) and 46(3).

Even with the restrictions just mentioned, the Convention grants specific performance on a wider scale than does the common law. As a concession to the common law, Article 28 provides that rules of national law withholding specific performance will prevail over the rules of the Convention. Thus, courts in the United States would still be subject to the limits on such remedies provided in Section 2–716 of the Uniform Commercial Code. *Cf.* UCC 2–709.

Article 29. Modification of Contract; Requirement of a Writing

Sales contracts sometimes provide that they may be modified only in writing. Article 29 gives effect to these private "statutes of frauds." The Uniform Commercial Code is similar (UCC 2–209(2)).

CHAPTER II. OBLIGATIONS OF THE SELLER

(Articles 30–52)

Introduction to Chapter II

Chapter II opens with a brief statement giving the essence of the seller's obligations (Art. 30). The remaining articles of the Chapter are grouped in three sections. Two sections define the seller's most important duties: The time and place for delivering the goods (Sec. I, Arts. 31–34); the quality of the goods and their freedom from third party claims (Sec. II, Arts. 35–44). The final section sets forth the basic remedies that are given to the buyer when the seller fails to perform his duties under the contract (Sec. III, Arts. 45–52).

The brief summary of Chapter II in Article 30 does not call for further discussion.

SECTION I: DELIVERY OF THE GOODS AND HANDING OVER THE DOCUMENTS

(Articles 31–34)

Article 31. Place for Delivery

When the contract, interpreted in the light of practices and usages, does not state where the seller should deliver the goods, the place of delivery is determined by Article 31. See also the Convention's rules on risk of loss in Article 67 and 69, *infra*.

Article 32. Shipping Arrangement

In international sales, the seller usually completes his obligation to deliver by "handing over the goods to the first carrier for transmission to the buyer." Art. 31, *supra,* and Article 67, *infra.* However, the seller also normally makes various arrangements with respect to carriage. Any provision of the sales contract (including usage and any practice between the parties) is decisive as to the seller's obligations in this regard; to the extent that there is no agreement with respect to shipping arrangements, Article 32 fills the gap.

Paragraph (1), requiring the seller to notify the buyer of the shipment, is similar to Section 2–504(c) of the Uniform Commercial Code. Paragraph (2), dealing with transportation arrangements, is similar to UCC 2–504. Paragraph (3) calls for cooperation between the parties with respect to supplying needed information concerning insurance. Similar rules on co-operation are set forth in the Uniform Commercial Code (2–311, 2–319(1)(c) and 2–319(3)).

Article 33. Time for Delivery

This article does not call for discussion.

Article 34. Documents Relating to the Goods

Article 34 responds to commercial practice in international sales that permits, and often requires, delivery of the goods to be effected by handing over documents (such as a bill of lading) that control the goods. Accord: UCC 2–310(b). *Cf.* UCC 2–505 and 2–507(2).

Article 34 also provides that the seller's right to "cure" a defective delivery of goods (Art. 37, *infra*) extend to the delivery of documents. The Uniform Commercial Code provides that a seller may cure a "tender or delivery," which may include the tender of documents (2–508(1); 2–504(b)).

SECTION II. CONFORMITY OF THE GOODS AND THE THIRD PARTY CLAIMS

(Articles 35–44)

Introduction to Section II

Articles 35 and 36 define the seller's obligations with respect to the quality of the goods. Articles 37–40 describe procedures that apply when goods are defective—the seller's privilege to cure defects in the goods (Art. 37) and the buyer's obligation to examine the goods and notify the seller of nonconformity (Arts. 38–40). Articles 41 and 42 define the rights of the buyer when the goods are subject to third party claims of ownership (Art. 41) and of rights based on patents, trademarks or other types of intellectual property (Art. 42). Article 43 requires the buyer to notify the seller of these claims; the concluding article (Art. 44) gives grounds for excusing a failure to notify the seller.

Article 35. Conformity of the Goods

Paragraph (1) of Article 35 emphasizes that the seller must supply goods of the quality provided in the contract. As mentioned earlier (Art. 9, *supra*) under the Convention the practices established by the parties and applicable trade usages help to determine the contractual obligations of the parties. Accord: UCC 1–205. The Uniform Commercial Code also emphasizes the importance of the contract (UCC 2–313).

Paragraph (2) of Article 35, like Sections 2–314 and 2–315 of the Uniform Commercial Code, gives effect to the buyer's basic expectations of quality. Paragraph 2(a), on fitness of goods for "the purposes for which goods of the same *description* would *ordinarily* be used," is similar to UCC 2–314(2)(c). Paragraph 2(b), on fitness for a particular purpose, is similar to UCC 2–315. Paragraph (2)(c), on conformity with a sample or model, is similar to UCC 2–313(1)(c). Paragraph (2)(d), on packaging, is similar to UCC 2–314(2)(e). Paragraph (3), on the effect of the buyer's knowledge of a lack of conformity, is comparable to UCC 2–316(3)(b).

Article 36. Damage to Goods: Effect on Conformity

Goods often arrive in poor condition because of damage that occurred after the risk of loss passed to the buyer. Paragraph (1) of Article 36 makes it clear that the seller is not responsible for defects that result from transit casualties which the buyer has assumed under the contract or under the Convention's rules on risk of loss (Arts. 66–70, *infra*). Paragraph (2) deals with the effect of contractual guarantees that goods will retain a specified quality for a prescribed period of time.

Article 37. Right to Cure Up to the Date for Delivery

Under Article 37 the seller, up to the agreed date for delivery, may remedy defects in the goods and thereby prevent destruction of the contract by "avoidance"—the remedy that in U.S. law is termed "rejection" (UCC 2–601) or "revocation of acceptance" (UCC 2–608). The "cure" provisions of Article 37 closely resemble those of UCC 2–508(1). *Cf.* Art. 48, *infra,* and UCC 2–508(2).

Article 38. Time for Examining the Goods

Article 38 provides rules on how soon the buyer "must examine" the goods. These rules are given legal effect by Article 39(1), which cuts off the buyer's rights if he fails to notify the seller of a nonconformity within a reasonable time after he "ought to have discovered" it. The rules on inspection and notice in Articles 38 and 39(1) are similar to the notice requirement in UCC 2–607(3).

Article 39. Notice of Lack of Conformity

Article 40. Seller's Knowledge of Non-Conformity

Article 41. Third-Party Ownership Claims to Goods

Article 42. Third-Party Claims Based on Patent or Other Intellectual Property

Article 43. Notice of Claim

One of the limits on the scope of the Convention is set by Article 4: "this Convention . . . is not concerned with . . . (b) the effect which the contract may have on the property in the goods sold." Thus, if a third person claims the goods because of a defect in the seller's title, the question whether the buyer is protected, as a good faith purchaser, against that third-party claim is not governed by the Convention but is left to applicable domestic law.

Article 41 addresses this question: When the seller supplies goods that are subject to a third-party claim, what are the rights of the buyer *against the seller?* Third-party claims "based on industrial property or other intellectual property" (e.g., a patent or copyright) are dealt with in Article 42.

The protection afforded the buyer under Article 41 is similar to the implied warranty of title provided by the Uniform Commercial Code (UCC 2–312(1)). The Code gives the buyer rights against the seller when a third person establishes a claim "by way of infringement or the like" (UCC 2–312(3)), but does not deal with the problems that arise when the buyer encounters an infringement claim in a country where the seller could not have anticipated that the goods would be used or resold. These problems are addressed in Article 42.

The notice provisions of Article 43 do not call for discussion here. *Cf.* Articles 39, 40 and 44, *supra*. (Article 43 does not set a fixed cut-off period for notice comparable to the two-year period in Article 39(2)).

Article 44. Excuse for Failure to Notify

As was mentioned under Article 38, the notice requirement of Article 39(1) is similar to that of UCC 2–607(3). However, Article 39(2) sets an outer limit for notice of two years unless the parties agree otherwise; the UCC states no fixed outer limit for notification. *Cf.* UCC 2–725 (limitation period for actions of four years after delivery). On the other hand, the Uniform Commercial Code extends to claims, including those for personal injury arising out of consumer purchases, where substantial delays in notification may be justified. As we have already seen, the Convention excludes substantially all consumer transactions (Art. 2(a)) and excludes all claims for death or personal injury (Art. 5). Article 44 of the Convention relaxes the notice requirement of Articles 39(1) and 43(1) to the extent of allowing the buyer to reduce the price (Art. 50) "or claim damages, except for loss of profit" when the buyer "has a reasonable excuse for his failure to give the required notice." This provision, however, does not remove the two-year outer limit for notification set by Article 39(2) or authorize a buyer, who has failed to give notice within a reasonable time, to exercise other remedies such as avoidance of the contract (Art. 49, *cf.* Art. 46).

SECTION III. REMEDIES FOR BREACH OF CONTRACT BY THE SELLER

(Articles 45–52)

Introduction to Section III

A. A Bird's-Eye View of the Section

The first two sections of Chapter II define the seller's duties; Section III defines the buyer's remedies when the seller is in breach.

Section III opens (Art. 45) with a general overview of the remedial system and indicates the relationship of different remedies to each other. *Cf.* UCC 2–711, 2–720. Article 46 states the buyer's right to compel performance by the seller. See Art. 28, *supra,* and UCC 2–716.

Three articles (Arts. 47–49) address the buyer's right to "avoid" the contract, a concept that includes the rejection of goods. *Cf.* UCC 2–601, 2–608. Article 47 empowers the buyer to fix an additional final period for the seller's delivery of the goods—a step that clarifies the buyer's right to avoid the contract for delay in delivery. Article 48 empowers the seller to "cure" defects in performance and thus forestall avoidance of the contract. *Cf.* UCC 2–508. Article 49 states the grounds on which the buyer may avoid the contract. *Cf.* UCC 2–608.

The section closes with three articles dealing with special situations—the buyer's right to reduce the price (Art. 50), the applicability of remedies to only part of the goods (Art. 51; *cf.* UCC 2–601(c), 2–608(1)) and deliveries that are too early or excessive in quantity (Art. 52; *cf.* UCC 2–601(c)). Although the remedy in Article 50 (reduction of price) has its origin in civil law concepts, its formula has been amended so as to approximate the common law right to deduct damages from the price (*Cf.* UCC 2–717).

B. Relationship to Other Parts of the Convention

Section III of the present chapter provides remedies that apply only to breach by the seller; Section III of Chapter III provides comparable remedies for breach by the buyer. These two sections are supplemented by remedial provisions in Chapter V that apply to both parties—*e.g.,* anticipatory breach (Sec. I), the measurement of damages, and interest (Secs. II and III), "exemption" from damages (Sec. IV) and the effects of avoidance of the contract (Sec. V).

C. General Comment

It is not feasible for this legal analysis to analyze in detail the remedial provisions of Articles 45–52. It must suffice to note that, with the encouragement of the United States delegation, UNCITRAL reviewed the 1964 Hague Convention (ULIS), unified and simplified its complex provisions, and thereby met the serious objections of the United States delegation to the 1964 Hague Conference.

CHAPTER III: OBLIGATIONS OF THE BUYER

(Articles 53–65)

Introduction to Chapter III

The structure of Chapter III is similar to that of the preceding chapter on Obligations of the Seller. Two sections state the buyer's duties: to pay the price (Sec. I, Arts. 53–59; *cf.* UCC 2–310(a), 2–507(1)) and to take delivery (Sec. II, Art. 60). The final section defines the remedies that are available to the seller when the buyer fails to perform these duties (Sec. III, Arts. 61–65; *cf.* UCC 2–703). These remedial provisions (like those in Chapter II) are supplemented by general rules on remedies in Chapter V (Arts. 71–88).

Many of the provisions of this chapter on the obligations of the buyer are mirror-images of provisions in the preceding chapter on the obligations of the seller.

CHAPTER IV: PASSING OF RISK

(Articles 66–70)

Introduction to Chapter IV

Casualty to the goods (*e.g.* by theft or fire) may occur in various settings—while the seller holds the goods before delivering them to a carrier or to the buyer, while the goods are in transit, while the buyer is examining the goods, or while the buyer holds the goods after rejecting them. Usually the loss will be covered by insurance. Allocating the risk of loss between seller and buyer should reflect considerations such as these: Which party is in a better position to evaluate the loss and press a claim against the insurer and to salvage or dispose of damaged goods? Who can insure the goods at the least cost? Who is more likely to carry insurance under standard commercial practice? What rules on risk will minimize litigation over negligence in the care and custody of the goods?

The United States delegates to the 1964 Hague Conference on Sales reported their disappointment that risk of loss was governed by concepts that were so abstract that results were unpredictable and unresponsive to commercial needs. In UNCITRAL, on the initiative of the United States and other delegations, these objections were met by a thorough overhaul of these rules. As a result, the 1980 Convention speaks of physical acts of transfers of possession—the "handing over" of the goods to a carrier or to the buyer.

Article 67 deals with the important issue of risk of loss in transit. When the contract (including the parties' established practices—Art. 9) does not solve this problem, the Convention, like the Uniform Commercial Code, provides the general rule that risk passes to the buyer when the goods are handed over to the carrier. Article 67 also echoes the Code in providing that the seller's retention of "documents controlling the disposition of the goods does not affect the passage of the risk." (See UCC 2–509(1)(a)).

Article 68 deals with contracts for the sale of goods that are already in transit when the contract is made, and provides that risk passes at the making of the contract unless the parties otherwise agree or the circumstances indicate an earlier time. The Uniform Commercial Code does not address this problem.

Article 69 deals, among other matters, with non-transit situations, and makes risk pass to the buyer "when he takes over the goods"—an approach that is similar to UCC 2–509(3). Finally, Articles 69(1) and 70 deal with the effect of breach of contract on risk; in both approach and result these articles are similar to the Uniform Commercial Code (UCC 2–510).

CHAPTER V. PROVISIONS COMMON TO THE OBLIGATIONS OF THE SELLER AND OF THE BUYER

(Articles 71–88)

This concluding chapter addresses special problems with respect to remedies for breach of contract. Section I, Anticipatory Breach and Installment Contracts (Arts. 71–73), is concerned primarily with protection against impending failure of counter-performance; a party who faces this problem may, in some circumstances, suspend performance (Art. 71; *cf.* UCC 2–609, 2–705) or avoid the contract (Art. 72; *cf.* UCC 2–610). Article 73 deals with similar problems that arise in contracts for the delivery of goods by installments (*Cf.* UCC 2–612). Section II (Arts. 74–77) provides rules for measuring damages. (*Cf.* UCC 2–706—2–710, 2–712 to 2–715, 2–723). Section III consists of a brief provision (Art. 78) allowing the recovery of interest on sums in arrears. Section IV, exemptions (Arts. 78–80), confronts the difficult question of excuse from liability when performance is prevented by an impediment (*e.g., force majeure*). (*Cf.* UCC 2-613, 2-615). Section V, Effects of Avoidance (Arts. 81-84), includes provisions on the restitution of benefits received under a contract that has been avoided (*Cf.* UCC 2-711 (1) & (3)). Section VI, Preservation of the Goods (Arts. 85-88), is designed to prevent the waste or deterioration of goods that have been rejected. *Cf.* UCC 2-602(2)(b), 2-603, 2-604.

PART IV. FINAL PROVISIONS
(Articles 89-101)

A. Introduction

Many of these provisions are ministerial. Articles 89 and 91 are administrative provisions commonly included in United Nations conventions. Article 90 deals with the relationship between the 1980 Convention and any other convention that "contains provisions concerning the matters governed by" the 1980 Convention. The most significant provisions in this part deal with permitted reservations and the Convention's entry into force.

(1) "Declarations" (Reservations)

Articles 92-96 specify those "declarations" (reservations) that may be made by Contracting States to modify their obligations under the Convention.

Article 92 permits a Contracting State to declare that it will not be bound by Part II (Formation of the Contract) or by Part III (Obligations of the Parties under a Contract of Sale). At the 1964 Hague Conference, contrary to the position urged by the United States, separate conventions were adopted on formation of the sales contract and on obligations under the contract. In UNCITRAL, the United States position was accepted. Because of the relationship between Parts II and III, it seems advisable for the United States to ratify the entire Convention without a declaration under Article 92.

Article 93 is designed to permit a declaration (reservation) by a Contracting State with a constitutional system different from the United States (e.g. Canada) that embraces territorial units in which "different systems of law are applicable in relation to the matters dealt with" in the Convention. As already indicated, the Convention applies only to international sales. In view of the Constitutional power of the United States federal government over foreign commerce (Constitution Art. I § 8) and the treaty power (Constitution Art. II § 2; Art. VI), a declaration by the United States pursuant to Article 93 would be unnecessary and inappropriate. In the absence of a United States declaration, the Convention will extend to all territories under the jurisdiction of the United States.

Article 94 seeks to meet the needs of States joined in economic communities (e.g. Benelux) by providing for reservations by two or more Contracting States "which have the same or closely related legal rules on matters governed by" the Convention. If two or more States make declarations under Article 94, the Convention will not apply to transactions among parties in these States but will, of course, apply to transactions that run between parties in these States and parties in other States. See Article I, *supra.* There is no need for the United States to make use of such a reservation.

Article 95 permits a Contracting State to declare that it will not be bound by Article 1(1)(b) which would make the Convention also apply "when the rules of private international law lead to the application of the law of a Contracting State." States that make this declaration would apply the Convention only when the seller and buyer have their places of business in different *Contracting* States (Art. 1(1)(a)). As noted under Article 1, *supra,* it is recommended that the United States ratify subject to this reservation; the reasons are set forth in Appendix 9 to this analysis.

Article 96 permits a declaration by a State that wishes to protect its domestic legislation that "requires contracts of sale to be concluded in or evidenced by writing," *i.e.,* a "statute of frauds." For the reasons given in the discussion of Articles 11 and 12 of the Convention, it is considered inadvisable for the United States to make use of the reservation permitted by this Article.

(2) Entry into Force

Article 99(1) provides that the Convention enters into force on the first day of the month following the expiration of twelve months after the tenth State has consented to be bound by the Convention. Article 99(2) governs the time when the Convention enters into force with respect to States whose consent to be bound follows that of the ten initial States.

ADDENDUM

PROPOSED UNITED STATES DECLARATION UNDER ARTICLE 95 EXCLUDING APPLICABILITY OF THE CONVENTION BASED ON ARTICLE 1(1)(B)

Under Article 1 the Convention will apply only if two basic requirements are met: (1) The sale must be international—i.e., the seller and the buyer must have their "places of business in different states," and (2) the sale must have a prescribed relationship with one or more States that have adhered to the Convention. This statement is concerned with the second requirement—the relationship between the Convention and one or more Contracting States.

The Convention, in subparagraphs (1)(a) and (1)(b) of Article 1, states two such relationships, either of which will suffice.

(a) *First,* under subparagraph (1)(a) the Convention applies when the places of business of the seller and the buyer are in different Contracting States.

(b) *Second,* under subparagraph (1)(b) the Convention would also apply:

(a) when the rules of private international law lead to the application of the law of a Contracting State.

At the 1980 Diplomatic Conference, delegates of the United States and several other countries proposed the deletion of the second of these grounds for applicability—subparagraphs (1)(b) of Article 1. This proposal was defeated; as a compromise, the Convention's Final Provisions (Part IV) provide in Article 95 that a Contracting State may, by reservation, declare "that it will not be bound by subparagraph (1)(b) of Article 1."

The United States, in signing the Convention, states that ratification subject to the Article 95 reservation was contemplated. This position, recommended by the American Bar Association, will promote maximum clarity in the rules governing the applicability of the Convention. The rules of private international law, on which applicability under subparagraph (1)(b) depends, are subject to uncertainty and international disharmony. On the other hand, applicability based on subparagraph (12)(a) is determined by a clear-cut test: whether the seller and buyer have their places of business in different Contracting States.

A further reason for excluding applicability based on subparagraph (1)(b) is that this provision would displace our own domestic law more frequently than foreign law. By its terms, subparagraph (1)(b) would be relevant only in sales between parties in the United States (a Contracting State) and a *non*-Contracting State. Transactions that run between the United States and another Contracting State are subject to the Convention by virtue of subparagraph (1)(a). Under subparagraph (1)(b), when private international law points to the law of a foreign *non*-Contracting State the Convention will not displace that foreign law, since subparagraph (1)(b) makes the Convention applicable only when "the rules of private international law lead to the application of the law of a *Contracting* State. Consequently, when those rules point to United States law, subparagraph (1)(b) would normally operate to displace United States law (the Uniform Commercial Code) and would not displace the law of the foreign *non*-Contracting States.

If the United States law were seriously unsuited to international transactions, there might be an advantage in displacing our law in favor of the uniform international rules provided by the Convention. However, the sales law provided by the Uniform Commercial Code is relatively modern and includes provisions that address the special problems that arise in international trade.

For these reasons it seems advisable for the United States to exclude applicability of the Convention under sub-paragraph (1)(b) by the declaration (reservation) permitted by Article 95. Fortunately, this position will not interfere with broad application of the Convention to international sales. Widespread adoption of the Convention can be anticipated; hence it is expected that eventually a substantial portion of United States international trade will involve other Contracting States and will receive the benefits of the Convention by virtue of subparagraph (1)(a) of Article 1. Moreover, parties who wish to apply the Convention to international sales contracts not covered by Article 9(1)(a) may provide by their contract that the Convention will apply.

[1] The instrument of accession by the Government of Argentina contains the following declaration:

(Translation) (Original: Spanish)

In accordance with Articles 96 and 12 of the United Nations Convention on Contracts for the International Sale of Goods, any provisions of Article 11, Article 29 or Part II of the Convention that allows a contract of sale or its modification or termination by agreement or any offer, acceptance or other indication of intention to be made in any form other than in writing does not apply where any party has his place of business in the Argentine Republic.

[2] The instrument of accession by the Government of Australia contains the following declaration:

"The Convention shall apply to all Australian States and mainland territories and to all external territories except the territories of Christmas Island, the Cocos (Keeling) Islands and the Ashmore and Cartier Islands."

[3] The instrument of accession by the Government of Belarus contains the following declaration:

(Translation) (Original: Russian)

"Belarus, in accordance with Articles 12 and 96 of the Convention declares that any provision of Article 11, Article 29 or Part II of this Convention that allows a contract of sale or its modification or termination by agreement or any offer, acceptance or other indication of intention to be made in any form other than in writing does not apply where any party has his place of business in Belarus."

[4] The instrument of accession by the Government of Canada contains the following declarations:

"The Government of Canada declares, in accordance with Article 93 of the Convention, that the Convention will extend to Alberta, British Columbia, Manitoba, New Brunswick, Newfoundland, Nova Scotia, Ontario, Prince Edward Island and the Northwest Territories;

The Government of Canada also declares, in accordance with Article 95 of the Convention, that, with respect to British Columbia, it will not be bound by Article 11 (b) of the Convention."

[5]The instrument of ratification by the Government of Chile contains the following declaration:

(Translation) (Original: Spanish)

"The State of Chile declares, in accordance with Articles 12 and 96 of the Convention, that any provision of Article 11, Article 29 or Part II of the Convention that allows a contract of sale or its modification or termination by mutual agreement or any offer, acceptance or other indication of intention to be made in any other form than in writing, does not apply where any party has its place of business in Chile."

[6]The instrument of approval by the Government of China contains the following declaration:

(Courtesy Translation) (Original: Chinese)

The People's Republic of China does not consider itself to be bound by subparagraph (b) of paragraph 1 of Article 1 and Article 11 as well as the provisions in the Convention relating to the content of Article 11.

[7]The instrument of ratification by the Government of Czechoslovakia contains the following declaration:

(Courtesy Translation) (Original: Czechoslovak)

"Pursuant to Article 95, the Czechoslovak Socialist Republic declares that it shall not consider itself bound by the provision of Article 1, paragraph 1, item (b), of the Convention."

[8]The instrument of ratification by the Government of Denmark was accompanied by the following declaration:

(Original: English)

"Upon ratifying the Convention, the Kingdom of Denmark declares:

"1) under paragraph 1 of Article 92 that Denmark will not be bound by Part II of the Convention,

"2) under paragraph 1 of Article 93 that the Convention shall not apply to the Faroe Islands and Greenland,

"3) under paragraph 1 cf. paragraph 3 of Article 94 that the Convention shall not apply to contracts of sale where one of the parties has his place of business in Denmark, Finland, Norway or Sweden and the other party has his place of business in another of the said states,

"4) under paragraph 2 of Article 94 that the Convention is not to apply to contracts of sale where one of the parties has his place of business in Denmark, Finland, Norway or Sweden and the other party has his place of business in Iceland."

[9] In accordance with Article 99(2), the Convention will enter into force for Ecuador on 1 February 1993.

[10] The instrument of ratification by the Government of Finland contains the following declarations:

(Original: English)

"1. With reference to Article 92, Finland will not be bound by Part II of this Convention (Formation of the Contract).

2. With reference to Article 94, in respect of Sweden in accordance with paragraph (1) and otherwise in accordance with paragraph (2) the Convention will not apply to contracts of sale where the parties have their places of business in Finland, Sweden, Denmark, Iceland or Norway."

[11] On October 3, 1990 the German Democratic Republic acceded to the Federal Republic of Germany.

The instrument of ratification by the Government of the Federal Republic of Germany contains the following declaration:

(Courtesy Translation) (Original: German)

"The Government of the Federal Republic of Germany holds the view that Parties to the Convention that have made a declaration under Article 95 of the Convention are not considered Contracting States within the meaning of subparagraph (1)(b) of Article 1 of the Convention. Accordingly, there is no obligation to apply—and the Federal Republic of Germany assumes no obligation to apply—this provision when the rules of private international law lead to the application of the law of a Party that has made a declaration to the effect that it will not be bound by subparagraph (1)(b) of Article 1 of the Convention. Subject to this observation the Government of the Federal Republic of Germany makes no declaration under Article 95 of the Convention."

In a note accompanying the instrument of ratification the Government of the Federal Republic of Germany stated that the said Convention shall also apply to Berlin (West) with effect from the date on which it enters into force for the Federal Republic of Germany.

The Federal Republic of Germany denounced, on 1 January 1990, the Conventions relating to the formation of contracts for the international sale of goods and the international sale of such goods, both done at The Hague on 1 July 1964. These denunciations shall take effect on 31 December 1990, and the present Convention will therefore enter into force for the Federal Republic of Germany on 1 January 1991, in accordance with paragraphs 2 and 6 of Article 99.

[12] In accordance with Article 99(2), the Convention will enter into force for Guinea on 1 February 1992.

[13] In a note accompanying its instrument of ratification, the Government of Hungary made the following declarations:

"It [Hungary] considers the General Conditions of Delivery of Goods between Organizations of the Member Countries of the Council for Mutual Economic Assistance/GCD

CMEA, 1968/1975, version of 1979/ to be subject to the provisions of Article 90 of the Convention;

It states, in accordance with Articles 12 and 96 of the Convention, that any provision of article 11, Article 29, or part II of the Convention that allows a contract of sale or its modification or termination by agreement of any offer, acceptance or other indication of intention to be made in any form other than in writing, does not apply where any party has his place of business in the Hungarian People's Republic."

[14]The instrument of ratification by the Government of Norway contains the following declarations:

(Original: English)

"1. In accordance with Article 92, paragraph (1), the Government of the Kingdom of Norway declares that Norway will not be bound by Part II of this Convention (Formation of the Contract).

"2. With reference to Article 94, in respect of Finland and Sweden in accordance with paragraph (1) and otherwise in accordance with paragraph (2), the Government of the Kingdom of Norway declares that the Convention will not apply to contracts of sale where the parties have their places of business in Norway, Denmark, Finland, Iceland or Sweden."

[15]The instrument of accession by the Government of the [Russian Federation] contains the following declaration:

(Translation) (Original: Russian)

"In accordance with Articles 12 and 96 of the Convention, the [Russian Federation] declares that any provision of Article 11, Article 29 or Part II of the Convention that allows a contract of sale or its modification or termination by agreement or any offer, acceptance or other indication of intention to be made in any form other than in writing does not apply where any party has his place of business in the [Russian Federation]."

[16]The instrument of ratification by the Government of Sweden contains the following declarations:

(Original: English)

"1. With reference to Article 92, Sweden will not be bound by Part II of this Convention (Formation of the Contract).

"2. With reference to Article 94, in respect of Finland in accordance with paragraph (1) and otherwise in accordance with paragraph (2) the Convention will not apply to contracts of sale where the parties have their places of business in Sweden, Finland, Denmark, Iceland or Norway."

[17]In accordance with Article 99(2), the Convention will enter into force for Uganda on 1 March 1993.

[18]The instrument of accession by the Government of [Ukraine] contains the following declaration:

(Translation) (Original: Russian)

"In accordance with Articles 12 and 96 of the Convention, [Ukraine] declares that any provision of Article 11, Article 29 or Part II of the Convention that allows a contract of sale or its modification or termination by agreement or any offer, acceptance or other indication of intention to be made in any form other than in writing does not apply where any party has his place of business in [Ukraine]."

[19]The instrument of ratification by the Government of the United States contains the following declaration:

"Pursuant to Article 95 the United States will not be bound by subparagraph (1)(b) of Article 1."

Appendix D

Seller and Purchaser Clauses for Foreign Trade

EXPORT CONTRACT TERMS AND CONDITIONS OF SALE*

1. GENERAL:

All quotations, offers to sell, proposals, acknowledgments and acceptances of orders by Seller are subject to the following terms and conditions, and acceptance by buyer is expressly limited to them.

2. CONTRACT OF SALE:

A binding contract of sale shall be entered into between buyer and seller, and shall become effective, upon the happening of any of the following:

(a) Buyer's written acceptance of a firm written proposal submitted by the seller;

---

*Courtesy of Bryan Sandler. This was taken from the Terms and Conditions of Sale for the Barry-Wehmiller Company, St. Louis, Mo., reprinted with their approval.

(b) Seller's separate written acceptance of buyer's purchase order or other document furnished by purchaser;

(c) Seller's acceptance of a sales agreement form prepared by Seller's authorized sales representative and executed by Buyer.

The contract of sale shall include all of the following terms and conditions. When the contract of sale is entered into by Seller's written acceptance of Buyer's purchase order or the document furnished by Buyer, Seller's acceptance is expressly limited to these terms and conditions, and any matters contained in any purchase order or other document furnished by Buyer which state terms additional to or which conflict with the following are deemed proposals for addition to the contract of sale, and do not become part of the contract of sale unless expressly and separately agreed to by Seller.

3. PRICES AND SPECIFICATIONS:

Prices and specifications quoted are valid for the stated period. Price quotations do not include any federal, state, local or other taxes, and Buyer agrees to pay or collect on account of the manufacture or sale of goods and performance of any services under this agreement. All licenses or other approvals required shall be obtained by Buyer, at Buyer's expense. Buyer shall promptly ship prepaid and without charge to Seller, for Seller's approval, Buyer's specified samples of containers and products to be handled by Seller's products. After the contract of sale becomes effective, specification changes requested by Buyer will be made only by separate written agreement, in which event the prices quoted in connection with the original specifications will be subject to change. Unless otherwise specified, Underwriters Laboratories approved electrical fixtures and electrical wiring are used, and wiring practices conform to the National Electric Code. Wiring to local standards will be furnished only if expressly incorporated in specifications and price quotations, accompanied by a copy of such local code.

4. SUPPLIES FOR DESIGN TESTING:

Buyer shall promptly ship prepaid and without obtaining Buyer's charge to Seller, for seller's approval, to make changes in the design and specifications of the Buyer's specified samples of containers, products sold hereunder, or of any component part, which changes do not affect the performance of the goods sold, and materials to be handled by Seller's products and other engineering information of Buyer required by the Seller for design and testing purposes.

5. NOTICE OF NON-CONFORMITY; BUYER'S REMEDIES:

Buyer shall give seller written notice of any claim for shortage, error, or other non-conformity of the products within thirty days after receipt at customer's designated delivery point, or be barred from any claim or remedy for such shortage, error, or other non-conformity. Except for warranty claims (which are governed exclusively by Section 8 below), Buyer's exclusive remedies for all claims arising out of the contract of sale shall be the right to return non-conforming products to Seller and, at Seller's option, to receive repayment of the purchase price or repair or replacement of non-conforming products or components.

6. WARRANTY

Seller warrants that the products sold hereunder are free from defects in material and workmanship when used in the manner and for the purposes for which designed, and in accordance with all instructions and directions for installation, operation and maintenance furnished by Seller, for a period of one year from receipt at customer's designated delivery point, or 2,000 hours of operation, whichever occurs earlier, subject to the following conditions:

(a) Buyer shall notify Seller in writing promptly upon discovery of facts giving rise to any claim under this warranty, stating specifically the nature of the claim, the date of the discovery of same and identifying by serial number and invoice the product involved. Failure to so notify Seller within ninety to one hundred eighty days after discovery of facts giving rise to the claim shall fully and completely relieve seller from any obligation under this warranty.

No claim under the terms of this warranty will be accepted by Seller unless and until the nature of the claim shall have been established to the satisfaction of an authorized representative of Seller, and no return of any product claimed to be defective will be accepted unless accompanied by a Returned Materials Authorization supplied by Seller. If a claim is accepted, Seller will issue a credit to Buyer against the invoiced price of repair or replacement. All returns shall be at Buyer's expense.

(b) Seller's obligations under this warranty are expressly limited to the repair or replacement, at seller's option, of any defective products or components determined by Seller as aforesaid to be defective under the terms of this warranty, and do not extend to any damages arising from any alleged act or omission of Seller, beyond the invoiced price of any product or component that is found by Seller to be defective under the terms of this warranty. All other remedies are expressly excluded.

(c) This warranty applies only to products properly used and maintained and is expressly non-applicable to any products or components which have been repaired, altered or changed other than in accordance with instructions and directions furnished by Seller and its authorized representatives or to any product which has not been operated or utilized in accordance with instructions or directions furnished by Seller, or which has been operated or treated in any matter which, in the reasonable judgment of Seller, adversely affects its reliability and performance.

(d) This warranty does not apply to normal wear or consumable parts. This warranty also does not apply to any product or component not manufactured by the Seller, and Buyer's sole warranty with respect to such items shall be that of the manufacturer, if any.

(e) THIS WARRANTY COMPRISES THE ENTIRE AND SOLE WARRANTY PERTAINING TO THIS PURCHASE AND PRODUCTS SOLD HEREUNDER. SELLER MAKES NO OTHER REPRESENTATIONS, WARRANTIES OR GUARANTEES OF ANY KIND, INCLUDING BUT NOT LIMITED TO, MERCHANTABILITY AND FITNESS FOR PURPOSE, WHETHER EXPRESS, IMPLIED OR ARISING BY OPERATION OF LAW, TRADE USAGE OR COURSE OF DEALING EXCEPT AS SET FORTH HEREIN. ANY OTHER REPRESENTATIONS, STATEMENTS OR PROMISE WARRANTIES OR GUARANTEES MADE BY ANY PERSON ARE UNAUTHORIZED AND ARE NOT BINDING UPON SELLER UNLESS SEPARATELY SET FORTH IN WRITING. Any descriptions of the products and any specifications, samples, models, drawings, diagram, engineering sheets or similar material used in connection with this are for the sole purposes of identifying the products not to be construed as warranties, either express or implied.

7. REMEDIES OF SELLER:

The contract of sale shall be governed by the law of the State of Missouri, and Seller retains all rights under the applicable law in addition to those expressly provided for herein. Buyer agrees to execute any documents at Seller's request with respect to creation and perfection of a security interest in the goods sold. If Seller is required to employ attorneys or engage in any legal proceedings to enforce its rights hereunder, buyer agrees to pay Seller's reasonable attorney's fees, cost and expenses incurred in connection with such enforcement.

8. REMEDIES OF BUYER:

Buyer shall give Seller written notice of any claim for shortage or error within ten days after receipt at customer's designated delivery point, which is agreed to be a reasonable time for discovery and the giving of such notice, or be barred from any claim or remedy for such shortage or error. Other than as expressly provided herein, Buyer's exclusive remedies for all claims arising out of the contract of sale shall be the right to return non-conforming products to Seller, at Buyer's expense and, at Seller's option, to receive repayment of the purchase price or components.

9. APPLICABLE LAW

This contract shall be governed by the law of the State of Missouri and the Uniform Commercial Code.

EXPORT CONTRACT TERMS AND CONDITIONS *OF PURCHASE**

1. GENERAL:

All quotations, offers to sell, proposals, acknowledgments and acceptances of orders by Buyer are subject to the following terms and conditions, and acceptance by buyer is expressly limited to them.

2. CONTRACT OF SALE:

A binding contract of sale shall be entered into between buyer and seller, and shall become effective, upon the happening of any of the following:

(a) Seller's written acceptance of a firm written proposal submitted by the Seller;

---

*This was taken from the Terms and Conditions of Sale for the Barry-Wehmiller Company, St. Louis, Mo., reprinted with their approval.

(b) Buyer's separate written acceptance of Seller's purchase order or other document furnished by purchaser;

(c) Buyer's acceptance of a sales agreement form prepared by seller's authorized sales representative and executed by Seller.

The contract of sale shall include all of the following terms and conditions. When the contract of sale is entered into by Buyer's written acceptance of Seller's purchase order or the document furnished by buyer, seller's acceptance is expressly limited to these terms and conditions, and any matters contained in any purchase order or other document furnished by Buyer which state terms additional to or which conflict with the following are deemed proposals for addition to the contract of sale, and do not become part of the contract of sale unless expressly and separately agreed to by Buyer.

3. PRICES AND SPECIFICATIONS:

Prices quoted are valid for the stated period. Price quotations do include any federal, state, local and other taxes, and seller agrees to pay or collect on account of the manufacture or sale of goods and performance of any services under this agreement. After the contract of sale becomes effective, specification changes requested by seller will be made only by separate written agreement, in which event the prices quoted in connection with the original specifications will not be subject to change.

4. SUPPLIES FOR DESIGN TESTING:

Seller shall not be responsible for buyer's changes in the design and specifications of the Seller's specified samples of containers, products sold hereunder, or of any component part, which changes do not affect the performance of the goods sold, and materials to be handled by Buyer and other engineering information.

5. SELLER'S REMEDIES FOR NON-PERFORMANCE:

Seller's exclusive remedy for non-performance by the Buyer is the return of the goods then shipped, or the price thereof for such goods shipped, or the difference between the purchase price and the cover price incurred by Seller. This is the exclusive remedy for Seller; no other remedies will be available to Seller for breach by the buyer, including those given under the UCC and the Convention.

6. WARRANTY

Seller shall not be able to exclude any warranties or obligations under the UCC or the Convention, without the prior agreement, in writing signed by both parties, for the exclusion of any warranties. Any attempt to exclude any warranty or obligation by seller shall not be given effect.

7. REMEDIES OF BUYER:

The Buyer's remedies include but are not limited to those that are incurred because of Seller's breach, for seller's non-performance and all consequential and incidental damages, including, but not limited to, damages incurred by any loss in production, sale due to loss of production, and any and all other expenses incurred by Buyer due to Seller's non-performance. Any attempt to limit Buyer's remedies by the Seller shall not be given effect and will be considered a material term and a counter-offer under the Convention. Buyer shall also be allowed to determine that the contract is void upon its sole determination. Buyer shall also be able to have Seller specifically perform if Buyer so wishes.

8. APPLICABLE LAW

This contract shall be governed by the law of the State of Missouri and the Uniform Commercial Code.

Appendix E

Rules and Procedures for Dispute Settlement

The Purchasing Manager should be aware of the possibilities for Mediation and Arbitration of any disputes he may encounter with others. This Appendix helps to further educate one on what is involved by setting forth the Rules and Procedures for Dispute Resolution of the American Arbitration Association.

They are reprinted with the permission of the American Arbitration Association* to provide greater understanding of these processes.

Rules and Procedures for Dispute Resolution
American Arbitration Association
140 West 51st Street
New York, NY 10020-1203
Main Number: (212) 484-4000
Fax: (212) 765-4874

By looking at the actual rules and procedures, there is both reinforcement of existing knowledge and a further gain in learning some of the details which one might formerly have questioned.

---

*© 1995, all rights are reserved by the American Arbitration Association. Reprinted with permission.

The American Arbitration Association has regional offices in the following cities:

Phoenix, AZ; Irvine, CA; Los Angeles, CA; San Diego, CA; San Francisco, CA; Denver, CO; East Hartford, CT; Washington, DC; Miami, FL; Orlando, FL; Atlanta, GA; Honolulu, HI; Chicago, IL; New Orleans, LA; Boston, MA; Southfield, MI; Minneapolis, MN; Kansas City, MO; Las Vegas, NV; Somerset, NJ; Garden City, NY; New York, NY; Syracuse, NY; White Plains, NY; Charlotte, NC; Cincinnati, OH; Cleveland, OH; Philadelphia; PA; Pittsburgh, PA; Nashville, TN; Dallas, TX; Houston, TX; Salt Lake City, UT; Seattle, WA

Contents

MEDIATION
Rules and Procedures

1. Agreement of Parties.. M-5
2. Initiation of Mediation M-5
3. Requests for Mediation M-5
4. Appointment of the Mediator................................... M-5
5. Qualifications of the Mediator M-5
6. Vacancies... M-6
7. Representation... M-6
8. Date, Time, and Place of Mediation M-6
9. Identification of Matters in Dispute M-6
10. Authority of the Mediator M-6
11. Privacy M-7
12. Confidentiality M-7
13. No Stenographic Record M-8
14. Termination of Mediation M-8
15. Exclusion of Liability M-8
16. Interpretation and Application of Rules M-8
17. Expenses M-8

Administrative Fees
Filing Fee M-9
Deposits... M-9
Refunds M-9

ARBITRATION
Rules and Procedures

1. Agreement of Parties A-5
2. Name of Tribunal A-5
3. Administrator and Delegation of Duties A-5
4. National Panel of Arbitrators A-5
5. Regional Offices A-5
6. Initiation Under an Arbitration Provision in a Contract A-5
7. Initiation Under a Submission A-6
8. Changes of Claim A-6
9. Applicable Procedures A-6
10. Administrative Conference, Preliminary Hearing and
    Mediation Conference A-7
11. Fixing of Locale A-7
12. Qualifications of an Arbitrator A-8
13. Appointment from Panel A-8
14. Direct Appointment by a Party A-9
15. Appointment of Neutral Arbitrator by Party-Appointed
    Arbitrators or Parties A-9
16. Nationality of Arbitrator in International Arbitration A-10
17. Number of Arbitrators A-10
18. Notice to Arbitrator of Appointment A-10
19. Disclosure and Challenge Procedures A-10
20. Vacancies A-10
21. Date, Time, and Place of Hearing A-11
22. Representation A-11
23. Stenographic Record A-11
24. Interpreters A-11
25. Attendance at Hearings A-11
26. Postponements A-12
27. Oaths A-12
28. Majority Decision A-12
29. Order of Proceedings and Communication with Arbitrator A-12
30. Arbitration in the Absence of a Party or Representative A-13
31. Evidence A-13
32. Evidence by Affidavit and Posthearing Filing of Documents or
    Other Evidence A-13
33. Inspection or Investigation A-14

34. Interim Measures.. A-14
35. Closing of Hearing.. A-14
36. Reopening of Hearing A-14
37. Waiver of Oral Hearing A-15
38. Waiver of Rules A-15
39. Extensions of Time.. A-15
40. Serving of Notice A-15
41. Time of Award A-15
42. Form of Award A-16
43. Scope of Award A-16
44. Award upon Settlement A-16
45. Delivery of Award to Parties A-16
46. Release of Documents for Judicial Proceedings............. A-16
47. Applications to Court and Exclusion of Liability........... A-16
48. Administrative Fees.. A-17
49. Expenses A-17
50. Neutral Arbitrator's Compensation A-17
51. Deposits... A-18
52. Interpretation and Application of Rules..................... A-18

Expedited Procedures
53. Notice by Telephone....................................... A-18
54. Appointment and Qualifications of Arbitrator.............. A-18
55. Date, Time and Place of Hearing A-19
56. The Hearing A-19
57. Time of Award A-19

Administrative Fees
Hearing Fees A-20
Postponement Cancellation Fees A-20
Processing Fees A-20
Suspension for Nonpayment................................. A-20
Hearing Room Rental....................................... A-21

Regional Office Listing................................. Back Cover

Commercial Mediation Rules and Procedures

As amended and in effect May 1, 1995

INTRODUCTION

In some situations, the involvement of an impartial mediator can assist parties in reaching a settlement of a commercial dispute. Mediation is a process under which the parties submit their dispute to an impartial person—the mediator. The mediator may suggest ways of resolving the dispute, but may not impose a settlement on the parties.

If the parties want to use a mediator to resolve an existing dispute under these rules, they can enter into the following submission.

> The parties hereby submit the following dispute to mediation administered by the American Arbitration Association under its Commercial Mediation Rules (the clause may also provide for the qualifications of the mediator, the method of payment, the locale of meetings, and any other item of concern to the parties).

If the parties want to adopt mediation as an integral part of their contractual dispute settlement procedure, they can insert the following mediation clause into their contract in conjunction with a standard arbitration provision.

> If a dispute arises out of or relates to this contract or the breach thereof and if the dispute cannot be settled through negotiation, the parties agree first to try in good faith to settle the dispute by mediation administered by the American Arbitration Association under its Commercial Mediation Rules before resorting to arbitration, litigation, or some other dispute resolution procedure.

The Neutrals

Mediators are qualified, experienced neutrals with an understanding of current legal and business practices. The parties select the neutral best qualified to hear their controversy.

Cost

The administrative fees of the American Arbitration Association and the compensation arrangements for the neutral are set forth in the particular resolution procedure agreed on.

Filing

A party may file a dispute with the AAA and request that the AAA invite the other party to join in a submission to mediation. The AAA will, upon request, provide a forum to do so. It is sufficient, however, to provide the information outlined below in a letter or by telephone. Upon receipt of this information, the AAA will contact the other party or parties to the dispute.

A party submitting a case for disposition must provide the AAA with the following:

- names of the parties to the case, including any court docket number;
- the alternative dispute resolution (ADR) procedure requested—e.g., mediation;
- the nature and the amount of the claim (a brief statement of the claim and the response of the other party or parties);
- desired qualifications of the neutral, if any;
- the preferred location of hearing; and
- addresses and telephone numbers of all parties, including counsel, if any.

If there is no agreement among the parties to submit the dispute to an ADR procedure, there is no charge to the filing party. If the matter settles as a result of AAA contact with the parties, the filing party will pay an administrative fee. If there is a submission to an ADR procedure, the current fee schedule in effect will apply.

Commercial Mediation Rules and Procedures

1. Agreement of Parties

Whenever, by stipulation or in their contract, the parties have provided for mediation or conciliation of existing or future disputes under the auspices of the American Arbitration Association (AAA) or under these rules, they shall be deemed to have made these rules, as amended and in effect as of the date of the submission of the dispute, a part of their agreement.

2. Initiation of Mediation
Any party or parties to a dispute may initiate mediation by filing with the AAA a submission to mediation or a written request for mediation pursuant to these rules, together with the appropriate Filing Fee (page M-9). Where there is no submission to mediation or contract providing for mediation, a party may request the AAA to invite another party to join in a submission to mediation. Upon receipt of such a request, the AAA will contact the other parties involved in the dispute and attempt to obtain a submission to mediation.

3. Requests for Mediation
A request for mediation shall contain a brief statement of the nature of the dispute and the names, addresses, and telephone numbers of all parties to the dispute and those who will represent them, if any, in the mediation. The initiating party shall simultaneously file two copies of the request with the AAA and one copy with every other party to the dispute.

4. Appointment of the Mediator
Upon receipt of a request for mediation, the AAA will appoint a qualified mediator to serve. Normally, a single mediator will be appointed unless the parties agree otherwise or the AAA determines otherwise. If the agreement of the parties names a mediator or specifies a method of appointing a mediator, that designation or method shall be followed.

5. Qualifications of the Mediator
No person shall serve as a mediator in any dispute in which that person has any financial or personal interest in the result of the mediation, except by the written consent of all parties. Prior to accepting an appointment, the prospective mediator shall disclose any circumstance likely to create a presumption of bias or prevent a prompt meeting with the parties. Upon receipt of such information, the AAA shall either replace the mediator or immediately communicate the information to the parties for their comments. In the event that the parties disagree as to whether the mediator shall serve, the AAA will appoint another mediator. The AAA is authorized to appoint another mediator if the appointed mediator is unable to serve promptly.

6. Vacancies
If any mediator shall become unwilling or unable to serve, the AAA will appoint another mediator, unless the parties agree otherwise.

7. Representation
Any party may be represented by persons of the party's choice. The names and addresses of such persons shall be communicated in writing to all parties and to the AAA.

8. Date, Time, and Place of Mediation
The mediator shall fix the date and the time of each mediation session. The mediation shall be held at the appropriate regional office of the AAA, or at any other convenient location agreeable to the mediator and the parties, as the mediator shall determine.

9. Identification of Matters in Dispute
At least ten days prior to the first scheduled mediation session, each party shall provide the mediator with a brief memorandum setting forth its position with regard to the issues that need to be resolved. At the discretion of the mediator, such memoranda may be mutually exchanged by the parties.

At the first session, the parties will be expected to produce all information reasonably required for the mediator to understand the issues presented.

The mediator may require any party to supplement such information.

10. Authority of the Mediator
The mediator does not have the authority to impose a settlement on the parties but will attempt to help them reach a satisfactory resolution of their dispute. The mediator is authorized to conduct joint and separate meetings with the parties and to make oral and written recommendations for settlement. Whenever necessary, the mediator may also obtain expert advice concerning technical aspects of the dispute, provided that the parties agree and assume the expenses of obtaining such advice. Arrangements for obtaining such advice shall be made by the mediator or the parties, as the mediator shall determine.

The mediator is authorized to end the mediation whenever, in the judgment of the mediator, further efforts at mediation would not contribute to a resolution of the dispute between the parties.

11. Privacy

Mediation sessions are private. The parties and their representatives may attend mediation sessions. Other persons may attend only with the permission of the parties and with the consent of the mediator.

12. Confidentiality

Confidential information disclosed to a mediator by the parties or by witnesses in the course of the mediation shall not be divulged by the mediator. All records, reports, or other documents received by a mediator while serving in that capacity shall be confidential. The mediator shall not be compelled to divulge such records or to testify in regard to the mediation in any adversary proceeding or judicial forum.

The parties shall maintain the confidentiality of the mediation and shall not rely on, or introduce as evidence in any arbitral, judicial, or other proceeding:

(a) views expressed or suggestions made by another party with respect to a possible settlement of the dispute;

(b) admissions made by another party in the course of the mediation proceedings;

(c) proposals made or views expressed by the mediator; or

(d) the fact that another party had or had not indicated willingness to accept a proposal for settlement made by the mediator.

13. No Stenographic Record

There shall be no stenographic record of the mediation process.

14. Termination of Mediation

The mediation shall be terminated:

(a) by the execution of a settlement agreement by the parties;

(b) by a written declaration of the mediator to the effect that further efforts at mediation are no longer worthwhile; or

(c) by a written declaration of a party or parties to the effect that the mediation proceedings are terminated.

15. Exclusion of Liability

Neither the AAA nor any mediator is a necessary party in judicial proceedings relating to the mediation.

Neither the AAA nor any mediator shall be liable to any party for any act or omission in connection with any mediation conducted under these rules.

16. Interpretation and Application of Rules

The mediator shall interpret and apply these rules insofar as they relate to the mediator's duties and responsibilities. All other rules shall be interpreted and applied by the AAA.

17. Expenses

The expenses of witnesses for either side shall be paid by the party producing such witnesses. All other expenses of the mediation, including required traveling and other expenses of the mediator and representatives of the AAA, the expenses of any witness and the cost of any proofs or expert advice produced at the direct request of the mediator, shall be borne equally by the parties unless they agree otherwise.

Administrative Fees

The Filing Fee

The case filing fee is to be borne equally or as otherwise agreed by the parties.

Additionally, the parties are charged a fee based on the number of hours of mediator time. The hourly fee is for the compensation of both the mediator and the American Arbitration Association and varies according to region. Check with your local AAA regional office for specific availability and rates.

There is no charge to the filing party where the AAA is requested to invite other parties to join in a submission to mediation. However, if a case settles after AAA involvement but prior to dispute resolution, the filing party will be charged a filing fee.

The expenses of the AAA and the mediator, if any, are generally borne equally by the parties. The parties may vary this arrangement by agreement.

Where the parties have attempted mediation under these rules but have failed to reach a settlement, the AAA will apply the administrative fee on the mediation toward any subsequent AAA arbitration, which is filed with the AAA within ninety days of the termination of the mediation.

Deposits

Before the commencement of mediation, the parties shall each deposit such portion of the fee covering the cost of mediation as the AAA shall direct and all appropriate additional sums that the AAA deems necessary to defray the expenses of the proceeding. When the mediation has terminated, the AAA shall render an accounting and return any unexpended balance to the parties.

Refunds

Once the parties agree to mediate, no refund of the administrative fee will be made.

Commercial Arbitration Rules and Procedures

As amended and in effect May 1, 1995

Introduction

Each year, many millions of business transactions take place. Occasionally, disagreements develop over these business transactions. Many of these disputes are resolved by arbitration, the voluntary submission of a dispute to a disinterested person or persons for final and binding determination. Arbitration has proven to be an effective way to resolve these disputes privately, promptly, and economically.

The parties can provide for arbitration of future disputes by inserting the following clause into their contracts.

> **Standard Arbitration Clause**
>
> Any controversy or claim arising out of or relating to this contract, or the breach thereof, shall be settled by arbitration administered by the American Arbitration Association under its Commercial Arbitration Rules, and judgment on the award rendered by the arbitrator(s) may be entered in any court having jurisdiction thereof.

Arbitration of existing disputes may be accomplished by use of the following.

> We, the undersigned parties, hereby agree to submit to arbitration administered by the American Arbitration Association under its Commercial Arbitration Rules the following controversy: (cite briefly). WE further agree that the above controversy be submitted to (one) (three) arbitrator(s). We further agree that we will faithfully observe this agreement and the rules, that we will abide by and perform any award rendered by the arbitrator(s), and that a judgment of any court having jurisdiction may be entered on the award.

The services of the AAA are generally concluded with the transmittal of the award. Although there is voluntary compliance with the majority of awards, judgment on the award can be entered in a court having appropriate jurisdiction if necessary.

The Neutrals

The American Arbitration Association maintains an international panel of trained and expert neutrals who are available to serve with distinction in the resolution of disputes. Counted among these seasoned professionals are attorneys, industry leaders, retired jurists and executives, who possess the substantive and discrete knowledge necessary for effective conflict management.

Cost
The American Arbitration Association shall prescribe filing and other administrative fees and service charges to compensate it for provision of administrative services. All fees in effect at the time the costs are incurred shall apply. Compensation for the arbitrator(s), unless otherwise agreed, is generally borne equally by the parties to the agreement. Check with your local AAA region office for specific availability and rates.

Administration
In order to facilitate expeditious and fair resolution of disputes, the Association is able to provide administrative services which may include:

- receipt and acknowledgment of claims and counterclaims;
- conduct of administrative conferences with parties and their counsel;
- preparation of lists of neutral arbitrators suitable to the specific dispute;
- supervision of the neutral arbitrator selection process;
- scheduling of meetings or hearings in AAA offices or at other mutually convenient facilities;
- management and facilitation of all communications between the parties and the arbitrator, including any arrangement for compensation of the neutral;
- determination as to whether or not a neutral may have a disqualifying relationship;
- ensuring that the settlement or decision of the arbitrator is achieved promptly and fairly.

Commercial Arbitration Rules and Procedures

1. Agreement of Parties
The parties shall be deemed to have made these rules a part of their arbitration agreement whenever they have provided for arbitration by the American Arbitration Association (hereinafter AAA) or under its Commercial Arbitration Rules. These rules and any amendment of them shall apply in the form obtaining at the time the

demand for arbitration or submission agreement is received by the AAA. The parties, by written agreement, may vary the procedures set forth in these rules.

2. Name of Tribunal
Any tribunal constituted by the parties for the settlement of their dispute under these rules shall be called the Commercial Arbitration Tribunal.

3. Administrator and Delegation of Duties
When parties agree to arbitrate under these rules, or when they provide for arbitration by the AAA and an arbitration is initiated under these rules, they thereby authorize the AAA to administer the arbitration. The authority and duties of the AAA are prescribed in the agreement of the parties and in these rules, and may be carried out through such of the AAA's representatives as it may direct.

4. National Panel of Arbitrators
The AAA shall establish and maintain a National Panel of Commercial Arbitrators and shall appoint arbitrators as provided in these rules.

5. Regional Offices
The AAA may, in its discretion, assign the administration of an arbitration to any of its regional offices.

6. Initiation Under an Arbitration Provision in a Contract
Arbitration under an arbitration provision in a contract shall be initiated in the following manner:

> (a) The initiating party (hereinafter claimant) shall, within the time period, if any, specified in the contract(s), give written notice to the other party (hereinafter respondent) of its intention to arbitrate (demand), which notice shall contain a statement setting forth the nature of the dispute, the amount involved, if any, the remedy sought, and the hearing locale requested, and

> (b) shall file at any regional office of the AAA three copies of the notice and three copies of the arbitration provisions of the contract, together with the appropriate filing fee.

> The AAA shall give notice of such filing to the respondent or respondents. A respondent may file an answering statement in duplicate with the AAA within ten

Rules and Procedures for Dispute Settlement 239

days after notice from the AAA, in which event the respondent shall at the same time send a copy of the answering statement to the claimant. If a counterclaim is asserted, it shall contain a statement setting forth the nature of the counterclaim, the amount involved, if any, and the remedy sought. If a counterclaim is made, the appropriate fee shall be forwarded to the AAA with the answering statement. If no answering statement is filed within the stated time, it will be treated as a denial of the claim. Failure to file an answering statement shall not operate to delay the arbitration.

7. Initiation Under a Submission
Parties to any existing dispute may commence an arbitration under these rules by filing at any regional office of the AAA three copies of a written submission to arbitrate under these rules, signed by the parties. It shall contain a statement of the matter in dispute, the amount involved, if any, the remedy sought, and the hearing locale requested, together with the appropriate filing fee.

8. Changes of Claim
After filing of a claim, if either party desires to make any new or different claim or counterclaim, it shall be made in writing and filed with the AAA, and a copy shall be mailed to the other party, who shall have a period of ten days from the date of such mailing within which to file an answer with the AAA. After the arbitrator is appointed, however, no new or different claim may be submitted except with the arbitrator's consent.

9. Applicable Procedures
Unless the AAA in its discretion determines otherwise, the Expedited Procedures shall be applied in any case where no disclosed claim or counterclaim exceeds $50,000, exclusive of interest and arbitration costs. Parties may also agree to using the Expedited Procedures in cases involving claims in excess of $50,000. The Expedited Procedures shall be applied as described in Sections 53 through 57 of these rules, in addition to any other portion of these rules that is not in conflict with the Expedited Procedures.

All other cases shall be administered in accordance with Sections 1 through 52 of these rules.

10. Administrative Conference, Preliminary Hearing, and Mediation Conference
At the request of any party or at the discretion of the AAA, an administrative conference with the AAA and the parties and/or their representatives will be scheduled

in appropriate cases to expedite the arbitration proceedings. There is no administrative fee for this service.

In large or complex cases, at the request of any party or at the discretion of the arbitrator or the AAA, a preliminary hearing with the parties and/or their representatives and the arbitrator may be scheduled by the arbitrator to specify the issues to be resolved, to stipulate to uncontested facts, and to consider any other matters that will expedite the arbitration proceedings. Consistent with the expedited nature of arbitration, the arbitrator may, at the preliminary hearing, establish (i) the extent of and schedule for the production of relevant documents and other information, (ii) the identification of any witnesses to be called, and (iii) a schedule for further hearings to resolve the dispute. There is no administrative fee for the first preliminary hearing.

With the consent of the parties, the AAA at any stage of the proceeding may arrange a mediation conference under the Commercial Mediation Rules, in order to facilitate settlement. The mediator shall not be an arbitrator appointed to the case. Where the parties to a pending arbitration agree to mediate under the AAA's rules, no additional administrative fee is required to initiate the mediation.

11. Fixing of Locale

The parties may mutually agree on the locale where the arbitration is to be held. If any party requests that the hearing be held in a specific locale and the other party files no objection thereto within ten days after notice of the request has been sent to it by the AAA, the locale shall be the one requested. If a party objects to the locale requested by the other party, the AAA shall have the power to determine the locale and its decision shall be final and binding.

12. Qualifications of an Arbitrator

Any neutral arbitrator appointed pursuant to Section 13, 14, 15, or 54, or selected by mutual choice of the parties or their appointees, shall be subject to disqualification for the reasons specified in Section 19. If the parties specifically so agree in writing, the arbitrator shall not be subject to disqualification for those reasons.

Unless the parties agree otherwise, an arbitrator selected unilaterally by one party is a party-appointed arbitrator and is not subject to disqualification pursuant to Section 19.

The term "arbitrator" in these rules refers to the arbitration panel, whether composed of one or more arbitrators and whether the arbitrators are neutral or party appointed.

13. Appointment from Panel

If the parties have not appointed an arbitrator and have not provided any other method of appointment, the arbitrator shall be appointed in the following manner: immediately after the filing of the demand or submission, the AAA shall send simultaneously to each party to the dispute an identical list of names of persons chosen from the panel.

Each party to the dispute shall have ten days from the transmittal date in which to strike names objected to, number the remaining names in order of preference, and return the list to the AAA. In a single-arbitrator case, each party may strike three names on a peremptory basis. In a multiarbitrator case, each party may strike five names on a peremptory basis. If a party does not return the list within the time specified, all persons named therein shall be deemed acceptable. From among the persons who have been approved on both lists, and in accordance with the designated order of mutual preference, the AAA shall invite the acceptance of an arbitrator to serve. If the parties fail to agree on any of the persons named, or if acceptable arbitrators are unable to act, or if for any other reason the appointment cannot be made from the submitted lists, the AAA shall have the power to make the appointment from among other members of the panel without the submission of additional lists.

14. Direct Appointment by a Party

If the agreement of the parties names an arbitrator or specifies a method of appointing an arbitrator, that designation or method shall be followed. The notice of appointment, with the name and address of the arbitrator, shall be filed with the AAA by the appointing party. Upon the request of any appointing party, the AAA shall submit a list of members of the panel from which the party may, if it so desires, make the appointment.

If the agreement specifies a period of time within which an arbitrator shall be appointed and any party fails to make the appointment within that period, the AAA shall make the appointment.

If no period of time is specified in the agreement, the AAA shall notify the party to make the appointment. If within ten days thereafter an arbitrator has not been appointed by a party, the AAA shall make the appointment.

15. Appointment of Neutral Arbitrator by Party-Appointed Arbitrators or Parties

If the parties have selected party-appointed arbitrators, or if such arbitrators have been appointed as provided in Section 14, and the parties have authorized them to appoint a neutral arbitrator within a specified time and no appointment is made within that time or any agreed extension, the AAA may appoint a neutral arbitrator, who shall act as chairperson.

If no period of time is specified for appointment of the neutral arbitrator and the party-appointed arbitrators or the parties do not make the appointment within ten days from the date of the appointment of the last party-appointed arbitrator, the AAA may appoint the neutral arbitrator, who shall act as chairperson.

If the parties have agreed that their party-appointed arbitrators shall appoint the neutral arbitrator from the panel, the AAA shall furnish to the party-appointed arbitrators, in the manner provided in Section 13, a list selected from the panel, and the appointment of the neutral arbitrator shall be made as provided in that section.

16. Nationality of Arbitrator in International Arbitration
Where the parties are nationals or residents of different countries, any neutral arbitrator shall, upon the request of either party, be appointed from among the nationals of a country other than that of any of the parties. The request must be made prior to the time set for the appointment of the arbitrator as agreed by the parties or set by these rules.

17. Number of Arbitrators
If the arbitration agreement does not specify the number of arbitrators, the dispute shall be heard and determined by one arbitrator, unless the AAA, in its discretion, directs that a greater number of arbitrators be appointed.

18. Notice to Arbitrator of Appointment
Notice of the appointment of the neutral arbitrator, whether appointed mutually by the parties or by the AAA, shall be sent to the arbitrator by the AAA, together with a copy of these rules, and the signed acceptance of the arbitrator shall be filed with the AAA prior to the opening of the first hearing.

19. Disclosure and Challenge Procedure
Any person appointed as neutral arbitrator shall disclose to the AAA any circumstance likely to affect impartiality, including any bias or any financial or personal interest in the result of the arbitration or any past or present relationship with the parties or their representatives. Upon receipt of such information from the arbitrator or another source, the AAA shall communicate the information to the parties

and, if it deems it appropriate to do so, to the arbitrator and others. Upon objection of a party to the continued service of a neutral arbitrator, the AAA shall determine whether the arbitrator should be disqualified and shall inform the parties of its decision, which shall be conclusive.

20. Vacancies

If for any reason an arbitrator is unable to perform the duties of the office, the AAA may, on proof satisfactory to it, declare the office vacant. Vacancies shall be filled in accordance with the applicable provisions of these rules.

In the event of a vacancy in a panel of neutral arbitrators after the hearings have commenced, the remaining arbitrator or arbitrators may continue with the hearing and determination of the controversy, unless the parties agree otherwise.

21. Date, Time, and Place of Hearing

The arbitrator shall set the date, time, and place for each hearing. The AAA shall send a notice of hearing to the parties at least ten days in advance of the hearing date, unless otherwise agreed by the parties.

22. Representation

Any party may be represented by counsel or other authorized representative. A party intending to be so represented shall notify the other party and the AAA of the name and address of the representative at least three days prior to the date set for the hearing at which that person is first to appear. When such a representative initiates an arbitration or responds for a party, notice is deemed to have been given.

23. Stenographic Record

Any party desiring a stenographic record shall make arrangements directly with a stenographer and shall notify the other parties of these arrangements in advance of the hearing. The requesting party or parties shall pay the cost of the record. If the transcript is agreed by the parties to be, or determined by the arbitrator to be, the official record of the proceeding, it must be made available to the arbitrator and to the other parties for inspection, at a date, time, and place determined by the arbitrator.

24. Interpreters

Any party wishing an interpreter shall make all arrangements directly with the interpreter and shall assume the costs of the service.

25. Attendance at Hearings

The arbitrator shall maintain the privacy of the hearings unless the law provides to the contrary. Any person having a direct interest in the arbitration is entitled to attend hearings. The arbitrator shall otherwise have the power to require the exclusion of any witness, other than a party or other essential person, during the testimony of any other witness. It shall be discretionary with the arbitrator to determine the propriety of the attendance of any other person.

26. Postponements

The arbitrator for good cause shown may postpone any hearing upon the request of a party or upon the arbitrator's own initiative, and shall also grant such postponement when all of the parties agree.

27. Oaths

Before proceeding with the first hearing, each arbitrator may take an oath of office and, if required by law, shall do so. The arbitrator may require witnesses to testify under oath administered by any duly qualified person and, if it is required by law or requested by any party, shall do so.

28. Majority Decision

All decisions of the arbitrators must be by a majority. The award must also be made by a majority unless the concurrence of all is expressly required by the arbitration agreement or by law.

29. Order of Proceedings and Communication with Arbitrator

A hearing shall be opened by the filing of the oath of the arbitrator, where required; by the recording of the date, time, and place of the hearing, and the presence of the arbitrator, the parties, and their representatives, if any; and by the receipt by the arbitrator of the statement of the claim and the answering statement, if any.

The arbitrator may, at the beginning of the hearing, ask for statements clarifying the issues involved. In some cases, part or all of the above will have been accomplished at the preliminary hearing conducted by the arbitrator pursuant to Section 10.

The complaining party shall then present evidence to support its claim. The defending party shall then present evidence supporting its defense. Witnesses for each party shall submit to questions or other examination. The arbitrator has the discretion to vary this procedure but shall afford a full and equal opportunity to all parties for the presentation of any material and relevant evidence.

Exhibits, when offered by either party, may be received in evidence by the arbitrator.

The names and addresses of all witnesses and a description of the exhibits in the order received shall be made a part of the record.

There shall be no direct communication between the parties and a neutral arbitrator other than at oral hearing, unless the parties and the arbitrator agree otherwise. Any other oral or written communication from the parties to the neutral arbitrator shall be directed to the AAA for transmittal to the arbitrator.

30. Arbitration in the Absence of a Party or Representative

Unless the law provides to the contrary, the arbitration may proceed in the absence of any party or representative who, after due notice, fails to be present or fails to obtain a postponement. An award shall not be made solely on the default of a party. The arbitrator shall require the party who is present to submit such evidence as the arbitrator may require for the making of an award.

31. Evidence

The parties may offer such evidence as is relevant and material to the dispute and shall produce such evidence as the arbitrator may deem necessary to an understanding and determination of the dispute. An arbitrator or other person authorized by law to subpoena witnesses or documents may do so upon the request of any party or independently.

The arbitrator shall be the judge of the relevance and materiality of the evidence offered, and conformity to legal rules of evidence shall not be necessary. All evidence shall be taken in the presence of all of the arbitrators and all of the parties, except where any of the parties is absent in default or has waived the right to be present.

32. Evidence by Affidavit and Posthearing Filing of Documents or Other Evidence

The arbitrator may receive and consider the evidence of witnesses by affidavit, but shall give it only such weight as the arbitrator deems it entitled to after consideration of any objection made to its admission.

If the parties agree or the arbitrator directs that documents or other evidence be submitted to the arbitrator after the hearing, the documents or other evidence shall be filed with the AAA for transmission to the arbitrator. All parties shall be afforded an opportunity to examine such documents or other evidence.

33. Inspection or Investigation
An arbitrator finding it necessary to make an inspection or investigation in connection with the arbitration shall direct the AAA to so advise the parties. The arbitrator shall set the date and time and the AAA shall notify the parties. Any party who so desires may be present at such an inspection or investigation. In the event that one or all parties are not present at the inspection or investigation, the arbitrator shall make a verbal or written report to the parties and afford them an opportunity to comment.

34. Interim Measures
The arbitrator may issue such orders for interim relief as may be deemed necessary to safeguard the property that is the subject matter of the arbitration, without prejudice to the rights of the parties or to the final determination of the dispute.

35. Closing of Hearing
The arbitrator shall specifically inquire of all parties whether they have any further proofs to offer or witnesses to be heard. Upon receiving negative replies or if satisfied that the record is complete, the arbitrator shall declare the hearing closed.

If briefs are to be filed, the hearing shall be declared closed as of the final date set by the arbitrator for the receipt of briefs. If documents are to be filed as provided in Section 32 and the date set for their receipt is later than that set for the receipt of briefs, the later date shall be the date of closing the hearing. The time limit within which the arbitrator is required to make the award shall commence to run, in the absence of other agreements by the parties, upon the closing of the hearing.

36. Reopening of Hearing
The hearing may be reopened on the arbitrator's initiative, or upon application of a party, at any time before the award is made. If reopening the hearing would prevent the making of the award within the specific time agreed on by the parties in the contract(s) out of which the controversy has arisen, the matter may not be reopened unless the parties agree on an extension of time. When no specific date is fixed in the contract, the arbitrator may reopen the hearing and shall have thirty days from the closing of the reopened hearing within which to make an award.

37. Waiver of Oral Hearing
The parties may provide, by written agreement, for the waiver of oral hearings in any case. If the parties are unable to agree as to the procedure, the AAA shall specify a fair and equitable procedure.

38. Waiver of Rules

Any party who proceeds with the arbitration after knowledge that any provision or requirement of these rules has not been complied with and who fails to state an objection in writing shall be deemed to have waived the right to object.

39. Extensions of Time

The parties may modify any period of time by mutual agreement. The AAA or the arbitrator may for good cause extend any period of time established by these rules, except the time for making the award. The AAA shall notify the parties of any extension.

40. Serving of Notice

Each party shall be deemed to have consented that any papers, notices, or process necessary or proper for the initiation or continuation of an arbitration under these rules; for any court action in connection therewith; or for the entry of judgment on any award made under these rules may be served on a party by mail addressed to the party or its representative at the last known address or by personal service, in or outside the state where the arbitration is to be held, provided that reasonable opportunity to be heard with regard thereto has been granted to the party.

The AAA and the parties may also use facsimile transmission, telex, telegram, or other written forms of electronic communication to give the notices required by these rules.

41. Time of Award

The award shall be made promptly by the arbitrator and, unless otherwise agreed by the parties or specified by law, no later than thirty days from the date of closing the hearing, or, if oral hearings have been waived, from the date of the AAA's transmittal of the final statements and proofs to the arbitrator.

42. Form of Award

The award shall be in writing and shall be signed by a majority of the arbitrators. It shall be executed in the manner required by law.

43. Scope of Award

The arbitrator may grant any remedy or relief that the arbitrator deems just and equitable and within the scope of the agreement of the parties, including, but not limited to, specific performance of a contract. The arbitrator shall, in the award, assess arbitration fees, expenses, and compensation as provided in Sections 48, 49, and 50 in favor of any party and, in the event that any administrative fees or expenses are due the AAA, in favor of the AAA.

44. Award upon Settlement
If the parties settle their dispute during the course of the arbitration, the arbitrator may set forth the terms of the agreed settlement in an award. Such an awards is referred to as a consent award.

45. Delivery of Award to Parties
Parties shall accept as legal delivery of the award the placing of the award or a true copy thereof in the mail addressed to a party or its representative at the last known addressed, personal service of the award, or the filing of the award in any other manner that is permitted by law.

46. Release of Documents for Judicial Proceedings
The AAA shall, upon the written request of a party, furnish to the party, at its expense, certified copies of any papers in the AAA's possession that may be required in judicial proceedings relating to the arbitration.

47. Applications to Court and Exclusion of Liability

(a) No judicial proceeding by a party relating to the subject matter of the arbitration shall be deemed a waiver of the party's right to arbitrate.

(b) Neither the AAA nor any arbitrator in a proceeding under these rules is a necessary party in judicial proceedings relating to the arbitration.

(c) Parties to these rules shall be deemed to have consented that judgment upon the arbitration award may be entered in any federal or state court having jurisdiction thereof.

(d) Neither the AAA nor any arbitrator shall be liable to any party for any act or omission in connection with any arbitration conducted under these rules.

48. Administrative Fees
As a not-for-profit organization, the AAA shall prescribe filing and other administrative fees and service charges to compensate it for the cost of providing administrative services. The fees in effect when the fee or charge is incurred shall be applicable.

Rules and Procedures for Dispute Settlement **249**

The filing fee shall be advanced by the initiating party or parties, subject to final apportionment by the arbitrator in the award.

The AAA may, in the event of extreme hardship on the part of any party, defer or reduce the administrative fees.

49. Expenses

The expenses of witnesses for either side shall be paid by the party producing such witnesses. All other expenses of the arbitration, including required travel and other expenses of the arbitrator, AAA representatives, and any witness and the cost of any proof produced at the direct request of the arbitrator, shall be borne equally by the parties, unless they agree otherwise or unless the arbitrator in the award assesses such expenses or any part thereof against any specified party or parties.

50. Neutral Arbitrator's Compensation

Unless the parties agree otherwise, members of the National Panel of Commercial Arbitrators appointed as neutrals will serve without compensation for the first day of service.

Thereafter, compensation shall be based on the amount of service involved and the number of hearings. An appropriate daily rate and other arrangements will be discussed by the administrator with the parties and the arbitrator. If the parties fail to agree to the terms of compensation, an appropriate rate shall be established by the AAA and communicated in writing to the parties.

Any arrangement for the compensation of a neutral arbitrator shall be made through the AAA and not directly between the parties and the arbitrator.

51. Deposits

The AAA may require the parties to deposit in advance of any hearings such sums of money as it deems necessary to cover the expense of the arbitration, including the arbitrator's fee, if any, and shall render an accounting to the parties and return any unexpended balance at the conclusion of the case.

52. Interpretation and Application of Rules

The arbitrator shall interpret and apply these rules insofar as they relate to the arbitrator's powers and duties. When there is more than one arbitrator and a difference arises among them concerning the meaning or application of these rules, it shall be decided by a majority vote. If that is not possible, either an arbitrator or a party may refer the question to the AAA for final decision. All other rules shall be interpreted and applied by the AAA.

Expedited Procedures

53. Notice by Telephone

The parties shall accept all notices from the AAA by telephone. Such notices by the AAA shall subsequently be confirmed in writing to the parties. Should there be a failure to confirm in writing any notice hereunder, the proceeding shall nonetheless be valid if notice has, in fact, been given by telephone.

54. Appointment and Qualifications of Arbitration

(a) Where no disclosed claim or counterclaim exceeds $50,000, exclusive of interest and arbitration costs, the AAA shall appoint a single arbitrator, from the National Panel of Commercial Arbitrators, without submission of lists of proposed arbitrators.

(b) Where all parties request that a list of proposed arbitrators be sent, the AAA upon payment of the service charge as provided in the Administrative Fees shall submit simultaneously to each party an identical list of five proposed arbitrators, drawn from the National Panel of Commercial Arbitrators, from which one arbitrator shall be appointed. Each party may strike two names from the list on a peremptory basis. The list is returnable to the AAA within seven days from the date of the AAA's mailing to the parties.

If for any reason the appointment of an arbitrator cannot be made from the list, the AAA may make the appointment from among other members of the panel without the submission of additional lists.

(c) The parties will be given notice by telephone by the AAA of the appointment of the arbitrator, who shall be subject to disqualification for the reasons specified in Section 19. The parties shall notify the AAA, by telephone, within seven days of any objection to the arbitrator appointed. Any objection by a party to the arbitrator shall be confirmed in writing to the AAA with a copy to the other party or parties.

55. Date, Time, and Place of Hearing

The arbitrator shall set the date, time, and place of the hearing. The AAA will notify the parties by telephone, at least seven days in advance of the hearing date. A formal notice of hearing will also be sent by the AAA to the parties.

Rules and Procedures for Dispute Settlement 251

56. The Hearing
Generally, the hearing shall be completed within one day, unless the dispute is resolved by submission of documents under Section 37. The arbitrator, for good cause shown, may schedule an additional hearing to be held within seven days.

57. Time of Award
Unless otherwise agreed by the parties, the award shall be rendered not later than fourteen days from the date of the closing of the hearing.

Administrative Fees

The American Arbitration Association shall prescribe filing and other administrative fees and service charges to compensate it for the cost of providing administrative services. The fees in effect at the time the costs are incurred shall be applicable.

A non-refundable filing fee shall be advanced by the initiating party or parties, subject to final apportionment by the arbitrator in the award.

The AAA may, in the event of extreme hardship on the part of any party, defer or reduce the administrative fees.

Expedited Procedures, outlined in Sections 53–57 of the rules, are applied in any case where no disclosed claim or counterclaim exceeds $50,000, exclusive of interest and arbitration costs. Under those procedures, arbitrators are directly appointed by the AAA. Where the parties request a list of proposed arbitrators under those procedures, a service charge will be payable by each party.

Hearing Fees
For each day of hearing held before a panel, an administrative fee is payable by each party.

There is no hearing fee for the initial hearing in cases administered under the Expedited Procedures.

Postponement/Cancellation Fees
A separate fee is payable by a party causing a postponement of any hearing scheduled before a single or multi-arbitrator panel.

Processing Fees
A processing fee will be assessed, per party, payable 180 days after the case is initiated, and every 90 days thereafter, until the case is withdrawn or settled or the hearings are closed by the arbitrator(s).

Suspension for Nonpayment

If arbitrator compensation or administrative charges have not been paid in full, the American Arbitration Association may so inform the parties in order that one of them may advance the required payment. If such payments are not made, the arbitrator may order the suspension or termination of the proceedings. If no arbitrator has yet been appointed, the AAA may suspend the proceedings.

Hearing Room Rental

The Hearing Fees described above do not cover the rental of hearing rooms, which are available on a rental basis. Check with your local office for availability and rates.

Cumulative Index

(Note: Page references to the Supplement are preceded by "S" and are in boldface)

A

A & M Produce Co. v. FMC Corporation, 171
ABA Business Law Section Task Force on Software Contracting, **S73–74**
Acceptance of an offer, 225, 253–79
  acceptance, defined, 254–56
  buyer's acceptance methods, 258–64
    in blank, 258–59
    buyer receives/accepts goods, 261–63
    payment, 264
    repeat terms of offer, 259–61
  CISG regulations, 563–65
  conduct of parties, formation of contract by, 269–70
  effective date of, 271–74
  manner of acceptance, controlling, 274–76
  proof of mailing acceptance, 276–79
  source of, 256–57
  supplier's acceptance methods, 264–68
    in blank, 264–66
    supplier begins to manufacture, 268
    supplier delivers goods, 266–68
    supplier repeats terms of offer, 266
Acceptance of goods, 401, 563–65
  defined, 606
  revocation of, 415–17
    wrongful revocation of acceptance, 417
Accepted goods, damages for breach in, 428
Accountability of agent, 77–78
Acknowledgments, 281–305
Actual authority, See Express (actual) authority
Advent Systems, Ltd. v. Unisys Corp., 459, 460
Age discrimination, **S8–9**
Age Discrimination in Employment Act (ADEA), **S8–9**

Agency contract, breach of, 93–94
Agency relationship, 31–38
  agency, defined, 32–33
  agent, 32–36
  assistant purchasing agents, appointment of, 37–38
  buyers, appointment of, 37–38
  principal, 32, 85–91
  purchasing officer, appointment of, 36–37
  termination of, 38
  third party, 32
  See also Agent
Agent, 32–36
  appointment of, 35–36
  breach of agency contract, 93–94
  and business use of an automobile, 110–19
  check signing, 124–26
  compensation of, 86–87
  contracts/purchase orders, execution of, 94–104
  criminal liabilities, 119–20
  dealing with, 58–61
  duties of, 69–83
    accountability, 77–78
    confidentiality, 79–81
    exercise of reasonable care, 74–77
    keeping the employer informed, 79
    loyalty, 70–73
    obedience to instructions, 73–74
    possession of skills/training, 82–83
  environmental hazards liability, 120–24
  indemnification of, 87
  liability for criminal acts of, 90–91
  note signing, 124–26
  personal liabilities of, 93–126
  reimbursement of, 87
  role in business, 34–35
  tort liabilities, exposure to, 104–7
Agreement of the parties, 201–2
Alternative dispute resolution, 26–28
  arbitration, 28
  mediation, 26–27
American Bar Association (ABA), Electronic Messaging Services Task Force, 468, 469, 471, **S73–74**
American Law Institute (ALI), 636, 637
American purchasing officer, and CISG, 618
Americans with Disabilities Act (ADA), **S8–16**
Antichain-store law. See Robinson-Patman Act
Anticipatory breaches, 612–13
Antitrust:
  association meetings, attendance at, 149–51
  liabilities, exemption from, 151–52
  major legislation, 127–31
  and purchasing officer, 127–52
  See also Specific legislation
Apparent authority, 45
  in Agency Law, 47–49
  and purchasing, 49–51
Arbitration, 28
  electronic interchange (EDI), 506
Article 2 (UCC), 11, 15
  executive summary, 641–57
  sales reform, 631–39
    scope of, 75–76
  study and reform, 636–39

Article 2A (UCC), 11, 439–47
  adoption of, 440–41, **S35–36**
  lease, defined, 444
  leases:
    damages, 447
    finance lease, 445–46
    remedies, 447
    sales and leaseback transactions, 446
    statute of frauds, 446–47
    types of, 445
  parts of, 442–43
  scope of, 444–47
Article 2B (UCC), 11, **S55–70**
Article 3 (UCC), 11, 16
Article 4 (UCC), 11, 17
Article 4A (UCC), 11–12
Article 5 (UCC), 18
Article 7 (UCC), 19
Article 9 (UCC), 18
ASEAN Free Trade Area, **S138, S147–50**
Asia Pacific Economic Cooperation, **S138–47**
  collective action plans, **S144–45**
  general principles, **S140–41**
  Osaka Action Agenda, **S142**
"As is" as disclaimer, 362–63
Assistant purchasing officers:
  appointment of, 37–38
  authority of, 46–47
  and purchase order signature, 96–97
Association meetings, attendance at, 149–51
Authority:
  agent, dealing with, 58–61
  apparent, 45, 47–49
  assistant purchasing officers, 46–47
  buyers, 46–47

defined, 39
emergency, 44–45, 103
express (actual), 40–43, 98
implied, 43–44
purchasing officer, 45–46
  dealing with, 67
scope of authority, exceeding, 100–104
supplier, dealing with, 61–67
written, advantages of, 41–43
See also Unauthorized procurement
Automobile use, 110–19, **S5–6**
  driving a company-owned automobile, 112–15
  driving your own, 110–12
  and government procurement officers, 118–19
  liability insurance, 110
  rentals, 115–18

B

Bankruptucy, **S45–53**
  executory contracts, **S48–53**
  types of, **S47–48**
Bank's duty, **S38–39**
Battle of the Forms, 281–305, 566–71
Beneficiary, letter of credit, 17
Bid bonds, 246–49
Bilateral contract, 201
Bills of exchange, 17
Bills of lading, 19
Blanket orders, 338–39
Breach of contract, 93–94, 612
  avoidance, effects of, 617–18
  by buyer, 609–11
  by seller, 592–603
  damages for, 613–15

Breach of contract *(cont.)*
  excuses, 616–17
  interest, 615
  preservation of goods, 618
Bribery, 163–67, **S33–35**
Brown v. Board of Education, 12–13
Bundled software, 457
Burlington Industries v. Ellerth, **S30–31**
Business entities, forms of, 34
Buyers:
  acceptance methods, 258–59
    in blank, 258–59
      buyer receives/accepts goods, 261–63
      payment, 264
      repeat terms of offer, 259–61
  appointment of, 37–38
  authority of, 46–47
  breach of contract by, 609–11
  obligations of, 603–4
  protective devices, 538–42
    applicable law/jurisdiction, 539–40
    bonds/escrows, 540–41
    retainage, 541
    supplier excuses, 541–42
    supplier selection, 538–39
  remedies, 423–31, **S45–53**
    damages for breach in accepted goods, 428
    damages for nondelivery, 427
    incidental and consequential damages, 428–30 (*see also* Consequential damages; Incidental damages)
    limitations on, 431–35
    liquidated damages, 430–31
    right to specific performance, 430
    substitute goods, 426–27
    warranty to supplier against infringement, 346–47

C

C.&F. destination, 389
Capable parties, 196–98
Case law, 12
Cash discounts, 374–75
CERCLA, 122
Certificate of Origin, **S117**
Certified purchasing managers (CPMs), 154–59
  National Association of Educational Buyers (NAEB), 155–58
  National Association of Purchasing Management, 158–59, 162–63
  programs, 154–55
Chapter 11 reorganization, **S52–53**
Checks, 17
Check signing, 124–26
Chief purchasing officer, and buyer/assistant purchasing officer authority, 47
China, See People's Republic of China, negotiating and contracting in
C.I.F./C.&F. net landed weights, 389
C.I.F. destination, 387–88
CISG, 542–57
  acceptance, 563–65
  and American purchasing officer, 618
  Battle of the Forms, 281–305, 566–71
  benefit of, 618

Index

breach of contract by buyer, remedies, 609–11
breach of contract by seller, remedies, 592–603
buyer obligations, 603–4
conformity of goods, 580–92
contract, avoidance of, 599–600
copyright infringement, 589–91
damages/interest, 613–18
dealing, usages/course of, 555–56
defined, 545–46
delivery, taking, 609
firm offers, 560–623
general provisions, 549–57
genesis of, 543–44
inspection of goods, time for, 586–87, 606–8
interpretation of, 549–50
items not covered by, 551
nonconforming acceptances, 281–305, 566–71
nonconformity of goods, notice of, 587–88
nonuniformity, 619
offer, definition of, 557–58
passing risk of loss, 611–12
patent infringement, 589–92
payment price, 604–8
performance of seller, 593–97
price reduction, 601–2
purchaser's remedies, 82–85
ratified countries, 543–44
revocable offers, 558–60
role of, 544–45
sale of goods, 571–77
seller's notice of intent to cure, 599
seller's right to cure after delivery, 597–99
sphere of application, 546–49
statements/conduct of a party, interpreting, 551–54
supplier's quality obligations, extent of, 585
supplier's right to cure, 585–86
third-party claims, 580–92
UCC compared to, 619–23
undelivered/nonconforming goods, 602–3
warranties in, 580–83
  disclaimer of, 583–85
warranty of title–third party claims, 588
Civil law, 6
Civil Rights Act of 1964, **S16–30**
Civil Rights Act of 1991, **S9–16**
Classical model, contract law, 513–15
Clayton Act, 129
Clean Air Act, 122
Clean receipt, 402
Clean Water Act, 122
Code Napoléon, 6
Collision damage waiver insurance, 116
Commercial bribery, 163–67
Commercial documents, 15–21
  bills of exchange, 17
  bills of lading, 19
  checks, 17
  Convention on International Sale of Goods, **S1**
  drafts, 16–17
  financing statements, 18–19
  freedom of contract, 19–21
  letters of credit, 17–18
  promissory notes, 16
  sales contract, 15–19
  security agreements, 18
Commercial law, 7–8

Commercial letter of credit, **S37–43**
Common law, 6–7
Company legal counsel, 13
Company-owned automobile, driving, 112–15
Comparative liability, 107
Compensation, **S78–79**
Compensation of agent, 86–87
Comprehensive Environmental Response, Compensation and Liability Act, See CERCLA
Computer Fraud and Abuse Act, **S66–67**
Computers, 455–65
　attribution procedures, **S67–70**
　digital signatures, **S68–69**
　disclaimers, 465
　electronic commerce, **S64**
　electronic notaries, **S70–72**
　E-mail, **S62**
　express warranties, 461–63
　implied warranties, 463–65
　purchase strategy, 455–61
　purchases and controversies, **S55–75**
　　Article 2B, **S55–70**
　　explicit exclusions, **S58–59**
　　"hub and spoke" approach to Article 2, **S56**
　　implicit limitations, **S60–61**
　　laws, legislative reform of, **S56**
　　licensing, **S57–58**
　　"shrink-wrap" licenses, **S64–66**
　software contracts, **S56–60**
　software viruses, **S66–67**
Confidentiality:
　agent, 79–81
　electronic data interchange (EDI), 500–501

Confirming bank, 18
Conflict of interest, 71–73
Conformity of goods, 580–92
Consent judgment, 132
Consideration, legal definition of, 199
Construction Associates, Inc., v. Fargo Water Equipment Co., 172–73
Consumer legislation, 5–6
Contingency fee arrangement, 25–26, **S3–4**
Contract law, 513–26
　classical model, 513–15
　　neoclassical model, 514–15
　Law Made model, 520–24
　obligation model, 524–26
　relational model, 517–20
　UCC model, 515–17
Contracts:
　avoidance of, 599–600
　execution of, 94–104
　legal signature, 95–97
　order-signing responsibility, delegating, 97–98
　scope of authority, exceeding, 100–104
　traditional contract law, 282–83
　　applying to a Battle of the Forms, 284–86
Contractual liability, 116–17
Convention on the International Sale of Goods, See CISG
Copyright infringement, 589–92
Corporations, 34–35
Counter-offers, 213–14
Counterpurchase, **S78**
Countertrade, **S77–78**
Credit, letters of, **S37–43**
Credit period, dating, 373

Credit terms, 371–75
  cash discounts, 374–75
  code provisions for, 371–73
  credit period, dating, 373
Criminal liabilities, agent, 119–20
Custom-designed software, 459

D

Damages:
  for breach of accepted goods, 428
  for breach of contract, 613–15
  CISG regulations, 613–18
  incidental and consequential, 428–30 (*see also* Consequential damages)
  liquidated, 430–31
  for nondelivery, 427
Data Processing v. L.H. Smith Oil Corp., 359, 360
Deep-Pocket Principle, 106
Delivery, 531–38
  final cost, determination of, 533
  payment options, 534–38
  taking, 609
  transit financing, 532–33
Delivery terms, 377–95
  C.&F. destination, 389
  C.I.F./C.&F. net landed weights, 389
  C.I.F. destination, 387–88
  enforcement methods, 392–95
    delivery clauses, 392–94
    liquidated damages, 394–95
  ex-ship, 389–90
  F.A.S. vessel, 387
  F.O.B. place of destination, 384–85
  F.O.B. place of shipment, 382–83

F.O.B. vessel, car or other vehicle, 385–87
in single lots/in several lots, 391
"no arrival, no sale," 390–91
shipment contract, duties of seller under, 383–84
time for shipment, 391–92
Uniform Commercial Code (UCC) provisions, 378–92
  code definition of "delivery," 378–80
  place of delivery presumed by code, 380–81
  standard delivery terms, 381–91
Destination contract, 384–85
Digital signatures, **S70–74**
Disabilities discrimination, **S9–16**
  accommodation, **S11–12**
  legal actions, **S13–16**
Discrimination:
  age, **S8–9**
  disability, **S9–16**
  national origin, **S18–19**
  pregnancy, **S16–18**
  religious, **S19–20**
  sexual, **S20–30**
Discrimination legislation
  Age Discrimination in Employment Act (ADEA), **S8**
  Americans with Disabilities Act, S8, **S9–16**
  Civil Rights Act of 1964 (Title VII), **S16–30**
  Civil Rights Act of 1991, **S9–16**
Doctrine of Promissory Estoppel, 249–52
  and firm offers, 562
Drafts, 16–17
Drawee, 17

Duration of offers, 214–25
  accepted offers, 225
  lapsed offers, 215–20
  rejected offers, 220–22
  revoked offers, 222–25
Duties of agent, 69–83

E

Electronic Communications Privacy Act (ECPA), **S95**
Electronic data interchange (EDI), 467–509
  acceptance of a document, 494–95
  agreement, absence of, 508–9
  appendix, 507–8
  arbitration, 506
  communicating through, 467–69
  confidentiality, 500–501
  defined, 467–68
  documents, 481–85
  Electronic Messaging Services Task Force (ABA), 468, 469, 471
    strategy employed by, 474–76
  entire agreement, 504
  Federal Rules of Evidence (FRE), 473–74
  forces majeure, 505
  foreign sourcing, 477
  garbled transmissions, 495–97
  governing law, 505
  limitation of damages, 505–6
  Model Agreement, 469, 471–72, 474–78
    applicability of, 476
    credit/copyright notice, 478
    rule of "acceptance" under, 276
  perquisites, 481–91

  receipt of transmission, 491–92
  recitals, 479–81
  security procedures, 488–90
  serverability, 504
  service contracts, 477
  signatures, 490–91
  system operations, 487–88
  termination, 503–4
  terms and conditions, 497–500
  third-party service providers, 485–87
  transaction terms, 497–503
  transmissions, 491–97
  UCC provisions, 469–73
  use of, 478–79
  validity/enforceability, 501–3
  verification of transmission, 493–94
Electronic Messaging Services Task Force, American Bar Association (ABA), 468, 469, 471
Electronic notaries, **S70–72**
E-mail, policies, S7, **S62**
Emergency authority, 44–45, 103
Emergency order form, 54–56
  advantages of using, 55–56
Environmental hazards liability, 120–24
  accountability, 123
  CERCLA (Comprehensive Environmental Response Compensation and Liability Act), 122
  federal environmental laws, 122–23
  Occupational Safety and Health Administration (OSHA), 121–22
  recent litigation, 123–24
Estimating quantity, 329

Ethics, 153–80
  anti-corruption rules, **S33–34**
  certified purchasing managers (CPMs), 154–59
  defined, 153–54
  gifts from suppliers, 159–66
  good faith, 174–79
  "grease" payments, **S35**
  new business ethics, 167–74
    imposing, 173–74
  purchasing code of, 154
  "reason to know" language, **S18–19**
  trade transactions, decency in, 180
European Community, **S34**
European Currency Unit (ECU), **S129**
European Monetary System (EMS), **S129**
European Union, **S34, S121–37**
  aims, **S123–24**
  Charter of Fundamental Social Rights of Workers, **S134**
  commercial rules, **S128**
  European Commission, **S124–28**
  European Court of Justice, **S126–28**
  European Currency Unit (ECU), **S129–30**
  structure, **S124–28**
  union passport, **S131**
  U.S.-EU relations, **S135–37**
  what it is, **S122–28**
Excess personal liability, 112
Exclusion of warranties, 360–64
  exclusion by course of dealing, 363
  limitation of remedies, 363–64
  term "as is" as disclaimer, 362–63
Executive branch, as source of law, 13

Executive summary, Article 2 (UCC), 641–57
Exhaustion of rights, **S131**
Exports, See Gatt-Uruguay Round
Express (actual) authority, 40–43, 98
Express warranties, 347–55
  advantage of, 353–54
  affirmation of fact/promise, 349–50
  computer purchases, 461–63
  description of goods as, 351–52
  sample/model as, 352–53
  sources/types of, 348–49, 354
Ex-ship, 389–90

F

Fair dealing, 178
Fair Employment Practice Agency, **S28–29**
Faragher v. City of Boca Raton, **S29**
F.A.S. vessel, 387
Federal Acquisitions Regulation System, 625
Federal environmental laws, 122–23
Federal Trade Commission Act, 129
Feng Shui, **S153**
Financing statements, 18–19
Firm offers, 243–45, 560–63
  and Doctrine of Promissory Estoppel, 562
  rejection of, 562–63
  F.O.B. place of destination, 384–85
  F.O.B. place of shipment, 382–83
  F.O.B. vessel, car or other vehicle, 385–87
Foreign suppliers/vendors, 529–623, **S77–79**

Firm offers *(cont.)*
  buyer's protective devices, 538–42
    applicable law/jurisdiction, 539–40
    bonds/escrows, 540–41
    letters of credit, 541
    retainage, 541
    supplier excuses, 541–42
    supplier selection, 538–39
  CISG, 542–57
  compensation, **S78–79**
  contract, formation of, 557–71
  counterpurchase, **S78**
  countertrade, **S77–78**
  delivery, 531–38
    determination of final cost, 533
    payment options, 534–38
    transit financing, 532–33
  inherent problems, 530–31
  revocable offers, 558–60
  switch trading, **S79**
  See also Convention on the International Sale of Goods (CISG)
Formation of contract:
  by conduct of parties, 269–70
  with foreign suppliers/vendors, 557–71
  and government procurement, 628
Forms, 281–305
Freedom of contract, 19–21
  contracts whose provisions can be varied by agreement, 21
  setting contract outer limits, 19–21
  "unless otherwise agreed" clause, 21
Functional model, contract law, 515–17

G

GATT-Uruguay Round, **S101–3**
  background, **S85–87**
  benefits to Americans, **S103–5**
  defined, **S101**
  historic, **S101**
  importance of trade to the United States, **S102**
  provisions of, **S102–3**
General Agreement on Tariffs and Trade (GATT). See GATT-Uruguay Round
Generalized System of Preferences (GSP), **S134–35**
Gifts from suppliers, 159–66
  bribery, 163–66
  intent, 161–62
Good faith, 174–79
  fair dealing, 178
  honesty in fact, 176–77
  making the contract, 179
  merchants and nonmerchants, distinction between, 176
  reasonable commercial standards, 177–78
  and Uniform Commercial Code, 192–93
Goods
  conformity of, 580–92
Government procurement, 625–39
  competition in, 627
  contract:
    formation of, 628
    modification of, 629
  government procurement officers:
    appointment of, 626
    authority of, 626–27
    automobile use, 118–19

offer, 628
   acceptance of, 630
   quality control, 629
   supplier selection, 627–28
Gratuities, and purchasing personnel, 165–66
Grease payments, **S33–35**

H

Hall v. T. L. Kemp Jewelry, Inc., 463
Harmonized Commodity Description and Coding System, **S133**
Hazardous Materials Transportation Act, 122

I

Immigration Reform and Control Act of 1986, **S19**
Implied authority, 43–44
Implied warranty:
   computer purchases, 463–65
   defined, 354
   of fitness for a particular purpose, 358–60, 464
   of merchantability, 355–58
Indemnification of agent, 87
Individual proprietorships, 34
Industralease Automated & Scientific Equipt. Corp. v. R. M. E. Enterprises, Inc., 172
Inspection of goods, 403–5
   time for, 586–87, 606–8
Installment contracts, 338
   avoidance in, 613
Interest, breach of contract, 615

International Chamber of Commerce, **S37–38**
International Monitary Fund (IMF), **S82**
International Standby Practices (ISP), **S41–42**
Invitation to do business, 210–13
Issuer, letter of credit, 17

J

Job description, purchasing officer, 36–37
Job discrimination, see Discrimination
Joint and several liability, 106–7
Judicial branch, as source of law, 12–13
Jurisdiction, 14

K

Kickbacks, See Bribery

L

Language, discrimination issues, **S18**
Lapsed offers, 215–20
Law:
   commercial, 7–8
   common, 6–7
   company legal counsel, 13
   jurisdiction, 14
   modern sources of, 12–14
      executive branch, 13
      judicial branch, 12–13
      legislative branch, 12
   origin of U.S. law, 6–7
   state laws, standardizing, 8–9

Law Made model, contract law, 520–24
Law Merchant, 7, 189
Lawner v. Engelbach, 463
Law of agency, See Agency
Leases:
   filing, 450–1
   unconscionability in, 449–51
Legal bills, **S3–4**
Legal counsel, 13, 23–28
   alternative dispute resolution, 26–28
      arbitration, 28
      mediation, 26–27
   class-action suit against itself, initiating, **S5**
   fees, categories of, 25–26, **S3–4**
   outside legal services, 24–26
   role of, **S1–4**
Legal custody of goods, 401
Legal signature, 95–97
Legal tender, 419
Legislative branch, as source of law, 12
Letters of credit, 17–18, 536, 541, **S37–43**
   Article 5 of UCC, revision of, **S37**
   Article 13(a), **S39**
   Article 14(c), **S39**
   payment types, **S37**
   standby, **S41**
   tips for buyers, **S40–41**
   waivers of discrepancies, **S39**
Liabilities:
   agent, 93–126
   principal, 88–91
Libel, 108–9
Licensed product, purchasing, 120
Life's necessaries, 197
Liquidated damages, 394–95, 430–31
Llewellyn, Karl, 5

Long-form promissory note, 16
Loyalty, of agent, 70–73

M

Maker, 16
Maritime Arbitration Commission (MAC), **S139–40**
Market expansion clauses, requirements contracts, 333–34
Mediation, 26–27
Merchantability, implied warranty of, 355–58
Merchantable, code definition of, 356–58
Merchant(s), 189–90
   nonmerchants compared to, 176
Mexico, See NAFTA
Misfeasance, 105
Model Agreement:
   EDI, 469, 471–72, 474–78
      applicability of, 476
      credit/copyright notice, 478
      rule of "acceptance" under, 276
Mutual consideration, 199–201
Mutuality of obligation, requirements contracts, 331–32

N

Nader, Ralph, 5
NAFTA, **S105–21**
   agricultural products, **S109–17**
   apparel, **S117**
   automobiles, **S109, S116**
   computers, **S109**
   customs administration/procedures, **S109–11, S117–20**
   defined, **S105–8**

De Minimus test, **S115–16**
disputes, **S107–8, S112**
duty drawbacks, **S110**
effects on U.S. business, **S120–121**
energy, **S109**
environment, **S110**
financial services, **S110**
free trade commission, **S107**
general information, **S105–9**
goals and objectives of, **S106–7**
government procurement, **S110**
history, **S105–6**
impact of, **S120–21**
importance of, **S120–21**
investment, **S110**
manufactured good, **S109–17**
Mexico, doing business in, **S105–12**
rules of origin, **S112–17**
Secretariat, **S107–8**
supplemental agreements, **S108**
textiles/apparel, **S110, S116**
U.S. business, effect of on, **S120–21**
National Association of Purchasing Management, code of ethics, 158–59, 162–63
National Labor Relations Act, **S26**
Negotiable Instruments Act, 8
Negotiation, and counter-offers, 213–14
Neoclassical model, contract law, 514–15
New business ethics, 167–74
imposing, 173–74
unconscionability, 168–69
case examples of, 171–73
unfair surprise, 169–71
New York Law Revision Commission, 5
"No arrival, no sale," 390–91

Nonconforming acceptances, 281–305, 566–71
Nonconformity of goods, notice of, 587–88
Nonfeasance, 105
Nonuniformity, 619
North American Free Trade Agreement (NAFTA), See NAFTA
Notice of rejection, 409

O

Obligation model, contract law, 524–26
Occupational Safety and Health Administration (OSHA), 121–22
Offers, 203–25
communication of, 207–9
counter-offers, 213–14
defined, 203
duration of, 214–25
accepted offers, 225
lapsed offers, 215–20
rejected offers, 220–22
revoked offers, 222–25
firm offers, 243–45
intent to make, 205–6
invitation to do business, 210–13
legal implications of, 204–5
sources of, 203–4
subject matter, identification of, 209–10
valid offer, essentials of, 205–10
Off-the-shelf software, 457
Older Workers Benefit Protection Act(OWBPA), **S8–9**
One-time requirements contracts, 327–28
Open-price contracts, 369–71, 604–5

Option contracts, 245–46
Oral contracts, 307–19
  defined, 307
  origin of law on, 308
  Section 2-201 (UCC), 309–19
  Statute of Frauds, 308–9
Order bill, 537
Orders, 281–305
Order-signing responsibility, delegating, 97–98
Organization for Economic Cooperation and Development(OECD), **S33–35**
Origin of law in U.S., 6–7
OSHA, See Occupational Safety and Health Administration (OSHA)
Outside legal services, 24–26

P

Partnerships, 34
Passing risk of loss, 611–12
Patent infringement, 589–92
Payee, 16
Payment, 264, 419–20
  options, 534–38
  place of, 605–6
  time for, 606–8
Payment for goods, 401
Perfect tender rule, 407
Performance:
  buyer's responsibilities in, 402–7
    acceptance decision, 405–7
    inspection of goods, 403–5
    receipt of goods, 402–3
    rejection of goods, 407–13
  defined, 399–401
  revocation of acceptance, 415–17

  right to adequate assurance of, 417–19
  of seller, 593–97
  special terms/conditions, suggested phraseology, 420–21
  steps in, 401
Permanent Editorial Board: Uniform Commercial Code (UCC), 636
  study group, 641–57
Personal liabilities of agent, 93–126, **S5–6**
Physical receipt of goods, 401
Place of payment, 605–6
Pregnancy, discrimination issues, **S16–18**
Price, 365–71, 604–8
  expressing, 365–67
  open-price contracts, 369–71, 604–5
  place of payment, 605–6
  price escalation clauses, 367–69
  time for payment, 606–8
Price-adjustment clauses, requirements contracts, 333
Price reduction, 601–2
Pricing arrangements, 339
Principal, 32, 85–91
  duties of:
    compensation of the agent, 86–87
    indemnification of agent, 87
    non-interference with agent's work, 87–88
    possess authority delegated to the agent, 85–86
    reimbursement of agent, 87
  liabilities of, 88–91
    liability for criminal acts of agent, 90–91
    vicarious liabilities, 88–90

Privileged communication, 80
Procurement:
    offers in, 203–25
    unauthorized, 50–58
    See also Unauthorized procurement
Promissory estoppel:
    defined, 249
    doctrine of, 249–52
Promissory notes, 16
Proof of mailing acceptance, 276–79
Purchase contract, 195–202
    legal contract essentials, 196–202
        agreement of the parties, 201–2
        capable parties, 196–98
        mutual consideration, 199–201
        valid subject matter, 198–99
    purchase, defined, 195–96
Purchase orders:
    execution of, 94–104
    legal signature, 95–97
    order-signing responsibility, delegating, 97–98
    scope of authority, exceeding, 100–104
Purchasing code of ethics, 154, **S33–35**
Purchasing ethics, See Ethics
Purchasing under World Trade Organization, See World Trade Organization
Purchasing law, sources of, 4–6
Purchasing manager
    liabilities of, regarding the staff, **S7–31**
        age discrimination, **S8–9**
        disability discrimination, **S9–16**
        legal remedies, **S27–31**
        national origin discrimination, **S18–19**
        pregnancy discrimination, **S16–18**
        religious discrimination, **S19–20**
        sexual harassment, **S20–26**
    role of, 3–4
Purchasing officer:
    and accepted offers, 255–56
    and agent duties:
        accountability, 78
        confidentiality, 81
        conflict of interest, 73
        possession of skills/training, 82–83
    antitrust liabilities of, 127–52
    appointment of, 36–37
    authority of, 45–46
    and bribery, 165–66
    and cash discounts, 374–75
    and consumer rights, 213
    and copyright/patent infringement, 591–92
    and destination contract, 385
    and employer's liability insurance, 117–18
    and environmental hazards liability, 120–24
    and exclusion of warranties, 361–62, 363
    and express warranties, 350–51
    and implied warranty of merchantability, 355–58
    and no-assignment clauses, 336–37
    and offer duration, 224–25
    and order-signing responsibility, 97–98
    and prompt promise to ship, 275–76
    and purchase order signature, 95–97
    and the Robinson-Patman Act, 139–49
        Section 2(c), 141–42
        Section 2(f), 142–49

Purchasing officer *(cont.)*
   and scope of authority, exceeding, 100–104
   and Section 2–201 (UCC), 319
   and Section 2–207 (UCC), 302–5
   and the Sherman Act, 131–39
   and supplier's immediate delivery upon receipt of purchase order, 263
   and tort liabilities, 107–10
   Trading Partner Agreement, 475–76
   and warranty against infringement, 346
Purchasing officers, and unpriced purchase offers, 370–71

Q

Quality, 341–64
   determination of, 341–42
   warranties, 342–64
      defined, 342
      exclusion of, 360–64
      express warranties, 347–55
      implied warranty of fitness for a particular purpose, 358–60
      implied warranty of merchantability, 355–58
      warranty against infringement, 344–47
      warranty of title, 343–44
Quantity, 323–39
   blanket orders, 338–39
   estimating, 329
   expressing, 324–25
   installment contracts, 338
   maximum/minimum quantities, 329–31

pricing arrangements, 339
requirements contracts, 325–27
   drafting, 328–37
   Section 2–306(1) (UCC), 327–28

R

Receipt of goods, 402–3
Refuse Act, 122
Reimbursement of agent, 87
Rejected offers, 220–22
   effective date of, 271
   Rejection of goods, 407–13
   notice of rejection, 409
   reasonable time, 408–9
   rejected goods remaining in buyer's possession, 410–13
   wrongful rejection, 417
Relational model, contract law, 517–20
Religious discrimination, **S19–20**
Remedies:
   buyers, 423–35
   limitations on, 363–64, 431–35
   time limitations, 434
Request for a quotation (RFQ), 211
Requirements contracts, 325–27
   assignability, 334–36
   determination of requirements, 331
   drafting, 328–37
   estimating quantity, 329
   length of period covered by, 332
   market expansion clauses, 333–34
   maximum/minimum quantities, 329–31
   mutuality of obligation, 331–32
   one-time, 327–28
   price-adjustment clauses, 333

Section 2–306(1) (UCC), 327–28
variety of products, 337
Resource Conservation and Recovery
    Act, 122
Respondeat superior, doctrine of,
    89
Restrictive endorsement, 16
Retainage, 541
Revocable offers, 558–60
Revocation of acceptance, 415–17
Revoked offers, 222–25
Right to adequate assurance of
    performance, 417–19
Robinson-Patman Act, 129–31,
    138–39
    and purchasing officers, 139–40
Rules of origin, **S117**

S

Safe Drinking Water Act, 122
Sale of goods, 571–77
    contract:
        avoidance of, 573–75
        fundamental breach of, 572–73
        modification of, 577
        notice, date of effective, 575
    delivery terms, 578–80
    documents required by contracts,
        580
    performance, applicability of
        remedy of, 575–77
    seller's obligations, 577–80
    time of delivery, 580
Sales contract, 15–19
Scope of authority, exceeding,
    100–104
Security agreements, 18

Security interest, 18
Security procedures, EDI, 488–90
Seller(s):
    breach of contract by, 592–603
    cure of nonconforming delivery,
        413–15
    notice of intent to cure, 599
    performance of, 593–97
    remedies, 435
    right to cure after delivery, 597–99
    Service contracts, EDI, 477
Sexual harassment, **S20–30**
    costs, **S25**
    identifying, **S22–26**
    legal remedies, **S26–30**
    occurrences, **S21**
    policies, **S24–25**
Sherman Act, 128–29, 158
    boycott, 136
    collusion, 136
    group buying, 137–39
    and purchasing officers, 131–39
    reciprocity, 132–34
Shipment contract, duties of seller
    under, 383–84
Short-form promissory note, 16
Shrink-wrap license, **S64–65**
Sight drafts, 17, 537–38
Slander, 108–9
Society for World-Wide International
    Funds Transfer (S.W.I.F.T.), **S42**
Special endorsement, 16
Split-fee billing, **S4**
Stare decisis, 12
State laws, standardizing, 8–9
Straight bill of lading, 19, 537
Substitute goods, 426–27
Superfund, See CERCLA

Suppliers:
  acceptance methods, 264–68
  in blank, 264–66
    supplier begins to manufacture, 268
    supplier delivers goods, 266–68
    supplier repeats terms of offer, 266
  gifts from, 159–66
  negotiations with, 186
  quality obligations, extent of, 585
  right to cure, 585–86
Switch trading, **S79**

T

Termination of agency relationship, 38
Third party, defined, 32
Third-party claims, 580–92
Third-party service providers, EDI, 485–87
Thirty-day drafts, 17
Three-day drafts, 17
Time for shipment, 391–92
Tips, and purchasing personnel, 166
Tort liabilities, 104–7
  defined, 104
  misconceptions of, 105–7
  and purchasing officer, 107–10
Toxic Substance Control Act, 122
Trade, importance of to the United States, S120–21. (*See* also Gatt-Uruguay Round)
Trade acceptance, 537–38
Trade secrets, 80
Trade transactions, decency in, 180

Trading Partner Agreement, 475–76
Transit financing, 532–33
Triangle Underwriters v. Honeywell, Inc., 457–58
Two-party paper, 16

U

Unauthorized procurement, 50–58
  correcting past evils, 56
  eliminating, 52–56
    emergency order form, 54–56
    occasional offenses, confirming, 57–58
  problems created by, 51–52
Unconscionability, 168–69
  case examples of, 171–73
  in leases, 449–51
Unfair surprise, 169–71
Uniform Bills of Lading Act, 8, 11
Uniform Commercial Code Official Text, 187
Uniform Commerical Code (UCC), 5, 183–93
  applicability of, 11–12
  Article 2, 11, 15, 631–39
  Article 2A, 439–47
  Article 3 (UCC) 11, 16
  Article 4 (UCC), 11
  Article 4A (UCC), 11–12
  Article 5 (UCC), 18, **S37–38**
  Article 7 (UCC), 19
  Article 9 (UCC), 18
  CISG compared to, 619–23
  content of, 10–11
  course of dealing, 190–91
  definitions, 186
  express legislated purposes/policies of, 184–86

federal enactment:
  allowing, 635–36
  state enactment, 633–34
genesis of, 9–12
and good faith, 192–93
good faith, importance of, 192–93
goods, defined, 187–89
learning, 186–92
merchants, 189–90
past changes to, 631–33
Permanent Editorial Board of, 636
references, 187
Section 2-201, 309–19
Section 2-205, 228–43
Section 2-207, 281–305
Section 2-306(1), 327–28
state-by-state enactment, 634–35
unconscionability, section on, 168
usage of trade, principle of, 191–92
Uniform Commercial Code (UCC)
  model, contract law, 515–17
Uniform Customs and Practice, **S37–38**
Uniform Negotiable Instruments Law, 8, 11
Uniform Sales Act, 8, 11
Uniform State Laws, National Conference of Commissioners on, 8, 9
Uniform Warehouse Receipts Act, 11
United Nations Convention on Contracts for the International Sale of Goods
Union passport, **S131**
Uruguay Round, See GATT-Uruguay Round
U.S. law, origin of, 6–7
"Unless otherwise agreed" clauses, contracts containing, 21

Unpriced purchase offers, and purchasing officers, 370–71
Usage of trade, principle of, 191–92

V

Valid offer, essentials of, 205–10
Valid subject matter, 198–99

W

Waiver of discrepancies, **S39–40**
Warranties, 342–64
  defined, 342
  exclusion of, 360–64
  express warranties, 347–55
  implied warranty of fitness for a particular purpose, 358–60, 464
  implied warranty of merchantability, 355–58
  warranty against infringement, 344–47
  warranty of title, 343–44
Warranty disclaimer, term "as is" as, 362–63
Whistle blowers, protection of, 119–20
World Trade Organization, **S81–152**
  Asean Free Trade Area, **S147–50**
  Asia Pacific cooperation, **S139–47**
  basic systems of purchasing, **S81–82**
  benifits to U.S., **S103–5**
  European Union, **S121–37**
  GATT, **S85–87**
  multilateralism, **S82–85**
  North American Free Trade Agreement (NAFTA), **S105–21**
  customs administration, **S117–20**
  defined, **S105–8**

World Trade Organization *(Continued)*
   impact, **S120–21**
   key provisions, **S109–12**
   rules of origin, **S112–17**
   regional cooperation in Asia, **S137–38**
   Uruguay Round impact, **S101–3**

WTO, **S87–91**
   basic principles, **S89–91**
   substantive rules, **S91–101**

Written authority, advantages of, 41–43

Wrongful revocation of acceptance, 417